Understanding Photoboo

Understanding Photobooks is a user-friendly guide to engaging with the photographic book—or, as it is widely known, the photobook. Despite its importance as a central medium in which many photographers showcase their work today, there is surprisingly little information on the mechanics of the photobook: what exactly it does and how it does it. Written for both makers and artists, this book will help you develop a better understanding of the images, concept, sequence, design, and production of the photobook. With an awareness of the connections between these elements, you'll be able to evaluate photobooks more clearly and easily, ultimately allowing for a deeper and more rewarding experience of the work.

Jörg Colberg is a writer, photographer, and educator. He is currently a faculty member at Hartford Art School's International Limited-Residency Photography MFA Program, which is the only program of its kind to focus on photobooks. Since its inception in 2002, his *Conscientious Photography Magazine* (http://cphmag.com) has become one of the most widely read and influential websites dedicated to contemporary fine-art photography. Colberg has published articles and essays in numerous photography and design magazines, including *British Journal of Photography*, *Creative Review*, *Chinese Photography Magazine*, and *FOAM Magazine*.

Understanding Photobooks

The Form and Content of the Photographic Book

Jörg Colberg

Routledge
Taylor & Francis Group
NEW YORK AND LONDON

First published 2017
by Routledge
711 Third Avenue, New York, NY 10017

and by Routledge
2 Park Square, Milton Park, Abingdon, Oxon OX14 4RN

Routledge is an imprint of the Taylor & Francis Group, an informa business

Library of Congress Cataloging in Publication Data
Names: Colberg, Jörg, author.
Title: Understanding photobooks : the form and content of the photographic book / Jörg Colberg.
Description: New York : Routledge, 2017. | Includes bibliographical references and index.
Identifiers: LCCN 2016008733 (print) | LCCN 2016009827 (ebook) | ISBN 9781138892712 (hardback) | ISBN 9781138892699 (pbk.) | ISBN 9781315709031 Subjects: LCSH: Photobooks. | Photography literature. | Art portfolios.
Classification: LCC TR501 .C65 2017 (print) | LCC TR501 (ebook) | DDC 745.593/8--dc23
LC record available at http://lccn.loc.gov/2016008733

ISBN: 978-1-138-89271-2 (hbk)
ISBN: 978-1-138-89269-9 (pbk)
ISBN: 978-1-315-70903-1 (ebk)

Typeset in Times New Roman PS
by Servis Filmsetting Ltd, Stockport, Cheshire

Contents

Acknowledgments

This book would not have been possible without the generous input by the photographers, critics, writers, designers, editors, binders, producers, publishers, booksellers, and collectors, with whom I have had the opportunity to interact over the past years. At the same time, it would not be the same without the students in my photobook classes and workshops, who have never failed to challenge my ideas of what a photobook might be or do.

The luxury of being a teacher includes not just being able to contribute to students getting a deeper understanding of a given topic. It also means being wrong some of the time, which provides the opportunity to learn something. Even though I worked very hard on this book, I am going to be wrong concerning some—hopefully not too many—of its aspects. Needless to say, any errors or mistakes present are entirely my own, and they have nothing to do with any of the individuals to whom I talked while preparing the manuscript.

The list of people who deserve thanks for their input is long, and I am running the risk of forgetting someone. Nevertheless, the book would have not been possible without the following people.

My colleagues and friends Robert Lyons and Michael Vahrenwald have been partners-in-crime in seeing through a large number of students at Hartford Art School. Their perspectives have been instrumental in me being able to approach both photography and photobooks in myriad ways. Thank you to both of them!

Michael also very expertly took the photographs of photobooks used herein (unless where otherwise noted). Mari Kon deserves thanks for assisting.

I am indebted to the photobook experts who found the time to answer my questions so I could use some of their words: Laia Abril, Adam Bell, Josef Chladek, Cristina de Middel, Alice Rose George, Hans Gremmen, Markus Hartmann, Beverly Joel, Sybren Kuiper, Dewi Lewis, Sue Medlicott, Colin Pantall, Gordon Stettinius, David Strettell, Awoiska van der Molen, Ramon Pez, Mariela Sancari, Hannes Wanderer, and Donald Weber. Thank you!

Thanks are also due to the following individuals for kindly providing photographs used in the book: Leonie Hampton, Gerry Johansson, Sjoerd Knibbeler, Joshua Lutz, Peter Puklus, Richard Renaldi and Seth Boyd, Tamara Shopsin and Jason Fulford, Donald Weber, and Jessica Adams, Alissa Schoenfeld, and Yossi Milo at Yossi Milo Gallery.

What a photobook is, or what we might want from it—it's a book filled with pictures, and it does … Well, what? Without having had countless discussions, agreements, and disagreements over the past years, I would not have been able to write this book. In particular, I'd like to thank Valentina Abenavoli, Christopher Anderson, Harvey Benge, Seth Boyd, Cristina de Middel, Doug Dubois, Peter Evans, Tony Fouhse, Mary Frey, Alice Rose

George, Jim Goldberg, Hans Gremmen, Markus Hartmann, Rob Hornstra, Gerry Johansson, Barbara Karpf, Hester Keijser, Erik Kessels, Hiroh Kikai, Misha Kominek, Anouk Kruithof, Sybren Kuiper, Gábor Arion Kudász, Dewi Lewis, Lesley Martin, Sue Medlicott, Arwed Messmer, Rafal Milach, Sean O'Hagan, Daigo Oliva, Colin Pantall, Peter Puklus, Richard Renaldi, Fette Sans, Jonathan Saunders, Michael Schäfer, Markus Schaden, Caroline Schilling, Joachim Schmid, Oliver Sieber, Steve Smith, Alec Soth, David Strettell, Katja Stuke, Mark Tomlinson, Peter van Agtmael, Geert van Kesteren, Awoiska van der Molen, Frank van Eykelen, Hellen van Meene, Geert van Kesteren, Willem van Zoetendaal, Hannes Wanderer, Caroline Warhurst, Donald Weber, and Thomas Weski.

This book would not have seen the light of day without Kimberly Duncan-Mooney's initiative. My sincere thanks to her! Thank you also to Anna Valutkevich, Galen Glaze, and Judith Newlin at Routledge! Thank you to Melissa Catanese who read a draft of the book and provided invaluable feedback!

Last of all, thank you to Karen, Jim, and all the furry friends for their love, and support.

CHAPTER 1

Introduction: What Is a Photobook?

1.1 General Considerations: What Is a Photobook?

A photobook is a book that is being viewed because of the photographs inside. In the world of photography, photographic books are widely referred to simply as photobooks, which is why this is the term of choice adopted here. Of course, you can treat any book that contains photographs this way. However, even though someone might appreciate, say, a cookbook for its images, most people would probably look at it specifically because of its recipes. Unlike most books, producing a photobook begins with the photographs; everything else, which might include copious amounts of text, is added later.

Within the general category "photobook," there are several subcategories. These include albums, catalogues, and monographs. Over the course of this book, only monographs are going to be discussed. Here is why.

As digital photography seems to have replaced its analog equivalent, albums have become outdated. Whereas in the past people would assemble their own photography albums by buying blank ones and then adding photographs to them, albums now mostly exist in digital form, as folders on computers or cell phones, or as "albums" on sites like Flickr or Facebook.

Conceptually, a photography album is a very specific photobook. It usually is made over time, reflecting, say, a person's or family's history. Its producer edits it by selecting some photographs over others. In all likelihood, an album mostly contains happier, noteworthy moments in life. In this sense, albums are items of personal propaganda. We would hardly expect to encounter pictures of unhappy moments in them. Crucially, albums are hardly ever made to be published. They are one-of-a-kind objects, and most certainly nobody would need any rules for how to make one.

A catalogue is produced around a photographer's retrospective or exhibition, regardless at what stage in her or his career it might be happening. It intends to work as a survey, giving its readers/viewers insight into a segment of the artist's creative career. There usually is no narrative arc beyond exploring the career or exhibition in a catalogue. For example, for museum exhibitions, a catalogue is usually published, which contains the photographs from the show plus essays, written by experts such as the curator(s). The photographer might be involved, but only to the extent that she or he is involved in the selection of the work in the exhibition itself. In a catalogue, the individual photographs matter individually. In particular, if you were to tear out a page of a catalogue, in all likelihood this would not disturb the overall function of the book much.

This leaves us with monographs. Please note that in the following, when the term "photobook" is used, it is meant explicitly to exclude albums and catalogues.

Instead of trying to define what monographs actually are, it might be better to discuss what they *do*. For a start, you couldn't easily remove a photograph or page from such a photobook without running the risk of dramatically altering the book. It is made to rely heavily on each photograph having its very specific place next to and right after and before another photograph. The photographs' placement and the overall design create the connective tissue between the images that makes the whole, the book, more than just a sum of its parts. In the preface of *Publishing Photography*, Dewi Lewis describes these types of photobook as books that "attempt to use photography as a medium of visual communication in its own right."[1] The description places the focus on photography, making it clear that it carries the bulk of the weight "in its own right." Whatever text there might be, in the majority of cases it will play a subordinate role in a book's overall attempt to communicate its message. This really is what makes the photobook medium special, and what makes it stand out from other books that use photography for mostly illustrative purposes. In other words, in most cases, a viewer exposed to a photobook should be able to understand the book's message solely by looking at the photographs. Needless to say, the role of text is determined by the photographic body of work in question, and we will see examples of how it can be treated throughout the course of this book.

1.2 Photobooks vs. Exhibitions

A very different engagement with photographs is provided by an exhibition. The differences between a photobook and an exhibition of the same body of work are important enough to spell them out.

For a start, in a large variety of ways the overall presentation of the photographs is very different. An exhibition operates in a specific space, in which the exhibition itself, in the form of the (framed) photographs, is installed. Its makers have to pay attention to the space and where and how to hang the photograph to achieve the desired effect. Much like in the case of a photobook, someone hanging an exhibition has to think very carefully about what to do with the photographs.

But this is where the similarities end. Unlike a photobook, an exhibition will have a limited lifespan. At the end of the exhibition, the photographs will be taken off the walls. Another exhibition will be installed. A photobook, however, has no such shelf life. Its life is determined by its physicality and by the way it is being treated. Stored and treated properly, it will exist for decades, possibly centuries. We can still look at photobooks whose ground-breaking exhibitions have long become inaccessible events of the past (think Walker Evans' *American Photographs* at the Museum of Modern Art in the late 1930s).

The viewer enters an exhibition space to look at photographs on its walls. Usually a photobook is brought into the viewer's own home, to become part of her or his own environment. The terms of engagement with a book, how and when and how often it is being looked at, is entirely determined by the viewer.

What is more, a photobook usually is an intimate object, to be looked at by a single person at any given time. This is the polar opposite of most exhibitions, where at the same time many viewers will enter what essentially is a clinically white space that offers few, if any, of the comforts known from someone's home.

It is helpful to think of exhibitions and photobooks as centering on different parts of the human anatomy. Photobooks live in the space between a person's hands and eyes. In contrast, exhibitions are constructed around the ground people can cover with their legs in a relatively short period of time. Relatively speaking, a viewer can be much closer or much further away from a photograph in an exhibition than in a photobook. Consequently, the sizes of photographs in exhibitions tend to be larger, often much larger, than in a book. These large photographs can only be seen in their totality from relatively far away (a few yards). Provided they are printed well, those very details can be appreciated by moving close to the prints on the wall.

The sheer physicality of a large print on a wall psychologically makes for a very different engagement with the photograph itself—compared with what can be contained in a photobook. Quite large photobooks do exist, but they are still relatively small compared with what many contemporary artists these days produce for the walls of art museums, galleries, or collectors' homes. See Figures 1.1 to 1.4 for two examples of exhibition views versus books presenting the same body of work. The two bodies of work in question, Lorenzo Vitturi's *Dalston Anatomy* and Sze Tsung Leong's *Horizons* differ in a variety of ways, resulting in very different exhibitions and books.

Just as the case of the photobook, there is no full control over how viewers will engage with an exhibition, how long they will spend with each picture, whether they will move from left to right or right to left, whether they will try to look at pictures individually or in groups. In the case of a photobook, however, its makers can control what viewers look at in which order much more closely than in an exhibition. In both cases, photographs that need to be seen next to one another will be placed accordingly. But the order in which spreads are contained in a book restricts the viewer's engagement much more than the order in which prints are hung on a wall.

All of these differences between an exhibition and a photobook are very important. A photography project can usually exist as both an exhibition and a photobook (even though some projects might lend themselves much more easily to one or the other). But its actual realization as a photobook or an exhibition will—actually *should*—be different. Photobooks simply aren't exhibitions. They are their own, unique medium centered on photography.

In the afterword to Lee Friedlander's *In the Picture: Self-Portraits, 1958–2011*, Richard Benson describes these aforementioned differences as follows:

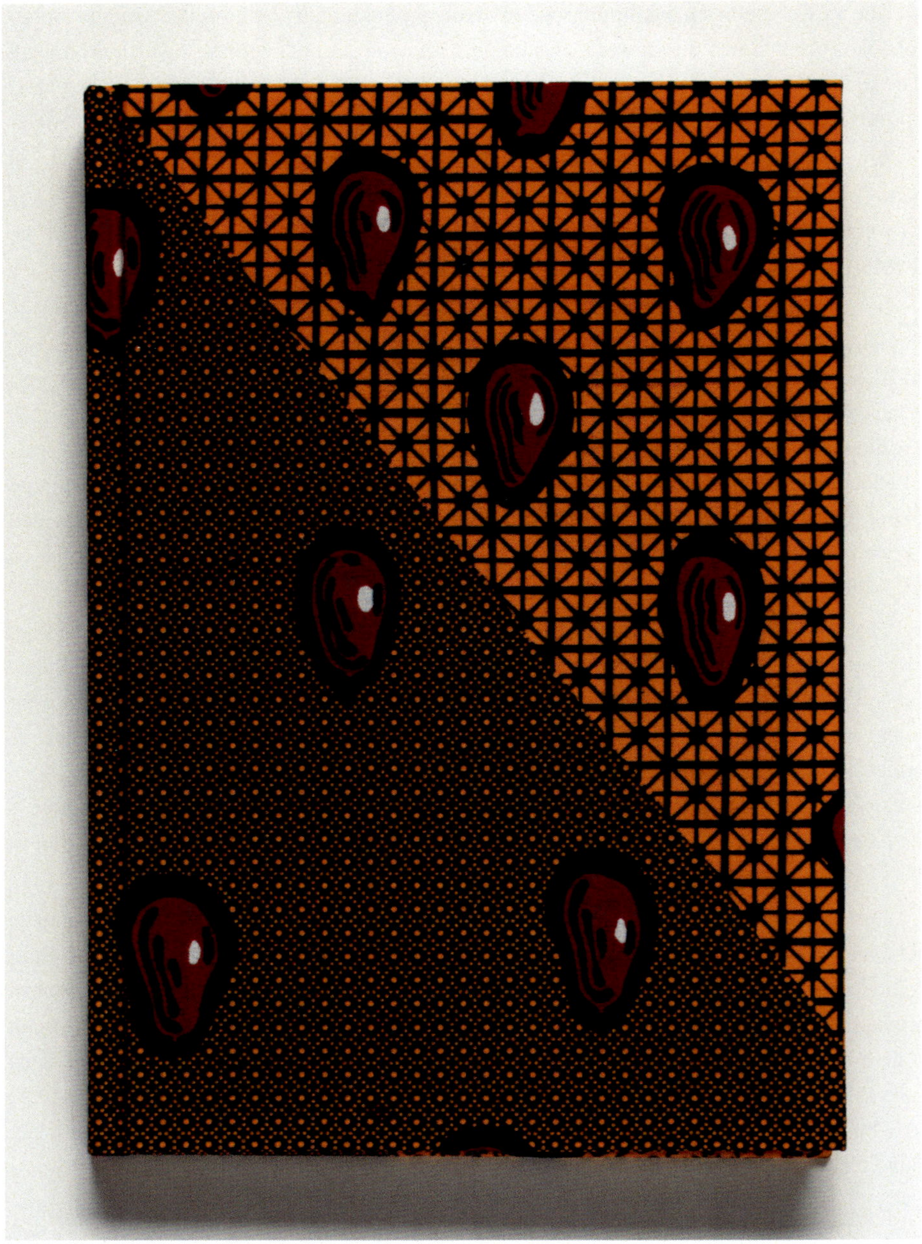

Figure 1.1 Cover of Lorenzo Vitturi's photobook *Dalston Anatomy* (this page), plus two spreads from the book (following page, top and bottom)

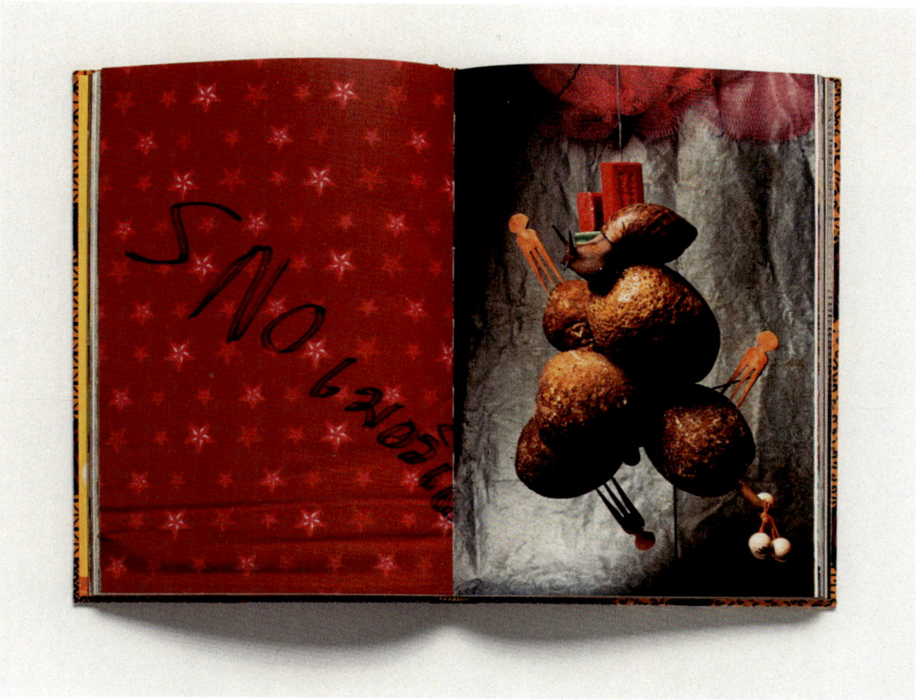

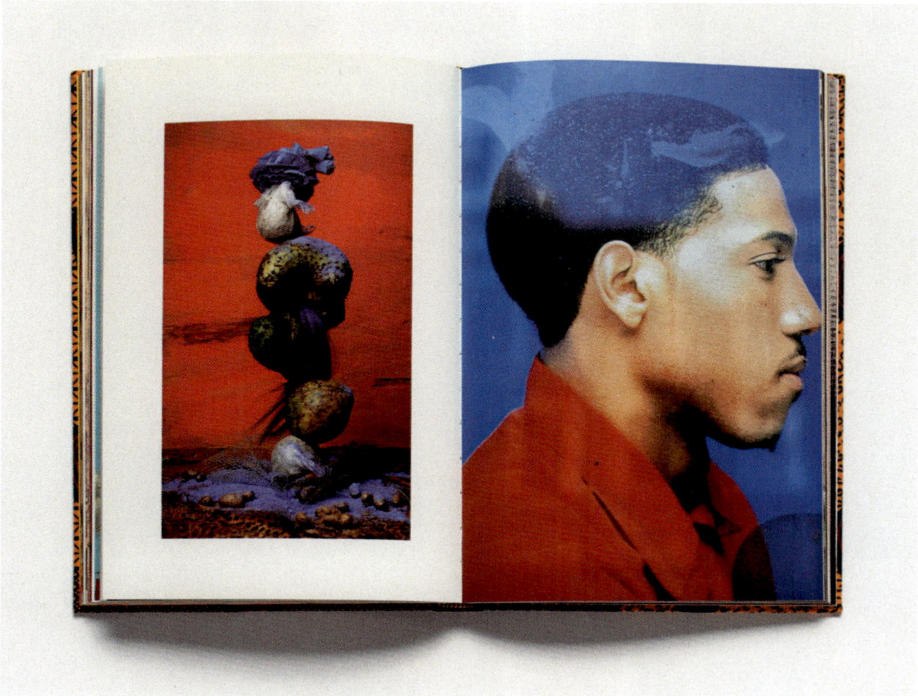

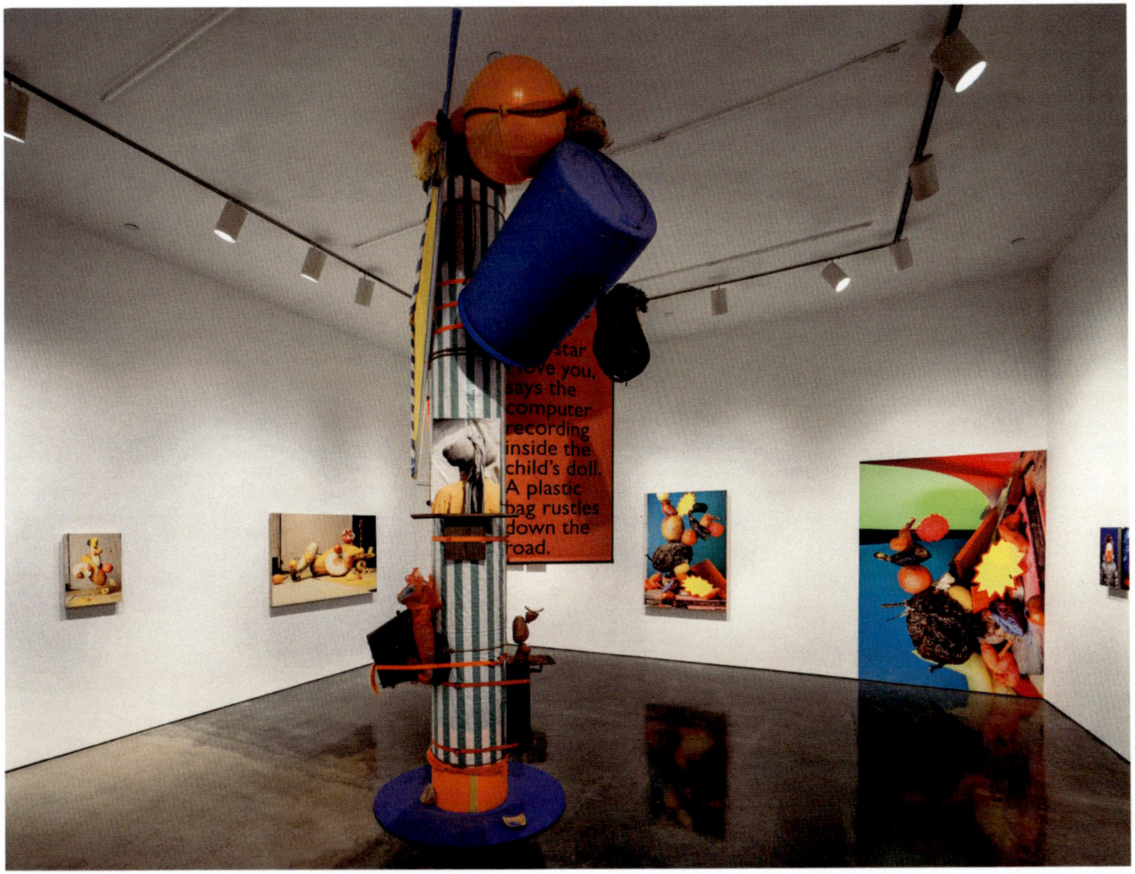

Figure 1.2 Installation view of Lorenzo Vitturi's *Dalston Anatomy* at Yossi Milo Gallery, New York City

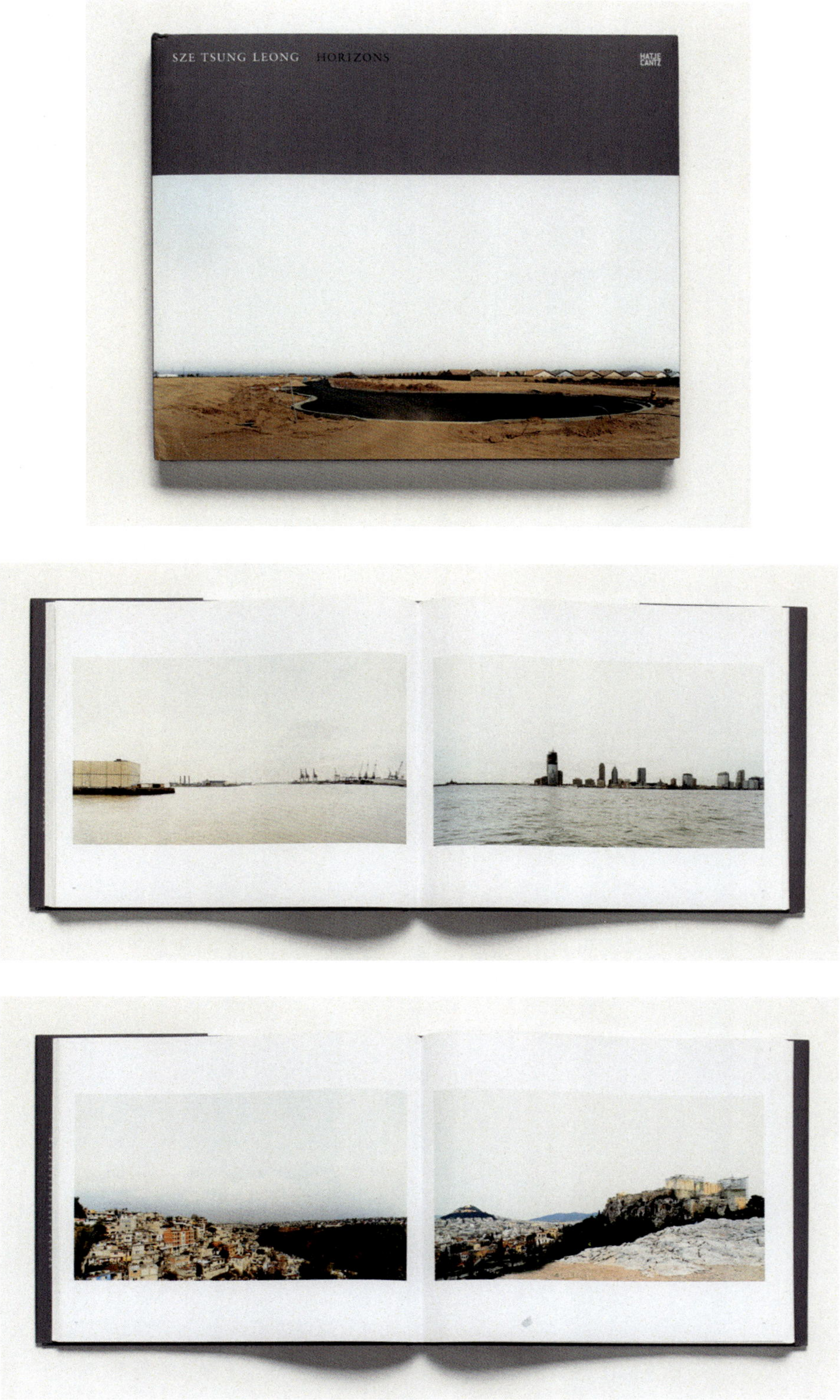

Figure 1.3 Cover of Sze Tsung Leong's photobook *Horizons* (top), plus two spreads (center and bottom)

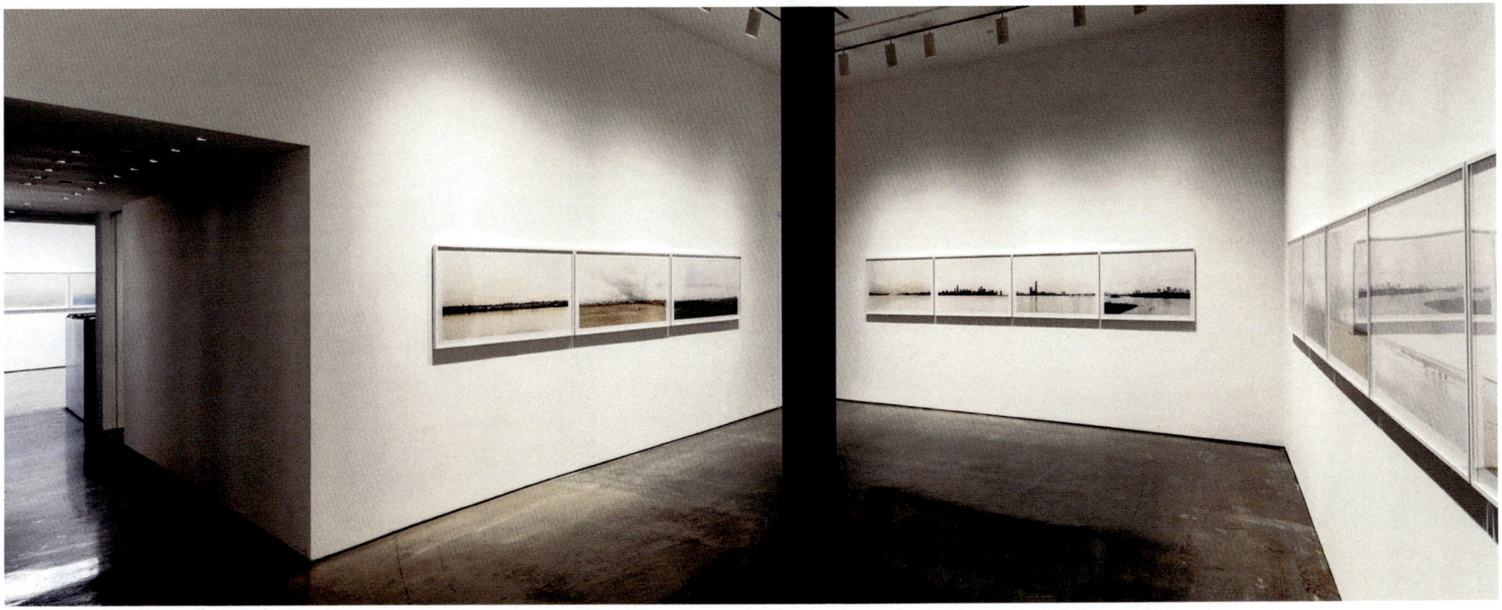

Figure 1.4 Installation view of Sze Tsung Leong's *Horizons* at Yossi Milo Gallery, New York City

> *The book became the ultimate venue for Lee [Friedlander], not the transitory one of the gallery show, where the pictures could only be seen for a short time, but instead a visual structure that lasted and could repeatedly reacquaint us with what we thought we already knew so well. In a mere instant, often no more than a hundredth of a second, a photograph can gather in an astounding mass of information. How naïve we are to think that we can see it all at first glance when hung on a wall or displayed on a computer monitor. The book solves this problem because we can look long and hard, without distraction, and return to it again and again. Photographs can become old friends, and like the best of them they can reveal themselves endlessly as we come to know them better.*[2]

Benson's case for the photobook as "the ultimate venue" for Friedlander can be seen as a general motivation for the medium. He clearly lays out what makes photobooks an established way to disseminate photography, allowing for a deep engagement with its audience.

1.3 The Photobook as an Object

To begin looking at photobooks in more detail, I now want to put the actual object itself into focus. A photobook is a book, and as such it has a large number of important properties that, while often overlooked, actually need to be considered and understood. Anyone wishing to understand the medium should spend a lot of time looking at photobooks. Much can be learned from how they are made.

Take a photobook, any photobook, from a shelf near you if possible, and open it. It really doesn't matter which one. Whichever book you picked, its specific properties will in all likelihood be different than those of another, in fact any other photobook you might own. Most photobooks are unique objects—even though at first glance, they all look so similar.

The fact that a photobook is an object, something to hold and to handle, is so obvious that it seems hardly worthwhile mentioning. But it is impossible to truly understand photobooks without this very simple and basic realization, especially since there result important implications from it.

Take the book you picked. I have no way of knowing any of its specific properties. Whichever book it is, it has a certain size and weight. It might be a fairly light softcover, or a heavier, larger hardcover. The cover will have a specific feel to the touch of your hands. There might be a dust jacket.

Open the book, and there are the first "pages." If it is a hardcover book, they are more noticeable, in the form of the so-called end paper. People usually don't consider these pages as anything important, because usually, but not always, they are ornamental (if even that). Often, the end paper is of a different paper stock than the bulk of the book. The end paper might have images on it, or a pattern, or maybe they are simply of one color, often not white. You will find the end paper at the very beginning and end of a hardcover book.

Turn the first page, and you will get to what you probably consider to be the real interior of the book (although I suspect that, from now on, you will actually pay more attention to the end papers as well).

When turning pages, you will notice that they move in specific ways in your hand. The paper will have a texture to the touch—it might be very smooth, or maybe it will be a little rough. It will also have a certain thickness, resulting in the pages turning easily or not so easily, in them folding over easily or not so easily. In all likelihood, the pages of your book will all be made from the same paper stock. But it is also possible that there is more than one paper stock.

None of what I have talked about so far has anything to do with the photographs in your photobook. But the size and weight of the book, whether it is a softcover or a hardcover, how the pages turn or resist turning, the feel of the paper to the touch—all of these properties play a role in how you view the book, however unconscious you might have been of them so far.

Think about the size. The size of the book determines how you can look at it. If you have a large and heavy hardcover book, it might be awkward, if not impossible, to place it in your lap or to hold it in front of you. You will require a table to look at the book. A small softcover, in contrast, can easily balance in your hands.

As before, none of this has anything to do with the pictures quite yet. Instead, what I have been talking about so far concerns the *physical experience of a viewer holding and looking at the book.* In contrast, an electronic form of the same book will miss all of these properties. It's just not the same thing, even if the pictures are the same.

In fact, given that our engagement with a computer screen is very different than with a book—regardless of whether we're talking about a desktop or laptop computer with a mouse and keyboard or a tablet computer that we operate by swiping its screen, photobooks and their electronic counterparts ("ebooks") are very different beasts. It is for this reason that ebooks will not be covered here.

The physicality of the photobook matters, not only because of how we interact with the book and experience it, but also because of the repercussions the materials have for the making of the book, and for how it is sold and perceived. For example, hardcover books usually are more expensive to produce, so they have to be sold for a higher price than softcover ones.

The price, along with the materials, has considerable influence on how we perceive the book. A cheap softcover book "feels" very different than a more expensive hardcover book. It must be handled differently, and psychologically, it feels more valuable, especially if the materials also feel precious. This is where the object photobook as a collectible enters. The value of collectibles is based on a large variety of factors, the monetary value merely being one of them.

The book will be printed on a glossy or semi-glossy or matte paper, which, in turn, will result in the photographs looking a certain way—apart from having a specific feel to the touch.

The way the photographs look is not only determined by what type of paper they are printed on, but also by the quality of the printing. Maybe your book was printed very well, and the pictures "shine." Maybe the printing was not that great, and if you look carefully, the pictures all lack some detail—the shadows (darker areas) might be a bit muddy, say, lacking detail.

And then there is all the rest: the text. There is a title page. There might be pages with an essay (or maybe more than one essay). These pages are usually either in the front of the book before the photographs or at the end, after the pictures. The text is laid out in a very specific manner, which, unless you are a graphic designer, you probably did not pay much attention to. There is, for example, the choice of font (or maybe fonts), the size of the font, the way the text is organized, etc.

When a photobook is made, each and every one of these many factors that I just outlined was considered. Someone had to make a decision about each and every one of them. As a viewer, you might not notice many of the choices made. If you are a photographer who wants to make a photobook, suddenly you are confronted with having to make all of those decisions. How can you possibly go about it? That is the subject of this book. Its goal is to teach you how to make a photobook in such a way that each of these decisions that have to be made has been carefully considered.

Even if you are not interested in making a photobook and just want to learn more about the medium, the following chapters will introduce photobooks to you in a way that will allow you to engage with them in a much more refined way. Maybe you are a collector, and you would like to get some pointers on what to look for in a book. Maybe you just want to learn what went into the making of a book, so you have a better understanding of how to appreciate it. Maybe you are a critic, and you want to gain a better understanding of the medium of the photobook.

Why does it matter, though, that every aspect of a photobook has been carefully considered? What is wrong with a shortcut here and there? Well, shortcuts in photobook making usually result in problems. Even if you are not aware of the shortcut, it is very likely that you will notice that something is "off."

For example, if the book was printed badly, the photographs will not look very good. They might be muddy, and they might feel lifeless. A common problem with so-called on-demand printing services such as *Blurb* is that the colors often are off. The whole book might have a slight green or magenta or red cast (or whatever other color might sneak in). A book that is supposed to be black and white might be slightly magenta in tone. As a viewer, you might not understand how the problem arose. But you will see the problem only too clearly.

There are many other common problems with photobooks. The binding might be flimsy. A softcover book might start to literally fall apart, with pages coming loose. A hardcover book might be impossibly hard to open and lay flat on a table. A book might be too heavy and unwieldy.

Apart from these various problems, all of which are related to the object and its materials, there are more. For example, you might own that photobook that you just can't look through in one sitting because you get bored after a while. Did it need to have that many pictures? Did it need to use such a boring format? Did it need to have, well … you might not be able to say what the problem is, but something is *off.*

All of these problems are usually the results of shortcuts, of decisions not made or made badly.

In contrast, when a photobook is made well, it is quite likely that you will not notice many of the great decisions that went into its making. That, ultimately, is the goal: while problems with photobooks are like hangnails that can be noticed even by those who do not know much about photobooks, many of the properties of perfectly made photobooks can only be appreciated by experts (designers, book binders, editors) or people who are aware of the various details to look out for.

But you do not have to be an expert to view and appreciate a photobook. You do not have to have a solid understanding of graphic design to notice how the text is laid out so attractively, making it easy to read. You do not have to be a bookbinding expert to notice the various small tricks employed to make the handling of the book easier. Having read this book, you will have a better understanding of what to look for without making you an expert in graphic design or bookbinding. You will be able to appreciate a photobook better not because you know exactly how it was made, but because you will know more about the various things to appreciate.

If you are a photographer intent on making a photobook, you will also not become an expert graphic designer or bookbinder. That cannot be the goal. Instead, you will have a lot of pointers how to approach all the various factors that lie outside your own expertise, seeking the help of professionals that know exactly what to do.

1.4 How to Approach Photobook Making

In light of the preceding, the goal of this book could be restated as follows: it will help photobook makers to understand the different aspects of photobook making, so they know what to focus on, what to spend time on, and—equally crucial—which pitfalls to avoid. Making a photobook requires a lot of time and effort. But the process does not need to be overly frustrating as long as there is clarity of what has to be done and how this can be achieved. Much like a photography project, the form of a photobook will reveal itself with time.

Given that time is a crucial part of the process, working with a computer is mostly detrimental to photobook making. If your idea of making a photobook is to work with, say, Adobe's *Lightroom,* using its book module, the very first thing you want to do is to shut off your computer before you proceed. At some stage during the process, computers do play a role in photobook making. But they come at the very end, when you know what your photobook is going to look like.

In much the same way, if you are using any of the on-demand services, whether it's *Blurb* or another company, stop doing that for a while. The severe quality problems aside, it is very hard to make a good photobook by placing images into a very small set of templates on a computer screen, having available a relatively small number of paper options, none of which is present at the actual moment when the book is laid out.

This is not to say that companies such as *Blurb* do not serve a purpose, even for those who want to make the kind of high-end photobooks discussed here. But just like with any tool, if you do not understand the outcome well enough and if the tool does not give you the options needed to properly work towards the outcome, you have to be very careful.

Over the course of the following chapters, all of which focus on particular aspects of this process, I am going to describe how this medium works and operates.

In addition, in the "In Focus" sections, I am going to look at a number of photobooks in detail, highlighting their important features. These investigations into photobooks are interspersed throughout this book. For these examinations, I have spoken with a variety of people who are working in the field of photobooks in very specific capacities, whether as editors, designers, producers, publishers, critics, or, of course, photographers. Given their different backgrounds, they will approach a photobook in often very specific ways. I will look at each photobook with the help of more than one expert. Taken together, they will provide further insight into each particular book.

Notes

1. Dewi Lewis and Alan Ward, *Publishing Photography*, Cornerhouse Publications, 1992, p. 7.
2. Lee Friedlander, *In the Picture: Self-Portraits, 1958–2011*, Yale University Press, 2011.

CHAPTER 2

The Photobook: Publishing and the Marketplace

2.1 Introduction

It is very important to understand the general environment photobooks "live in," in particular what aspects of publishing need to be understood and where photobooks can be found. While some of those aspects are fairly well known, others tend to be neglected when photobooks are being discussed. Photographers publishing a book, whether by themselves or with a publisher, often end up being surprised and then overwhelmed by some of the challenges they have to face. None of these challenges is insurmountable—quite on the contrary. But being aware of problems that—often inevitably—will appear is crucial.

2.2 The Market

To begin with, even the most art-oriented, avant-garde photobooks are ultimately objects that enter the marketplace. They are made to be enjoyed by their viewers, and the way those viewers get access to them is by buying them (if they are given as a gift, someone else buys them). As a consequence, photobooks are subject to the rules of their market. This is extremely important for a large variety of reasons that I will attempt to outline over the course of this chapter.

I don't mean to argue, however, that market considerations should trump anything else. They shouldn't. It would be straightforward to argue that as a photobook maker, you need to think about your audience first. Now, whether or not you call it "market" or "audience" doesn't really matter much, as long as you realize that if you produce a photobook, unless it's being done in a way that makes it qualify as an artist's book (typically meaning edition runs of ten or fewer), then besides (hopefully) a piece of art you will also have an object that you need to find viewers for. Who are these viewers? How can you reach them? These two questions lie at the core of thinking about audience and the market, respectively.

In this chapter, I will focus on the aspect of market. In the following chapter, which looks at photobooks' underlying concepts, I will discuss the aspect of audience. I do not mean to imply that one is more important than the other. Given the logic with which this particular book is arranged, it simply makes most sense to talk about the market first, before going into the details of how to specifically make a book. Market or publishing aspects often are not at all or barely understood by photobook makers, and I believe it is important to be aware of what world one is about to enter with one's book before making it. So what is this world like? How does it operate?

There is a large variety of photobook publishers, ranging from large publishing houses that produce photobooks along with all other kinds of books (such as Taschen or Phaidon), to larger, well-established photobook/art book publishers (such as Aperture, Steidl, or Hatje Cantz), to medium sized and smaller publishers, to self-publishers. Book publishing is a complex business, in which, at least currently, books are being produced in large numbers first before they are being sold.[1] For most books, it is very hard to predict whether the number of produced books, the print run or edition, is actually going to sell. In other words, publishers typically produce a book and then hope for the best, doing all kinds of things to make sure it will sell. We will see later in this chapter what is usually done to sell a book.

Imagine you run a publishing business. You will have a number of employees, whose salaries you need to pay (on top of your own). You will produce a number of copies of a book, for which the printer and binder each will send you invoices once they're done with their work. The idea of a serious publisher that hopes to stay in business will be to sell enough copies of the book to cover expenses. That really is the bottom-line goal for any publisher, including self-publishers (which we'll get to later), unless there is an independent, other source of income available.

Given you don't know whether there will be 1,000 people who will buy the book, producing 1,000 copies essentially is a bit of a gamble, with a fair amount of risk involved. If the book doesn't sell, the business is not going to get out of the red. Most publishers deal with this risk by publishing more than one book at a time (time here usually roughly meaning a season—catalogues are usually produced for different seasons). So there will be, let's say ten different books instead of one. If a publisher manages to diversify the books in a sufficient way, enough books will sell so that the income from the sold books covers all the costs. This could mean that one book becomes a bestseller, maybe even requiring further editions, or that three or four books sell well … But in all likelihood it will also entail some books just not selling well (if at all).

Most photobook publishers have established their specific formula of how to deal with the risk of publishing, and their catalogues indirectly reflect that formula. In other words, they know fairly well what might sell or what might not sell, and they publish books accordingly. Given that most publishers have established a particular brand, the different catalogues look different. Aperture's book publishing is different than Steidl's, say.

A first consequence of a publisher knowing which book they can sell is that if a photographer engages with them their book might get rejected. Rejections of book proposals by publishers happen for all kinds of reasons. An important one is that a publisher decides that based on its roster of already published books, taking on one that poses a risk simply isn't worth it. It's a business decision, based on business concerns, and it might not say much, if anything, about the artistic merit of the photography in question. Galleries operate in very similar ways.

If the owner of a gallery thinks she or he will be unable to sell a body of work, she or he will in all likelihood be unwilling to accept the artist in question to the gallery's roster.

If a book "comes out of a void and the context isn't too promising, meaning exhibition in a well-known museum or good school or great topic, then most publishers will turn it down," says Markus Hartmann, a longtime photobook expert, who formerly was publishing director at Hatje Cantz and now works as an editor, curator, exhibition organizer and small publisher. "They shy away from the risk. And that's totally fine with me. The question not only is how much the production of a book costs. It also is: how much of the publisher's capacity is being used up with the book? How much time—my own or time of my paid employees—is being used up? If I only sell 300 copies that doesn't make financial sense." In other words, if you operate as a business, you cannot afford to ignore very basic business considerations.

That said, reality still often is a little bit more complex. "We publish what we respond to," says Dewi Lewis of the eponymous British publishing company, which each year produces around 20 books. "We know we should think about things in a sensible commercial way, but more often than not we publish solely because we believe in the work." That belief in the work comes down to the following, according to Lewis: "I'm generally looking for projects which I feel have an international appeal—but by that I mean that they contain elements that reflect our shared humanity and shared experience—not that they necessarily involve international issues. I'm also looking for projects that I feel need an audience—in that they have something to communicate beyond a small circle of family and friends." And there are risks taken, albeit on a limited scale: "Each year we probably publish at least two to three books where we ignore all the financial realities. To do these we have to be pretty confident that other titles will generate the income we need. And so the list needs to achieve a sort of balance." As it turns out, determining edition sizes is a tricky business. Lewis again: "In reality, the edition size is at best an educated guess—but one that we, like most publishers, frequently get wrong. Over the years we've probably become more cautious with numbers and my own position is that I would prefer to reprint rather than hold vast stock in a warehouse. Financially, large runs appear to make more sense, but only if you can sell them." "Only if you can sell them"— the key point.

On the continuum of publishers there are bigger ones than Dewi Lewis Publishing and smaller ones. Candela Books is associated with the eponymous gallery, founded and run by Gordon Stettinius who notes "my projects will probably number one or two in any given year. And even given my stature as a small publisher, I am presented with a lot of work in a given year," with the result that "the odds are somewhat long when you could call me with a book dummy." Stettinius is upfront with photographers who approach him: "The questions I will have artists answer deal mostly with helping me understand where they are in their careers and what type of audience have they developed." There are reasons for him asking questions such as "Who is the audience for your work?" or "How many shows are upcoming in the next two to three years, especially with museums or in major markets?" Stettinius: "I ask all this not because I personally care about the glossy aspects of a resume but because my distributor will gauge their interest and projections, in part, by how popular the work might be, by how many market intersections the work might bring together. If the distributor is not excited about the work, then I will have to do the majority of the marketing and PR, something which I am not really cut out to do as someone who runs a couple of small businesses." This is an important aspect of publishing, especially for smaller (or self-) publishers: know what you want to be in charge of, know what needs to be done by others.

Photobook publishers are often described as gatekeepers, who for obscure reasons act in that capacity, keeping many great photobooks from being published. As is obvious from either Dewi Lewis' or Gordon Stettinius' descriptions of their approaches, this essentially is an unfair characterization of what publishers actually are or do. In a sense, a publisher is a gatekeeper who prevents a book from being made that they're certain they can't sell. Publishers aren't charities, so to expect them to act as anything other than businesses misses their point entirely. Of course, this does not mean that photobook publishers are only businesses. Most publishers are run by people deeply committed to photography and what can be done with photographs in book form. And those people will take on risks, knowing that they can afford to publish, let's say one or two books a year where they don't know whether it will sell. But to remain in business, to be able to stick around and produce what they believe to be good photobooks means having a level-headed view at the bottom line. That's the reality of photobook publishing. Any publisher who violates this basic property will find itself out of business sooner or later.

Actually, most serious and dedicated publishers produce photobooks not because they are unaware of the many challenges, but in spite of them. If you are not 100 percent committed to getting a product made that is a hard sell, you probably do not want to enter the world of publishing. And ultimately, there always are motives that go way beyond the books themselves and that have more to do with their art, and their artists. Based in Berlin, Germany, Hannes Wanderer is owner of both the shop 25books and of Peperoni Press, a small photobook imprint. For him, making a book is not just about the objects alone: "Since I develop all books with the artists from beginning to end, I have to develop a personal interest in the work, which extends across the whole process, from layout to printing to presentation at fairs, festivals, and in book shops." Instead, there is this investment that goes beyond money and time, and that directly aims at helping worthwhile projects gain visibility: "I judge the success of a book not using the edition size and sales, but by whether or not a strong body of work can be made visible at the right spots, triggering discussion. Fred Hüning's books *einer*, *zwei*, and *drei* were each published in an edition of 100 copies, but the photographs were then shown worldwide as part of Susan Bright's exhibition *Home Truth*. That's fantastic." Wanderer's comment not only affirms his deep commitment to the photographers whose works he produces in book form, it also clearly lays out a truth about photobooks that is often overlooked: a photobook might simply also be a vehicle to get the work into the right hands, to then result in exhibitions, print sales, or whatever else.

I already mentioned the print run or edition size of a photobook. In addition to publishers getting criticized for ultimately rejecting the vast majority of books pitched to them, they are often also criticized for printing what look like small numbers of photobooks. Why are editions of photobooks so small, given that novels or cookbooks or nonfiction writing deal with much larger numbers?

I already spoke of the market, so you can probably guess the answer: photobook publishers produce an edition size that they are confident they can sell. Remember, you need to pre-produce the books before you can sell them. If you have 10,000 books made instead of 1,000, you will not only have the extra costs, you will also have to store those books somewhere. And then you have to find ten times the number of people willing to buy the book.

Here's another reality of photobook making: Most photobooks will never sell 10,000 copies, let alone even 1,000. That is why most photobook publishers will keep edition sizes small (compared with the print runs of bestselling novels or nonfiction books). The drawback is that when a book does sell out, its price will skyrocket on the secondary market (unless the publisher decides to issue a second edition).

Over the past decade, the world of photobook publishing has changed considerably. "Ten years ago," Chris Boot, executive director of Aperture, observes, "there were, by my estimate, about 40 publishers around the world that a photographer needed to persuade to take on their book if they were going to get a book out on the marketplace. And that has completely changed. Now—it's a glib truism—all photographers are publishers."[2] Boot's statement has important—and obvious—repercussions in the form of an explosion of self-publishing. In a sense, however, self-publishing is not all that different from producing a book with a publisher, given that the underlying process and concerns are pretty much identical. The only aspect missing is having to get a book accepted for publication. It is for that reason that I am focusing so much on what publishers do, given that self-publishers have to take on a lot of additional roles, many of which photographers often only find out about once they are in the process of producing their own book.

How much things have changed even over the last two decades becomes obvious from an example given by Markus Hartmann: "I remember in the late 1990s, early 2000s I made the first books with Peter Bialobrzeski, and we produced 4,000 or 5,000 copies of *Neon Tigers*. Back then, he wasn't that well known at all. He was unknown. The first edition sold out after a year, so we printed a second one and sold that out, too. With that book he became known nationally and internationally. It's amazing what goals you can reach with a good book if it is made by the right publisher at the right time. The book helped his career a lot. But he then added a few other good books. These days, you would approach the same project and the same book probably with an edition of 1,500. If they sell out, you produce a second edition." How could this possibly be? The answer might be quite simple, notes Hartmann: "I'd say that now we have an incredible oversupply in terms of the sheer number of titles being published every year—clearly too many books for a market that is shrinking or stagnating as far as potential buyers are concerned." Could this really be the case, given there is so much excitement about the photobook these days?

While speaking to a large number of people in preparation for this book, I noted a growing sentiment that the sheer number of published books might, in fact, constitute an unsustainable bubble. After all, the main question is whether there are in fact buyers for all of the books published. Michael Mack, founder of the eponymous British publishing house, is concerned about the boom: "It's self-sustaining in terms of sales—there may be 500 people around the world who all know what's being published; they all buy a copy and that's the print run. In practical terms, there is no way you can print a thousand copies and make a return on it unless you're pricing it ridiculously high. So, commercially, I don't understand what is underpinning and sustaining these projects."[3] Of course, whether or not the boom is going to be self-sustaining or not will reveal itself with time. David Strettell, owner of New York City-based specialty bookshop Dashwood Books (who also published books under his own, eponymous imprint) confirms Mack's estimate, albeit in a more upbeat way: "I'd guess there isn't much more than a few hundred photobook buyers worldwide that you could call 'collectors' looking at new books, most of them genuinely enjoying the collecting process with an element of speculation in their buying habits. However, the titles being championed are often produced in editions of less than a thousand copies, so this small but motivated group can buy up a significant portion." And the rest of the books are then sold through shops like his own: "The rest of the sales come through specialist retailers like myself who are informing a broader audience looking for what's new and being interested in photography or just responding to something inspiring or beautiful." Given the vastly expanded interest in the medium photobook, even a contraction of the market is unlikely to put the genie back into the bottle.

2.3 Buying Photobooks

Despite their popularity, photobooks cannot be as easily bought as one would naïvely imagine. For a start, physical bookshops have been under a lot of pressure over the past decades, first through competition from chain bookshops, and then through the emergence of online retailers such as Amazon.com, which, in turn, has put enormous additional pressure on the business as a whole. In the United States, smaller independent bookshops have mostly been displaced by chain bookshops or online retailers. In places like Germany, which have stricter rules about, say, discounting books, there are a lot more smaller shops left.

But the existence of small or even chain bookshops does not translate into photobooks being available there. Chain bookshops might carry photobooks by the likes of Annie Leibovitz or Ansel Adams, artists known beyond the often rather narrow confines of the world of photography, or books distributed via D.A.P. (Distributed Art Publishers). Small bookshops might carry some of those books, but usually at even more reduced a rate. Physical bookshops, in other words, are unlikely places to find photobooks—unless they are specialty photobook shops, of which there exist a number across the globe. Such shops include Dashwood Books in New York City, Le Bal in Paris, or 25books in Berlin. In addition, photobooks can also be found in museum shops or in places like the International Center for Photography's bookshop in New York. Lastly, fairs such as Offprint (Paris) or the Art Book Fair (New York) offer a chance to find photobooks.

If you live in a city with such a specialty photobook shop, you have a good chance of encountering a fairly large, yet certainly not necessarily representative selection of photobooks, including both self-published books and books produced by small or large publishers. As a self-publisher, your role includes contacting such stores to see whether they would carry your book or renting a table at a fair to sell it there.

The internet has certainly contributed massively to democratizing the photobook market. It doesn't matter much whether you're a large publisher or a self-publisher working out of your own home, you can sell your photobook(s) online. In theory, this is an obvious and easy way to sell a book, because anyone interested in the book can—ideally—just click on a link, provide address and payment information, and the book will arrive in the mail. For example, a former Brazilian student of mine told me how excited he was when he received his first orders from India and Japan. In addition, many specialty photobooks stores will also sell books online, and there are dedicated online photobook sellers such as Photobookstore.co.uk.

But again, the devil is in the details. It's one thing to offer a book for sale on one's website. It's quite another to have people actually come to the website to look. Photobook makers often spend considerable amounts of time on social media (Facebook etc.), trying to spread word of their books. There are websites dedicated to listing self-published books such as *Self Publish, Be Happy*[4] or *The Independent Photobook*[5] (full disclosure: I cofounded the latter). But large parts of the experience that a visitor of a bookshop has are absent from the internet. It has become customary to display photobooks online either through selected spreads (such as in this book) or through videos where someone will quickly turn a book's pages. But still, to buy a physical object such as a photobook more or less sight unseen is not ideal.

"Because of the time I spend on the computer each day," notes Josef Cladek, "the net is my main source and inspiration of what to buy." A photobook aficionado based in Vienna, Austria, Chladek has been creating a virtual bookshelf of his collection online.[6] "Looking at books online is frustrating. It's totally different than the end product. Even when I order books, I'm often surprised how small or big they are when they arrive. This is one reason I started the virtual bookshelf, to actually see the different sizes of books compared to each other." In addition to seeing the books on a virtual shelf online, the site's visitor can "open" a book, to get detailed publishing information, plus a series of selected spreads. Part of the reason for this system is sheer fancy: "Even for me it's a resource because I have no proper order in my library. Sometimes, I have to look up the thickness or the color of the spine, which helps me to find the book on the actual bookshelf. This was the main reason for the site, because I don't want to order books alphabetically or by color or whatever else to be able to find them. They're stored the way they arrive or based on my mood." But for anyone visiting Chladek's site, there is a plethora of information, which certainly can make deciding whether or not to buy a certain book easier.

2.4 More on the Photobook Market(s)

David Strettell sums up the conundrum the photobook market has been having to deal with over the past few years as follows: "The photobook market has changed a great deal over the past ten or 15 years. The number of books being produced has grown exponentially, but the sizes of print runs have been dwindling as the trend for tiny publishers producing photobooks in short editions has gained a lot of critical interest, and as a result these books are often sold out within weeks of being released." A much increased number of books, with shrinking edition sizes—at least mathematically speaking the total number of sold books might not be changing much.

But there are other, more in-depth ways of looking at the photobook market. "There is no such thing as *the* market," says Hannes Wanderer, who in his role as book publisher and bookseller knows the state of things from more than one angle. "There is a diffuse mix of different markets with differently operating actors that pursue different interests and goals." Photographers concerned about their book might not need to know the details of these different markets, but it's important to be aware of them. According to Wanderer, there are three markets: the regular book market, the independent market, and the collectors' market.

The regular book market is tied closely to how books have been made, shipped, and sold for many years, with publishers selling their books in shops (including chains or online retailers such as Amazon) via a distributor. Up until the arrival of Amazon, the market operated following pretty clear-cut mechanisms, including, crucially, what is known as the bookseller discount: if you buy a book at a physical bookshop, a fraction of the money you pay—roughly speaking half—will go to the bookseller. It's simple to see how the arrival of Amazon, with its reduced prices, has put considerable strain on this system (the details differ in different countries, depending on the underlying rules and regulations of the book markets). In the US, people would simply stop buying a book at a shop if they could get it online for less, thus destroying large parts of the physical book-selling business.

As a photographer, you might be tempted to think that none of that concerns you much. But if you make a photobook, chances are you will need to be aware of these underlying mechanisms. If you work with a publisher, your publisher will take care of things, of course. But if you self-publish your book, and you want to sell it through specialty bookshops such as Strettell's Dashwood Books or Wanderer's 25books, you will have to agree to the bookseller discount. This brings us to Wanderer's second market, the independent market, covering small and self-publishers (both of which usually don't work with distributors—those that do can be thought of as operating in the regular market as well). "The main problem is that there are no distribution procedures in place," says Wanderer, "and the work of physical and online booksellers is being made hard or even impossible." There turn out to be a multitude of problems associated with this, many of which essentially boil down to photographers (or small publishers) being unaware of standard business practices. As noted earlier, bookshops make their money through the bookseller discount. If the discount is too low, if, in other words, the bookseller won't make enough money from a possible sale, s/he is unlikely to carry the book. Furthermore, given the lack of a distributor, especially self-publishers often completely neglect the aspect of shipping their books, resulting in high costs, which, in turn, result in decreased sales. Even worse is an unawareness of other standard business practices, such as being able to properly pack and ship books (resulting in damaged books, which a bookshop cannot sell at all or only at a reduced price), to deal with customs in the case of international shipping, or to simply write a proper invoice. These are all very basic problems that can easily be overcome with very little work. A photographer self-publishing her book needs to do basic research covering these aspects before selling her books (for example, research suitable packing materials and preorder them before offering books etc.).

But what is putting considerable strain on small specialty bookshops like his own 25books, says Wanderer, are aggressive attempts by small publishers or self-publishers to sell books: "There are discounts, bundles, free shipping worldwide, Christmas discounts, exclusive signed copies, and many more. For booksellers it then quickly becomes unfeasible to offer such books." This really replicates the Amazon problem: why should anyone buy a book at Dashwood Books or 25books if they can get it online for less? Obviously, as a small or self-publisher, you do not need to work with these shops. You can sell your books only online, and that's fine. But these kinds of specialty bookshop are well known, and many of them are in locations that allow for thousands of visitors. Having your book at Dashwood Books or 25books will give it a visibility and added credibility that you cannot get from offering it only on a website. Wanderer is not too upbeat about the prospects of photobooks without specialty shops: "I doubt that without these book sellers the publishers' networks will suffice to create a lasting business." It would be tempting to conclude that, of course, someone with a bookshop would argue this way. But Wanderer also publishes books and thus looks at things from more than one angle.

Lastly, there is the collectors market, for which Wanderer appears to have limited appreciation: "It is easy to understand the increases in price of old out-of-print books. However, many books are being marketed as collectors' items even when they are being published, with a small edition size, signed and numbered copies, available only for a short period of time. That only results in buyers who are not interested in the actual content of a book. This development moves the focus of books away from content, quality, and engagement with the book." Anyone perusing lists of newly published photobooks usually can easily detect books made for this particular market, especially if the price point is quite high.

That said, things are probably a little bit more complex than Wanderer would have it. For example, offering a special edition of a photobook—along with the regular one—often is a fantastic way for a photobook maker to recoup fairly large fractions of the production costs. For example, it is straightforward to sell, say, ten or 20 copies of the final book along with a signed and numbered print (or maybe more than one) in a custom-made box or container, for a relatively high price to collectors. Many photographers or smaller publishers follow this route, given that the possible income can be considerable. There merely is an added product for the collectors market that, crucially, does not compete with the product for the other market the book might find itself in. For Mike Brodie's *A Period of Juvenile Prosperity*, published by Twin Palm Publishers, TBW Books, which is run by Paul Shiek (who also manages Brodie), produced a limited edition: "The book comes repackaged in a screen printed dust jacket printed on 75 lb. butcher. The jacket design originates from Brodie's handwritten notes from the afterword of the book itself. Book comes housed in a screen printed and signed slipcase referencing again, the simplest and most common of materials, unfinished chip board. In the back of the book you will find a 9 x12 in. C-Type print. Printed on Kodak F-Surface paper. Signed and numbered on verso."[7] There are 75 copies, and they're being sold for $1,000 each. Clearly, the limited edition is in no competition with the regular edition of the book. This kind of approach can be very useful for self-publishing photographers.

2.5 Aspects of Photobook Publishing

Let's now look at the different aspects of photobook publishing. Some of them are going to be covered in the following chapters. Anyone interested in making a photobook, whether working with a publisher or on her or his own, needs to be aware of these various aspects, because they all have to be dealt with.

Photobook publishing essentially can be divided into two separate stages, the production stage and the post-production/market stage. This book is looking into the production stage in detail in the following chapters, covering the most important of its challenges. The different aspects of the post-production stage are equally important, and they mostly concern business/market problems.

The following tasks have to be addressed during the production stage. The combination of those tasks will result in a set of photographs being transformed into a photobook in the form of the actual objects, in whatever edition size:

- Defining the core concept of the book
- Editing the source photographs
- Sequencing the edit
- Production of the text component(s)
- Design of the book: Layout of photographs, design of text components
- Decision making: Materials, printing, and binding
- Preprinting file preparation
- Printing (including, ideally, press checks)
- Binding

All of these bullet points are going to be covered in full detail over the course of the following chapters.

Assuming all of these steps have been completed successfully, we now have a photobook, or rather a large number of identical photobooks, waiting to be picked up at a bookbinder. Obviously, people don't go to bookbinders to buy books. This brings me to what I called the post-production/market stage. Its various steps are:

- Transportation of books to (a) warehouse(s)
- Transportation of books to bookshops (where applicable)
- Advertising the book
- Selling the book

Photographers who self-publish their book often completely underestimate the time and effort involved in this stage. Publishers, in contrast, have specific and well-defined procedures to deal with it.

To begin with, the printed books have to be stored somewhere (a warehouse). Given that the photobook market is an international market, there often are warehouses in different continents. Books are relatively expensive to ship. It is easier (and cheaper) to send 500 copies in a container from, say, Europe to the US than to send 500 copies separately to people buying one. High shipping costs are a very good deterrent for possible buyers.

Given that many of the problems of the post-production stage are of a logistical nature, many publishers work with separate companies that specialize in this particular type of business. These companies are called distributors. In a nutshell, a distributor will take care of the transportation of books (getting them to—mostly larger/chain—bookshops), and it will also be engaged in the promotion.

Much like publishers, distributors are businesses—as are bookshops. In fact, everybody involved in the making of a book—the printer, binder, publisher, distributor, bookseller—will want to get a fraction of the final price of the book. So one can think of the final price of a book as the sum of all these different parts: production costs plus distributions costs, and whatever might be left then would be the profit (which in the case of a publisher would be used to essentially subsidize other books). Dewi Lewis: "A key problem is that if you follow the traditional sales model—selling through shops and using a distributor and sales reps—then the return from the retail price is pretty low. We work on the basis of receiving an average return of 35% of the retail price. And, of course if you end up with unsold copies then the effective return is much less than 35%." If the retail price of a book is, for example, $50, 35 per cent of that would be $17.50. "For me," Gordon Stettinius notes along the very same lines, "the margin involved with producing these books is pretty lean. It is done more with an eye towards contributing to the discussion of fine art photography that I enjoy." As I noted earlier, while aware of the bottom line, publishers really care about photography.

"The ideal would be to sell everything direct," says Lewis, "and avoid these high discounts. If we could make such a model work then we could achieve viability on much smaller print runs and thereby reduce the risk element." Stettinius seconds the sentiment: "I am happy to sell the books through my online store or through book signings because I can then realize a respectable profit on those books I sell." Increasingly, photobook publishers are moving towards such models, so that their books might be listed on Amazon.com, but under the "Marketplace," and then sold not at the kinds of discount the site has become well known for, but for the regular list price. But again, things are a little bit more complex according to Stettinius: "The actual visibility for my books depends more upon the size and reach of my distributor, D.A.P./ARTBOOK. The distributor and major bookstores will move the majority of my books and their involvement allows me to produce larger runs and push my per unit costs down a bit." There is no disagreement with Lewi about the advantage of direct sales: "Anyone who buys their copy of our book from a publisher directly, rather than from the bigger online entities, is doing that publisher a kindness." This is, coincidentally, the situation self-publishing photographers find themselves in, as we will see in the next section. According to Stettinius, the stakes go beyond simple market arguments: "Independent publishing is collectively responsible for a staggering number of new titles and continuing opportunities out there. If independent publishers cannot stay afloat, then we are back to only a few corporate and institutional players telling us what we should be paying attention to." This sums up the essential struggle of the larger photobook publishing business.

2.6 Working with a Publisher vs. Self-Publishing

Photobook publishers have a very good understanding of how the different publishing components work together. A photographer working with a publisher will not have to worry about production or distribution of her or his book. At the same time, working with a publisher will result in a loss of control over the final book. A publisher might insist on a different edit or design or maybe different cover, or on a smaller (rarely larger) edition size, on a more cheaply made book, etc.

Photographers will frequently bemoan this loss of control and consequently self-publish their books. Self-publishing a book means having to take care of all these different aspects of production and distribution that I outlined earlier. This is absolutely doable. At the same time, the amount of time and effort needed to distribute (aka sell), let's say, 1,000 books can be immense. Seen that way, the gain of control comes at the often considerable extra cost of a lot of work that has to be done after the book is made—a part of self-publishing that usually is completely ignored.

What is more, photobook publishers know their market quite a bit better than photographers. They know how to market a book, they know what has a higher chance of selling, and what should be avoided. Thus, photographers who are interested in approaching publishers should spend time looking at their catalogues and at actual books made by them. This will give them an idea what to (roughly) expect in terms of the materials, the design, the print quality, etc. A publisher who for example mostly works with very well-established older photographers shooting in black and white is probably less likely to publish a New Formalist color book by an emerging artist. It makes very little, if any, sense for a photographer to approach publishers for which the proposed book would clearly not fit into the overall program of photobooks established over years. This kind of information can be obtained easily by looking at publishers' back catalogues, many of which can found online. As is almost always the case, doing the proper research before venturing out and approaching people is most important for photographers.

As we have seen already, working with a publisher has advantages and disadvantages. Even though in the first half of the twenty-first-century's second decade self-publishing has become all the rage, part of its appeal is based on a profound if not misunderstanding then at least underestimating what publishers actually do.

Things usually become truly tendentious once the question of money is being brought up. It has become common for many publishers to ask photographers to contribute money to enable the production of a book. There is no general consensus among publishers how this topic is approached, however. There are publishers that will always ask for money, there are publishers that might ask for money, and there are publishers that do not ask for money from their photographers.

From what I can tell, at least in the United States a lot of photographers are under the impression that a) a publisher will always cover all the costs and b) that there will be a financial profit for them at the end. Neither a) nor b) is always the case. In fact, it's common for publishers to ask for financial support, and photographers should not expect to make money from their photobooks at all. Of course, in an ideal world publishers wouldn't ask for money, and a lot of money would be made with photobooks. We do not live in such an ideal world, unfortunately.

"In Germany," observes Markus Hartmann, "I think most photography students have heard that they have to invest money, and that they have to be happy when they get accepted by a publisher. And they approach things right away with the mindset that they have to cover part or all of the costs." This might, in fact, be in line with a historical trend. According to Hartmann, "it's not a new topic that books have to be financed. There is a nice small book by Francis Haskell, *The Painful Birth of the Art Book*. Expanded from a talk he gave, Haskell traces the history of the art book back to the seventeenth century. He proves that the art book has always depended on sponsors and patrons who supported it." Given that this topic presses so many buttons, it might help to take a step back even further and look at more parts of the larger picture. For a start, photographers often spend considerable amounts of time and money on their work. This includes, for example, the costs of their photographic equipment (cameras, lenses, film or storage media etc.) and the costs of whatever post-processing tools are used, whether they are in a darkroom (chemicals, paper, etc.) or not (in which case there are computers, printers, ink, possibly a scanner etc.).

If a photographer has an exhibition of her or his work, it is not uncommon for the exhibition space (whether it is a commercial gallery, a museum, or any other such space) to expect her or him to cover at least a part of the printing and framing of the work. Printing and framing photographs can run up fairly high bills. Of course, it would be nice if there weren't any costs associated with publishing a book (or getting it published). But the reality is that, just as in any other area of photography, there are. Seen that way, a publisher asking for a contribution to the production costs is not that different from a commercial gallery asking the photographer to cover parts (if not all) of the costs of printing and framing.

What is more, unlike exhibitions photobooks have a long lifespan. They literally go out into the world, bringing a very important part of a photographer's work into the homes of complete strangers. It is not too far fetched to think of them as the photographer's ambassadors. Seen that way, they are also promotional tools for a photographer. No direct connection can be easily made, but someone familiar with a photobook might decide to, for example, buy a print or hire the photographers for an assignment. Promotional tools, of course, should be part of a photographer's arsenal, and they tend to cost money. "If you have a printed book," notes Markus Hartmann, "something like that just works a lot better than using an email and a PDF. Emails just pass by. But when there is a nice book on the table people enjoy looking at it. That's the big advantage of the book—it simply doesn't disappear somewhere on a hard drive, never to be looked at again." And this is not just some general theory. Hartmann approached Markus Brunetti's body of work *Facades* in this way, producing a book, yet using it strictly as a promotional tool: "We said there would be no distribution. You can only buy the book at an exhibition or directly with us, provided you find us. Every once in a while someone would research the book online and place an order. But we managed to sell 1,500 books this way, using exhibitions and direct distribution. There was no book seller discount, so we made the full amount of money. Originally we thought we would have to invest a few thousand euros, seeing it as advertising. But in the end, we actually made a little money. We didn't get rich, but it worked a whole lot better than I expected." Selling 1,500 copies of a book that is not available in bookshops and that was not generously promoted online is quite a feat.

The promotional aspect aside, the real question behind the aspect of money in publishing should not be: why is this publisher asking for money? It should be: given the publisher is asking for money, what am I getting in return? Remember, publishers are businesses—and not charities. We all might have some idea about how the world should be run. But the reality of how it is run, meaning here: how a publisher can survive as a business in an incredibly tough and tricky market, cannot be ignored.

Dewi Lewis is upfront about how his publishing house deals with this issue: "These days we finance around 50/60 per cent of the cost but this varies from minimal or no input on some titles to 100 per cent on others." The main reason is very obvious and simple: "The bottom line is quite simply that I'm not in a position to risk the $400k to $500k or so that we spend on production each year." But as before, the details are complex. For a start, for Lewis funding plays no role in the initial approach: "Our starting point is always the project and not whether it has funding. In an average year we turn down dozens of approaches which are funding led." Given photobooks are objects in a marketplace, very basic considerations of how marketplaces operate apply: "If we publish someone like Martin Parr, Anders Petersen, Pentti Sammallahti, or Simon Norfolk then we don't need any funding as these are commercially viable projects. We can do a sufficiently large print run and we have a reasonable guarantee of sales. The difficulties arise with emerging photographers. The print runs must be much more cautious and even then everything is a risk. The shops are much more nervous about taking copies and there is no reservoir of 'followers' of the photographer." As has become clear from the above, publishers build photographers' audiences.

Dewi Lewis' assessment of the overall situation is apt: "The reality is that the majority of photobooks are now funded in one way or another. This is unlikely to change and it is a scenario that does cause me concern. It creates an uneven playing field—with emerging photographers without access to financial resources at a critical disadvantage." How this situation can be improved is unclear.

If a publisher asks for a financial contribution, instead of expecting such a contribution to be non-existent, a photographer might want to ask whether it is worth it, given what is being delivered in return. As I outlined earlier, publishers do provide a lot of services and expertise that a self-publisher would have to cover her or himself.

Of course, a photographer might still decide to self-publish her or his book. But this decision should be based on a cost–benefit analysis and not on moral indignation and/or unrealistic expectations. Self-publishing and working with a publisher also need not be necessarily completely independent. As a promotional tool, a book can be relatively cheap, compared with its potential impact—especially if high-quality digital technologies are used. In that case, the "possibility of being able to print a small edition for 1,000 or 2,000 euros should be a shot in the arm for the self-publishing scene." says Markus Hartmann. "I can sell those books to friends, acquaintances, and family, and I have copies I can send to publishers, book sellers or collectors." And it's important to keep in mind that a photobook in this case would not just be like a promotional item like a postcard. Instead, it is its own piece of art. A photobook clearly can wear more hats than just one.

There is one more aspect of publishing that has not been mentioned, yet, and that is the question of cachet. Publishers all have their own reputation that is informed both by their history and by how the topic publishing itself is being viewed. As I mentioned earlier, in the early 2010s self-publishing has become the model that attracts most attention. But there is no guarantee this situation will not change. For example, in the 1970s, photobooks published with a financial contribution by photographers were commonly belittled as "vanity publishing." How things have changed! Forty years later, self-publishing, the ultimate form of vanity publishing, is being celebrated as the most daring way to publish photobooks!

A photographer thinking about publishing a book needs to take the topic of cachet into consideration. Maybe self-publishing comes with considerable extra costs, and it might require a lot of extra work and time, but maybe that all is offset by the cachet gained? But then a well-known publisher might want to work with her or him, and one cachet (self-publishing) is replaced by a different one (a well-known publisher that might have a very impressive history).

As before, there is no single answer to how to go about this topic. Every photographer needs to come to her or his own decision about how to publish their book. That decision needs to be based on a cost–benefit analysis. This is what photobook publishing comes down to. As a result, a much more realistic approach to photobook publishing for a photographer would be to assume that a) there will be costs (which can be considerable) and b) the resulting photobook will not make any money.

How or whether photobooks will make money for a photographer is a tricky question that depends on all kinds of parameter. Realistically speaking, most photobooks will not sell their whole edition. There might or might not be money made in return. Instead of entering an unknown quantity into the cost–benefit analysis, it seems much simpler to assume the profit will be zero. That way, any financial analysis will not rely on unforeseeable, uncertain results. And if there is a profit, then it will be a real profit.

2.7 How to Approach Publishing as a Photographer

The preceding should have made clear that photobook publishing contains a large number of aspects that are not discussed much in photobook reviews or articles, or even in most of the various books about photobooks. As is obvious from the fact that a lot of photobooks get published, none of the challenges outlined above is insurmountable. The key for any photographer who is interested in publishing her or his book, either with a publisher or not, is to be as prepared as possible.

It is important to realize that if there is a difference between the two modes of publishing, that difference certainly is not necessarily apparent from photobooks themselves. Self-published books often are just as professionally produced as those by the best publishers; and, sadly, there are commercial publishers whose output compares to the worst of self-publishing. What this means for photographers is that quality itself has disappeared as a criterion for making a decision how to proceed. Any quality can be had—it's only a matter of paying careful attention to the details of a chosen mode of publishing, and to—often—having the financial resources available.

The following chapters are going to cover most of the relevant photographic aspects of photobooks. As for the non-photographic aspects, those concerning the business aspects, they were briefly outlined above. Regardless of which route a photographer decides to take (working with a publisher or self-publishing), unless she or he already has experience with the journey it is most important to speak to as many people who have already followed the route as possible.

Most publishers are very open and upfront about what exactly is going to be entailed in working with them. A photographer should be prepared to ask as many questions as possible to find out about details that are unclear. At the same time, it is important to find the right balance between trying to enforce aspects of the desired book and being open to suggestions or demands by the publisher. For example, if a publisher insists on a different title for a book or on a different cover image, this is usually based on having published books before. The choice of cover image can make a huge difference, given that people approach books they don't know based on their first appearances.

This is not to say that publishers are always right. Neither are photographers. Dogmatism is very likely going to cause huge problems along the line of the production, especially if it is coming from an inexperienced photographer. Actually, dogmatism might not even lead to a situation where there are clashes with a publisher. Dewi Lewis: "Very few projects arrive as perfectly formed book dummies. And from my own perspective I am not that interested in projects in which I can't have a creative input. As a publisher who also designs a large percentage of our output, I see my role as working with the photographer at every stage of the process. Often if I feel that a photographer is not open to our input then it can be a very strong reason not to take on a project." One of the benefits of working with a publisher, especially a very experienced one, is that there exists a repository of knowledge that can massively improve what a photographer considers to be a good book.

"My way or the highway" thus is probably the worst possible attitude to have for a photographer working with a publisher. After all, publishers have a vested interest in preserving their business (certainly not the photographer's over their own). If a publisher wants to publish a book in exactly the way in which it is being presented by a photographer, that's great. But photographers are well advised to be very open to suggestions or requests for change.

In the case of self-publishing, a photographer might want to approach other photographers who have published a book this way. Given a self-publisher needs to take care about a lot more aspects of a book than a photographer working with a publisher, it makes no sense diving blindly into what is a pretty tricky territory. Why repeat the mistakes other people have already made? Why not avoid pitfalls that can be avoided with a little bit of research?

Avoiding well-known pitfalls is especially important for self-publishers, given that the number of people working on the book usually is much smaller than in the case of producing a book with a publisher. Often, one person—the photographer—attempts to do everything at the same time, and this can be a recipe for disaster. This is not to say that a single person cannot be a good photographer, editor, designer, writer, producer, and bookseller at the same time. But most people simply are not able to wear that many hats. And there really is no reason why anyone should. For any photobook, says Markus Hartmann, the "question of format is decisive: what does the topic require? And then, in accordance with the topic, decisions have to be made about the choices of paper, binding, layout and design, and text. Through their education, photographers often have a semi-creative background and want to do everything themselves. And there are cases where this works out. But in the majority of cases it would have been better to get together with a designer or publisher to get input." Given there are so many professionals easily available, however, possibly at a cost, there is no reason for photographers to try to do it all on their own.

To provide an example of another one of the big problems of self-publishing, the issue of selling and especially shipping a book usually is completely underestimated. For a book to arrive in the same state it was sent in it needs to have been packed carefully. This is especially true for international shipping. A very common problem is created by dented corners, for example. Corners dent easily, unless the book is packed properly, and a customer might simply want to return the damaged book and get an undamaged replacement, especially if she or he is a collector. Of course, the issue of packaging materials can be solved easily. Given a book's size is known, packaging materials—in the form of boxes or customizable cardboard mailers—can be ordered easily. But self-publishers often do not consider this aspect until the binder delivers the books.

A related problem is caused by shipping costs, especially if a book is sent internationally. The photobook market is spread out over various continents, and shipping books is expensive: even though books are usually not overly big, they are quite heavy, given their size. This often results in fairly large shipping costs. To give an example, if someone in Germany, say, wants to order a book from the US, and the book costs $30, with $15 shipping costs, the potential buyer might be discouraged: why pay so much extra just for shipping? In much the same fashion, shipping within the US can be expensive. Needless to say, this problem can be solved by a self-publisher by factoring part of the shipping costs into the final price of the book and by then offering lower shipping rates. The same book selling for $40 is, of course, more expensive, but $5 shipping from the US to Germany is a steal! And within the US, books can be sent via media mail, which is quite cheap.

What this amounts to is a careful consideration of all the variables—production costs as well as shipping costs—into the final price of a book. This is exactly the kind of calculation that publishers always do, simply because they know what they are dealing with. Self-publishers, however, are on their own. Thus, asking other self-publishers for advice is a very good step towards identifying and solving unforeseen problems.

Cristina de Middel's *The Afronauts* is one of the major success stories of a self-published photobook. Released in 2012 in an edition of 1,000 copies, the book very quickly became highly sought after and sold out eventually. The reality behind the story provides some good lessons. Self-publishing, de Middel notes, " was the logical thing to do after all the work and time spent in the project, but I had no clue of what it meant and the huge amount of work that selling the book one by one [entailed.] [...] I never thought of contacting a publisher because I didn't know anyone and it made no sense to ask for help when you can do it by yourself, no? I was very optimistic and had nothing to lose (other than money) so I didn't think about it very much." De Middel worked with designers Laia Abril and Ramon Pez (who later produced *The Epilogue*, which we will start looking into in the next chapter). She was aware of the pitfalls of making the book, yet unprepared for the stages thereafter: "I understand the production process always has problems with the printer, the paper or what not, but most of the time you can solve them with more time, more money or both. But the distribution and the promotion is the real unavoidable nightmare for self-publishers." Promotional aspects always are complex for any artist, requiring time (and often money). But "it took me almost two months to be able to send most of the books," de Middel eventually found out: "I had absolutely no strategy and that is why it was such a mess!" This is not necessarily bad news for self-publishers, however, since distributing and/or selling a book can be outsourced. De Middel: "My advice is to hire someone who is comfortable with doing it, give that person a percentage of the benefit and forget about it. Basically get someone who can do what distributing companies do for publishing houses but at a small scale." One would probably need to add that smaller edition sizes reduce the problem in scale. But the basic underlying challenges remain. They can be solved—by a photographer simply doing everything themselves, but s/he has to be prepared to spend considerable amounts of time on aspects such as writing invoices, tracking shipments, dealing with the post office and/or shipping companies etc.

The considerations just examined expand the list of tasks a self-publisher has to deal with as follows:

- Defining the core concept of the book (covered in Chapter 3)
- Editing the source photographs (covered in Chapter 4)
- Sequencing the edit (Covered in chapter 4)
- Production of the text component(s) (covered in Chapter 3)
- Design of the book: Layout of photographs, design of text components (covered in Chapter 5)
- Decision making: Materials, printing, and binding (covered in Chapters 3 and 6)
- Preprinting file preparation (covered in Chapter 6)
- Printing (including, ideally, press checks) (covered in Chapter 6)
- Binding (covered in Chapter 6)
- Transportation of books to (a) warehouse(s):
  In all likelihood, self-publishers are not going to have a warehouse available, in which they can store their books. They might use their studio space (if they have one) or their own home. Transportation from the binder to whatever space is being used can usually be easily arranged by the binder.
- Transportation of books to bookshops (where applicable):
  Chain bookstores work with distributors, and many distributors are very unlikely to work with self-publishers. So it often falls on the self-publishers to send their books to whatever

bookshop is willing to sell it. In most cases, these are going to be the shops that specialize in photobooks, such as, for example, Dashwood Books in New York or 25books in Berlin. It is up to the self-publisher to contact the shops, see whether they will carry the books, arrange for the split in the sale price, the book-seller discount (50:50 is very common), and arrange for books to be shipped (or brought) to the shops.

- Advertising the book:

  Advertising/promoting a photobook is an incredibly important part of making one especially for self-publishers. Unlike in the case of publishers where buyers often check the catalogues or are on mailing lists, especially first-time self-publishers start out from scratch. Promotion of the book can entail a large mix of activities, such as promotions on social media online (Facebook, Twitter, etc.), attending photobook fairs (which usually incurs costs in form of traveling, accommodation, and, of course, the cost charged by the fair), sending out review copies to critics, writers, and/or bloggers who might cover the book etc.

- Selling the book:

  To some extent, the internet has leveled the playing field as far as selling books is concerned. While chain bookstores are unlikely to be willing to carry many, if not most self-published books (then again, chain bookstores mostly don't carry photobooks anyway), there is very little difference between what a publisher and self-publisher can do online. Self-publishers can use Amazon.com through its "Marketplace" (note that Amazon.com will specify the shipping charges!). Books can also be sold through websites, with payment systems such as PayPal making monetary transactions relatively straightforward.

Most of the aspects of selling photobooks online are simple to figure out. In terms of the logistics, determining the shipping costs *a priori* is important (otherwise, the sale of books can easily turn into cutting into what little profit was to be had), as is finding the right reliable shipping materials (boxes or mailers, bubble wrap, etc.). The key to all of this is to investigate all the options beforehand, so that once the book is listed online, selling and shipping a book becomes little more than a routine transaction.

As indicated already, over the course of the following chapters, the actual making of a photobook will be looked into in a lot of detail. There is a reason, however, why I decided to spend two full chapters on aspects of photobooks that for a lot of photographers are more like an afterthought: The process of making a photobook, whether in collaboration with a publisher or as a self-publisher, involves a lot more aspects than are usually being discussed. It is extremely important to be aware of them (especially in the case of self-publishing), because they have repercussions for the object photobook as a whole.

For example, even such a simple property as the size of a book has obvious repercussions. It might conceptually make sense to create a very large photobook for a body of work. But such a very large book then might not fit into the kinds of bookshelf most people have in their homes. Where are potential buyers going to store the book? This might appear to be a trivial concern, but it is not. On top of that, a very large book is likely to be problematic in terms of how it can be shipped. Taken together, an oversize book might simply sell less well because people don't know where to put it and because the shipping costs are too large.

In much the same fashion, many of the aspects of photobooks that are going to be discussed in the following chapters might have some repercussions that go beyond the basic concept of the book, whether it is elaborately produced books requiring a high price tag (which will reduce the number of people who can literally afford buying it) or being hard to handle (ditto), softcover books looking or feeling more cheap than hardcover books, or whatever else.

It's most important to realize that a photobook maker is unlikely to be able to make the perfect book that is going to appeal to everybody. There is such a large variety of tastes and preferences that aiming for the perfect book is a futile endeavor. Just to give one example, some people really object to photographs being printed across the gutter (center) of a book (more on book terms in Chapter 3). Of course, one can avoid doing that, but that might then result in a more conservative layout, which will make those unhappy who prefer something different.

The idea can thus never be to make a book that makes everybody happy (an impossible goal). Instead, the idea should always be to produce a book that comes as close as possible to conveying the concept of the work best.

But even in that case, it is likely that the final book will be made with a set of compromises, given there will inevitably be restrictions. For example, the desired printing might end up being prohibitively expensive, so a cheaper printing, resulting in a loss of quality, might be necessary. Or a book might not lie fully flat when opened given the choice of binding. Or instead of using a lot of gatefolds, there will be none to keep costs under control. There are many other such compromises a photographer might have to make, simply to produce a book that while not perfect is truly the best possible book, given all the various restrictions.

It is incredibly important for photographers to not only be aware of how the process of making a photobook will inevitably entail making compromises, but to also engage in the process with an open mindset. Being firmly stuck on unrealistic expectations is the worst possible approach to making a photobook.

Given we now know a lot more about photobooks—what they are, how they are made and sold, and what environments they live in—now it is really time to look into how to make one. In the following chapter, I am going to start by looking into how to start thinking about a book, given a finished body of work.

Notes

1. It is conceivable that book publishing is going to move to an on-demand model in the future, where a book might be only printed and bound after a customer decided to buy it.

2. Quoted from Liz Jobey, "Why photobooks are booming in a digital age," *Financial Times*, February 27, 2015, accessed April 20, 2015, at http://www.ft.com/intl/cms/s/2/be1fd978-bceb-11e4-a917-00144feab7de.html.
3. Ibid.
4. http://www.selfpublishbehappy.com/.
5. http://theindependentphotobook.blogspot.com/.
6. http://www.josefchladek.com/.
7. Quoted from TBW Books' website, accessed June 23, 2015, at http://www.tbwbooks.com/specialeditions/brodie-juvenile-prosperity-2-case-book-print.

A. In Focus

Laia Abril—*The Epilogue*

Telling stories with a combination of pictures and text has a long tradition in the history of photography. While the time of the traditional photojournalistic essay in print form for the most part has passed, its tools have been adapted and used in many documentary photography projects. There is, after all, only so much photographs can show, and for everything else you might need text—especially if the story does not allow for a completely open-ended set of interpretations. In photobook form, documentary photography has been enjoying a renaissance, in part because the book is an ideal vehicle for such stories.[1] A recent standout example of a book of this kind is *The Epilogue* by photographer Laia Abril, which was developed in close collaboration with and designed by Ramon Pez.

The book tells the story of the life and death of Mary Cameron ("Cammy") Robinson, a young woman who suffered from an eating disorder and then died because of it. As its title indicates, the book does the job after the fact, with its main character gone, using a variety of different materials such as photographs taken by Abril, archival photographs and materials from the family archives (which are either reproduced through photographs or at times as facsimile pieces inserted into the book), and text in the form of longer transcripts of conversations with family members and friends (only their words are given) and short captions. There is no explanatory text by Abril or a third-person writer, so the viewer/reader has to piece together the story by following and connecting what is given.

Abril found Cammy's family after a lot of research. "I suppose that the fact that I had overcome ten years of bulimia myself, and have lost several friends along the way," she says, "did made her [Cammy's mother] feel that I would quickly understand the complexity of the story that I was going to face." And it quickly became obvious that the story was more complex: "I realized that the focus of my work was no longer just the victim, but also the collateral victims—her family, her friends, her teachers, therapists; they had come to the fore. It was the first time I was going to tell the story of

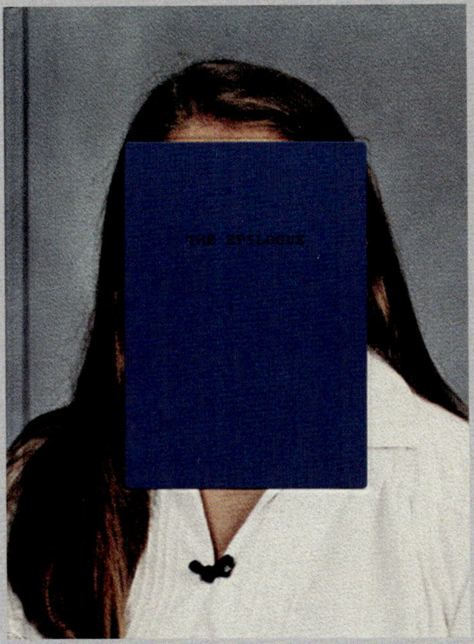

Figure A.1 Front cover of Laia Abril—*The Epilogue* (Dewi Lewis, 2014). Listing the photographer's name only on the spine and back, the cover of *The Epilogue* sets the tone for what is to come inside. The title hints at what the viewer/reader is going to be confronted with—a story after the fact, and the blue box obscuring the photograph of a young woman stands for the search for her identity

someone without hearing her voice: it would become a puzzle to explain who Cammy was through the memories of their loved ones." The use of archival materials almost came naturally: "I saw clearly that the vernacular materials would be key to explain the story of someone who is no longer with us." In other words, while at the time of this writing the use of archival/vernacular material is widely spread in the world of photobooks, here it was very clearly driven by the strong purpose of telling the story, or in Abril's words "to engage with and understand 26 years of someone's life from the point of view of over ten different people." That's a lot to carry for a book, 26 years of a life cut short so tragically.

Abril found inspiration for the way the story was to be told in other forms of media such as cinema or literature. In part, this strategy is driven by a desire to get the viewer/reader emotionally invested. Abril: "The book never says that Cammy has bulimia until (in terms of narrative time) the family knew she had a problem (around 16 to 17 years). The reader has doubts about what's going on. Meanwhile, the family lived with their own doubts. So you empathize with the anguish of that discovery by 'living it with them'." That investment is key to the book for the photographer because there always is the issue of people judging: "The only way I can make people not judge is by forcing them to empathize with the characters. A very good way to do that is through brutal honesty. The family opens all doors and tells you: '*this is what you get*'. That disarms you and makes you connect more deeply. The design of the book makes that possible, making you feel that what you have in your hands is a part of them. The object translates feelings and expectations." In other words, the book is about transporting an experience. Every part of the book, every decision made, is in service of this objective. "Nothing is random or pure aesthetics, everything has a reason." says Abril. "Sometimes, it is more rational, sometimes, it's more emotional. The trifolds not only break the narrative as every fatal event breaks someone's life. But they also hide something: Cammy's first diagnosis, the place where she had her first seizure, the fact that no one wanted to live with her because she had another seizure at home while living with her friends, her death. Bulimia is an illness about hiding things and pretending that 'everything is fine.' This was another way to put that on the table." So of course, it is a bit surprising to see trifolds introduced fairly late into the book, but they follow a strict logic in terms of the time line of events and conceptually as well.

"The book was published by Dewi Lewis," says Abril, "because they understood right away that this project was a research/documentary piece which I wanted to be as accessible as possible in order to get as many people as possible to look at it. So they did their best for that to happen." As we have seen in Chapter 2, for Dewi Lewis, his publishing is driven by faith in the work in question. In this particular case, having interacted with Abril over a period of time, he was convinced it would make for a great book: "It's not a subject that I knew much about or had any personal experience of, yet it was clear as the project developed that the story was being told with great conviction and integrity." The different added elements such as facsimile documents and the trifolds could have easily been a problem, because, in Lewis' words, "often designers have limited knowledge of book production issues and come up with proposals which are only workable at huge additional cost." Here, this problem did not arise. Lewis: "Ramon and I discussed his ideas in a very open way. It was clear to me very early on that he had an excellent knowledge of book production and fully understood how to add interesting elements to a book in the most cost effective way." So clearly, the book was driven by its concept, with the design elements aiming at telling the story. However, everything was produced with eventual costs in mind. In other words, there was a close collaboration between different parties (photographer, designer, publisher). While each was interested in making the best possible book, they each also knew about possible restrictions at their ends, making sure the other parties would be accommodated.

The book's reception by critics and viewers shows its makers' approach was indeed correct. "What is most admirable about the book," according to critic and writer Adam Bell, "is that it handles a tragic and all too invisible disease with compassion and honesty. It's easy to tell a sad story, but hard to do it well." His perception of the book reflects the book's underlying concept, coming from someone only exposed to the story through the object itself: "As readers, we're forced to uncover the secrets at the heart of the story, which draws us closer. The tension between what is purposely revealed and obvious, and what is withheld and we need to uncover mirrors the tragic

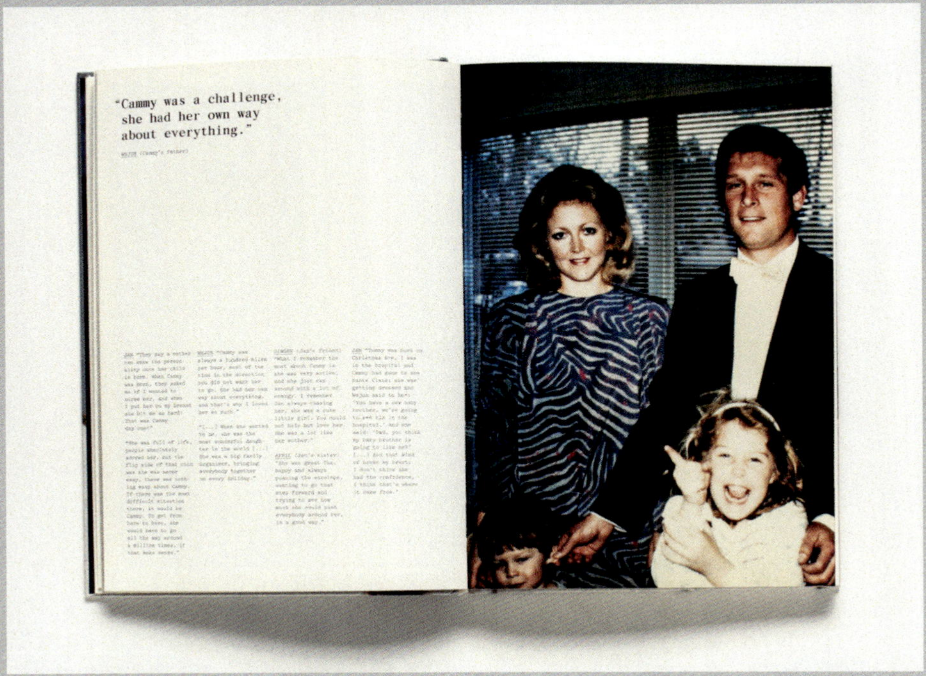

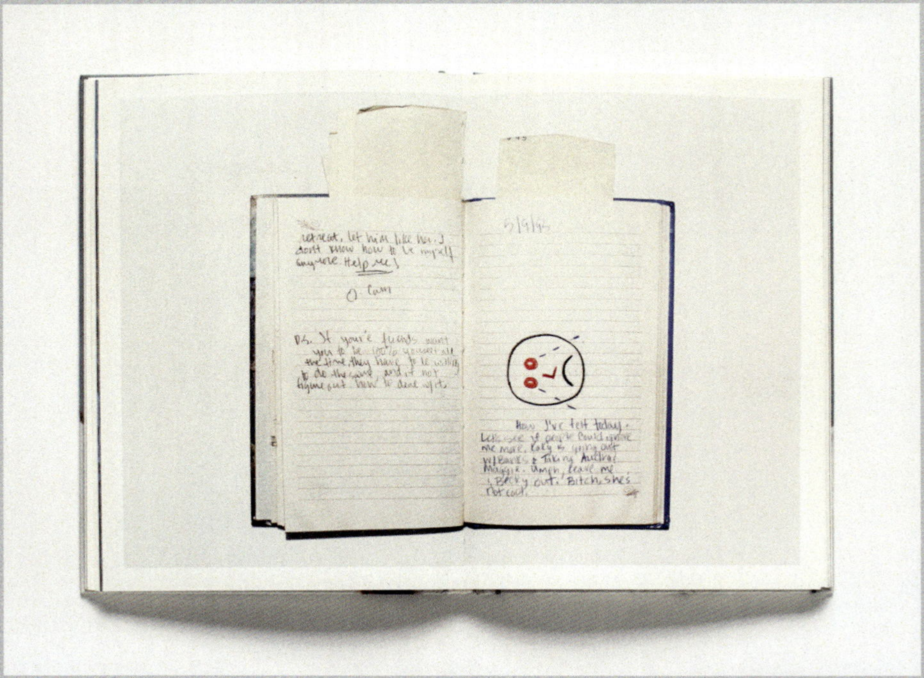

Figure A.2 Selected spreads from Laia Abril—*The Epilogue* (Dewi Lewis, 2014). These spreads demonstrate the variety of the material used in the book to tell the story. It includes photographs by Abril showing family members or friends (top right), photographs from the family's archives (top left and bottom right), photographs of the young woman's personal items (bottom left and right), and facsimiles

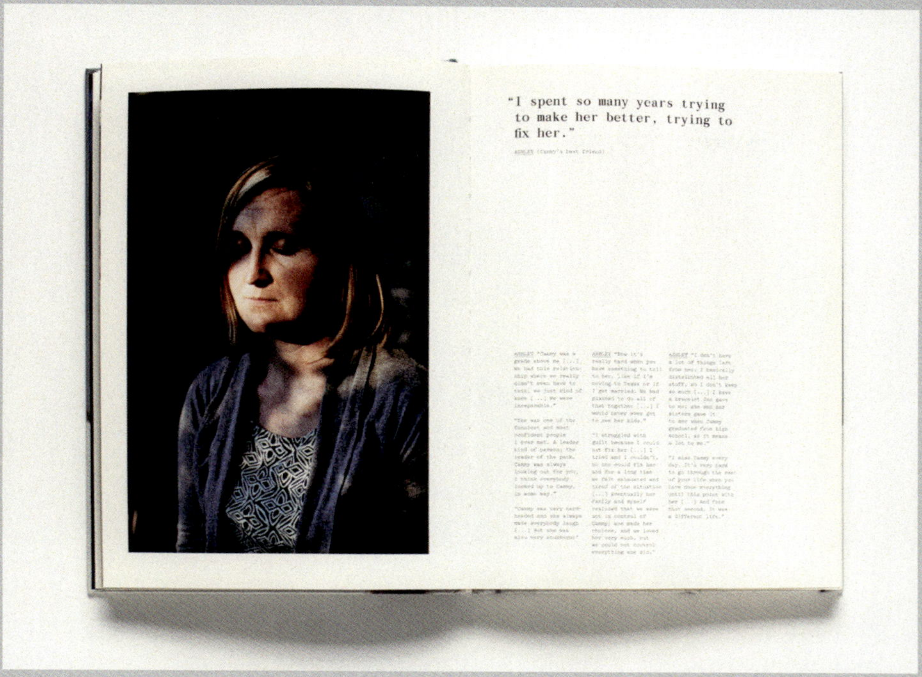

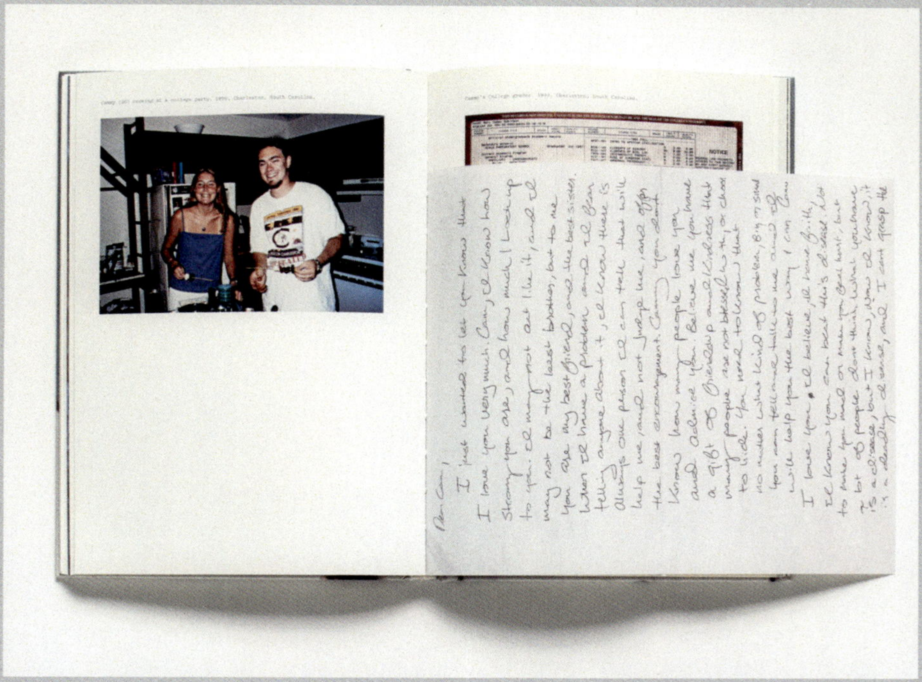

of such items attached to the book (bottom right). In addition, there is text in the form of transcripts of conversations Abril had with family members and friends (top left and right). The story is being told exclusively using these types of material, without any additional text by Abril or any third party other than short explanatory captions

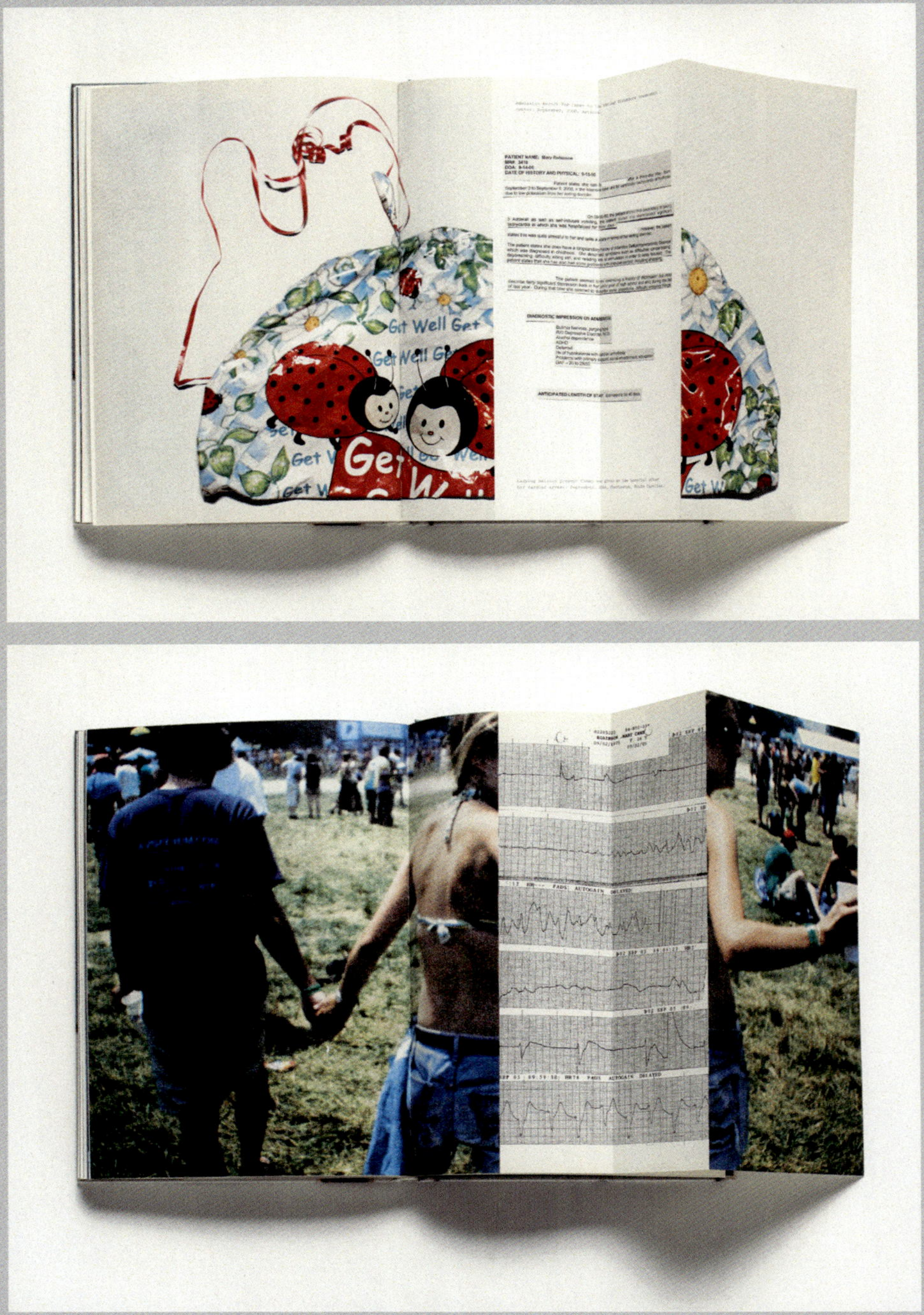

Figure A.3 Selected spreads from Laia Abril—*The Epilogue* (Dewi Lewis, 2014). In the later part of the book, coinciding in the time line with physical breakdowns of the young woman, trifolds are introduced. The first one (top image) shows a deflated balloon given to the young woman after her first cardiac arrest. Inside, parts of the medical admission record, listing, amongst other things, the medical diagnosis. The last one (bottom image) shows an archival photograph, with a medical chart from the day her heart gave out inside

nature of the disease at the heart of the book. Relaying moments of physical, mental or personal difficulty, the physical breaks and folds in the pages also seem to parallel psychic breaks within Cammy's life, as well as emotional ruptures in the book's narrative." And for Bell the book succeeds for the same reasons it does for me: "I think what is most surprising is that despite knowing the devastating outcome the end is so deeply affecting and sad. It's not a story or issue most people want to deal with or acknowledge directly, but it is handled with sensitivity and compassion, and never feels exploitative." Critic and writer Colin Pantall agrees, bringing a very personal background to the book: "I remember reading it at a time when one of my daughter's friends was (and still is) in a clinic for children with eating disorders. It's a really tragic thing. So I came from that very, very personal direction. The book struck a chord through that." Many people I have spoken with have asked whether *The Epilogue* is a photobook, given the amount of text. Being too dogmatic about what is a photobook and what isn't probably doesn't serve the discussion too well. Clearly the text does play a crucial role here. Pantall: "The images are kind of mood pieces. They're setting a particular suburban tone of childhood and family, with a tone of loss that comes through. There is the text in the interviews, and together with the pictures you get a photobook that goes beyond photography. When I was reading it I looked at it as a very personal study of eating disorders. I learned something from that, about how sudden and unexpected the young woman's illness was." Accordingly, for him *The Epilogue* is "a book that goes beyond photography, which is always a good thing." Pantall's assertion might only hint at what photobooks can aspire to, especially documentary ones—provided they are done well.

Note

1. Magazines in large parts of the world are unlikely to commission and run such stories any longer. The photobook has thus become a valuable outlet for this kind of storytelling.

CHAPTER 3

From Pictures to a Book: General Considerations

3.1 Introduction

In light of the preceding chapters, it should be clear that it is extremely important to think of a photobook as more than being a receptacle for photographs. Of course, photobooks are that, given that they contain photographs. But they can be—and I would argue: should be—a lot more. Here is a list of all the different hats a photobook has to wear:

- A photobook ideally presents a fully realized version of a photographic body of work in the form of a very specific object (see Chapter 1). As such, the experience of looking at the book, whether in one or repeated sittings, conveys as much as possible (hopefully everything) the photographer aimed at including in her or his pictures.

  This means that the object's properties are used to contribute to this experience. As we saw in Chapter 1, books are very specific objects, with very specific limitations (such as, for example, only one spread being visible at any given time). So the object "book" places restrictions on the possible presentation. The makers of a photobook have to take these restrictions into consideration and work with (or sometimes around) them to achieve the desired effect.

- A photobook is a commodity that exists in a very specific marketplace (ideally both online and in the real world in the form of bookshops). As such a commodity, a photobook has to compete with all the other books that are also available.

  In a bookshop, a photobook has to grab a customer's attention in multiple ways. First, a customer has to locate the book next to all the other ones on display. Second, the customer then has to get hooked, usually based on a very short timespan—however long it takes people to leaf through a book.

  Online, the situation is comparable, albeit slightly different. On the internet, people cannot easily look through books. Electronic reproductions of a book, whether a PDF or a video, are just that, electronic reproductions, which at best *approximate* the experience of looking at the actual object. At the same time, the browsing experience of online stores usually is also very different, given that every book is presented in exactly the same way, with the same size picture, the same length description, etc.

- A photobook also is a type of commodity that exists in the collectors' market. The collectors' market overlaps with the regular market, but there are different aspects at play. For a start, many collectors favor high production values. A book that has a very high price point might be well beyond what most people would be able (and willing) to buy, but it might easily be within a collector's budget. While most people won't care that much about whether there are only 100 or 1,000 copies available, for a collector the edition size might matter quite a bit, especially if there is a chance that the edition might be sold out eventually, in which case the price of a single book might rise considerably.[1]

All photobooks are subject to these different types of consideration once they are made, regardless of whether or not their makers thought about them beforehand. This is not to say that every photographer should produce a book that, say, specifically caters to collectors. But it is important to keep the various roles photobooks play in mind during every stage of the production, starting right when thinking about what a photobook of a body of work could be. In particular, considerations of the marketplace will inevitably have an influence on how the book is going to be made.

That said, the main focus of a photobook should always be to carry the work inside, to bring its viewer an experience that conveys the artist's intentions with the body of work in question. Given that a book's properties were discussed only briefly in Chapter 1, before proceeding, some important book terms need to be introduced, so we can assume familiarity with them throughout the rest of this book.

3.2 Important Book Terms

The world of books uses a large arsenal of terms to describe their various properties. It is not necessary for a photographer to know all them. However, it is important to have a good understanding of the most important and most commonly used ones. In alphabetical order, the most relevant terms are:

Folio: If you take a single sheet of paper and fold it in half, you get a folio. By construction, a folio has four pages.

Fore edge: The side of the book opposite the spine.

Gatefold: A gatefold adds a fold-out page. When unfolded, the spread is made up of the page without the gatefold plus the front of the unfolded gatefold. Once opened, the spread enlarges to the page without the gatefold plus the opposing page (which previously was covered by the gatefold) plus the back of the now unfolded gatefold. In the case of gatefolds on both sides, the situation changes accordingly.

Gatefolds offer a variety of properties. First, they allow for an additional engagement with the object book. The viewer not only has to simply turn pages, she or he also has to unfold and refold extra pages. Second, by construction, a gatefold offers an opportunity to hide and reveal information. Third, a gatefold changes the number of pages in a spread from two to three. An alternative way of thinking about this is to say that there are two spreads, one with two, one with three pages. Fourth, and this is somewhat related to the previous aspect, a gatefold offers additional space, which often is used in books depicting landscapes for more panoramic views. Last, while gatefolds are attractive for these aforementioned reasons, they come with two major disadvantages: they usually are a lot more expensive to produce (the use of gatefolds is likely to increase the production cost of a book often by a fairly large amount), and the folding pages lend themselves to dog-earing especially if the gatefold runs all the way into the gutter.

Gutter: The central area of an opened book where two opposing pages meet.

Hardcover book: A hardcover book has rigid covers, in the form of (usually) covered boards. The boards are typically covered with cloth or paper. [*Compare*: Softcover book.]

Head: The top of the book.

Perfect binding: A commonly used cheap industrial process, by which a set of pages is bound by applying a thick layer of glue at the spine. A cover is then added (also with glue). Apart from being cheap, perfect binding does not require signatures (which work with a multiple of four pages, see below). However, because of the glue at the spine, perfect bound books cannot be opened to lie flat, and information very close to the gutter can easily be inaccessible. While usually associated with softcover books, perfect binding can also be used to make hardcover books.

Signature: A set of stacked folios. Many books are produced with a set of signatures being bound. Signatures often arise after the printing process when a single sheet of paper is being folded multiple times, with extraneous material getting trimmed off. It is important to keep in mind that the number of pages for any type of signature is a multiple of four. The simplest signature, a single folio, has four pages. A signature with two folios has eight pages. Etc.

Smyth sewing: A commonly used commercial process to bind a set of signatures into a book. A machine will sew through the signature's fold and attach the signatures together, often with an added layer of glue for extra stability. An important advantage of Smyth sewing is that a book produced this way can open/lie completely flat.

Softcover book: A softcover book has flexible covers, usually in the form of a card stock that is thicker/heavier than the paper used for the main pages. [*Compare*: Hardcover book.]

Spine: The cover's spine is the only part visible when a book is stored on a shelf. It usually provides information about the artist, the title of the book, and the publisher. In terms of the binding, the spine covers the area where the folios that make up the book are bound.

Spread: A pair of two opposing pages.

There are a lot more terms and details that can get taken into consideration. These terms provide the minimum requirement for a photographer to understand what needs to be thought about.

Additional aspects might provide extra bells and whistles. But those bells and whistles might eventually add a level of ornamentation that is not necessary for the basic concept of the book, and they can be thought about at a later stage (with the help of specialists such as designers or bookbinders).

3.3 The Concept

I personally think that the most important aspect of a photobook is its concept. Without a concept, it is very hard to make a good photobook. A photobook's concept is tied to both the concept of the underlying body of work and to how the book itself functions.

As explored in Chapter 1, a photobook is the translation of a set of photographs into the form of a book. The book's physical properties provide restrictions on what can be done in book format. It is important to see how the concept of the body of work in question can be translated into this very specific form of presentation.

Using the term "concept" can easily feel like an overly intellectualized approach to making a book. In fact, there is a complementary approach to turning a set of photographs into a book. Instead of thinking about the concept first, a good initial question is: assuming the perfect book can be made for the body of work in question, what kind of experience will the viewer have when she or he looks at the book?

It is probably easier to consider the desired experience, because we all know and remember experiences with photobooks in our libraries. In part, the experience goes back to the handling of a photobook, as described in Chapter 1. In addition to the book causing very specific experiences simply through its physical properties, there are the photographs themselves (plus possibly some text), which do the bulk of the work. For your photobook, what do you want this experience to be?

Thinking about the viewer's experience is a good idea because we all are familiar with looking at very different photobooks. By "different" I here mean both the general form and, of course, their content. The vast majority of photobooks are unique because of their content and because of the way that content is presented. Two different books might cover the same or a very similar subject matter, but given the differences in the photographers' style and in the way the books are put together, in all likelihood we are unlikely to confuse one with the other.

So there are different things coming together here: the photography in question, the form of the book. The experience of looking at the book is determined by both. And this is something anyone interested in making a photobook and anyone looking at photobooks needs to keep in mind. With an existing book, the question posed earlier transforms into: How does this book give me the experience that I am having right now? In particular:

- What does this book do?
- What is it telling me?
- How is it telling me that?
- What are the pictures telling me, and what does the way the book is put together tell me?

3.4 Concept and Audience

In the preceding section, I discussed a photobook's concept in terms of the experience it provides for its viewers. The most basic questions center on what the photographs are telling its viewers and how they are doing it in the context of a book. Answers for these questions can, in fact *should*, probably be found by considering the book's desired or intended audience. To think of an audience might be straightforward, but I often have the feeling that the question of audience comes as an afterthought (at best) for many photographers and photobook makers. What is more, even attempts to find an audience are often done in a manner that suggests the photographer did not spend much time on considering the question: what is my audience?

In the day and age of social media, considerable literal and especially virtual ink is being spilt on the fact that photographers will have to "get their work out there" (to phrase it in a way often heard). How do you do that? Common solutions by business and social media consultants typically focus on the tools, which usually means a set of promotional materials that are to be disseminated in a variety of ways. There obviously is nothing wrong with that. But problems arise when the materials are being used shotgun style: you bombard as many people as possible in the hope that something will stick with someone. In other words, you might hit your target, while essentially sending out spam to everybody else. That's not a good approach. While the various aspects of marketing and promotion are clearly beyond the scope of this book, the general problem of trying to think about one's audience is not at all: what kind of audience does a photobook have? Who might be interested in the book?

The main reason why these questions are extremely important does not concern merely the book's eventual promotion. It also concerns the finding and shaping of the concept. Even in the relatively small world of contemporary fine-art photography there exist multiple audiences, covering such diverse groups as, for example, museum curators, photographers with MFA degrees, commercial photographers, people who are interested in photography, and many more. Of course, there is considerable overlap between these groups. But there also are important differences that a photobook maker needs to keep in mind. To begin with, these different groups have different degrees of visual sophistication. They each are trained (or, as in the case of people who are interested in photography, but who are not professionally engaged in the field, are not trained) to read photographs in specific ways. They also consider photographs in different types of context, using different approaches and sets of background knowledge or training. Just to make this very clear, I do not mean to imply that one group is somehow superior to another. That's not the point at all. Instead, the point is to realize that a book's target audience can, or actually should determine its concept, the way it provides answers to the questions posed at the end of the preceding section.

This boils down to the following questions: given my intended target audience how can I make a book that does the job of reaching that audience well? What are the basic conventions my audience is not only used to, but is, in fact, expecting? And: given my target audience and the resulting restrictions for my book, what are the odds of reaching someone who is not included in that audience? Photographers often fret over small edition sizes and a general inability to reach an audience outside of the narrow confines of contemporary photography. But given that most photobooks are made for an audience that is able to understand visually very complex stories this might not be so surprising. I certainly do not mean to argue that photobooks should necessarily be made for as large and wide an audience as possible. Every photobook will have to find its proper form and audience. But if a photographer is interested in reaching a very large audience, possibly including many people who usually do not spend much time with contemporary photography, then the photobook needs to be accessible. It cannot be overly complex. It might need text that helps viewers understand it.

So a photographer interested in making a photobook should really consider the target audience. The target audience will determine the concept. But to some extent it will also determine factors such as materials, the form (size etc.), even the final price point. Seen this way, zines, for example, are photobooks with a very specific audience. In form, zines often look like very sloppily made photobooks. But to focus on the form misses the point, because zines are made for a very specific audience, usually with very specific concepts in mind. In other words, concept, audience, and form are closely interconnected, and the same is true for every photobook. It's very important to keep this in mind. Thinking about the audience thus is not only a prerequisite for the eventual promotion of the book. It also is extremely important to consider the various aspects that determine the book, and it might help tackling the often tricky question of what the concept might or should be.

3.5 Narrative

A term that is often discussed when talking about photobooks is "narrative." What is commonly misunderstood is that the term "narrative" both means "story" (as in: *what* is the story that is being told here?) and the process or technique of telling a story (as in: *how* is the story being told?). So when thinking about narrative, a book maker needs to be clear about which one of those different meanings is supposed to be addressed. If there is a story in the book, then that story needs to be told in some way, possibly in that unique way that does it best. But the story itself is not the same as the way it is being told. It is very important to keep these two aspects of a photobook apart: what is the story? How is this story being told?

Do all photobooks have to have a story? Actually, no. Of course, in the very broadest terms, all photography is about *something*. So in these very broadest terms, there probably is some sort of story that applies for any body of work. But it is counterproductive to focus on the idea of a story too much, if it is very broad. Let me give you a couple of examples to make this point clearer.

Laia Abril's *The Epilogue* focuses on the story of a young woman who died as a consequence of her eating disorder, and on how family and friends are dealing with it. That is a very specific story that has a clear beginning (the birth of the young woman), and a very clear and touchingly sad outcome (the young woman's death). The book uses photographs and text to tell that story, to explore what could have been responsible for this tragic situation with its very sad ending.

Sze Tsung Leong's *Horizons* features a series of landscapes that are photographed in such a manner that their horizons will line up, with the book essentially presenting a very long—constructed—portrait of our planet by looking at landscape photographs taken all over the world (see Figure 1.3). There is no story here that is even remotely comparable to what can be found in *The Epilogue*. Instead, the book alludes to ideas such as beauty and to how our constructed environments resemble one another (or not) and are offset against pristine ones.

Given that *The Epilogue* has a very clear story, its makers had to think about how to tell the story in such a way that a viewer (and reader—there is a lot of text) would grasp it. In contrast, the makers of *Horizons* mostly had to contend with aesthetic considerations, making sure the different landscapes would line up in such a way that there would be a flow to be experienced for a viewer. Those are two very different kinds of problem. Only in the broadest sense *Horizons* has a story.

Thus, the issue with narrative in a photobook does not boil down to "Do I have to have a story in my book?" (a question I frequently get asked). Instead, it is: "Do I have a story that is being told in my work?" If there is none or if the general story is very broad, there is no need to worry about having one in the book.

It is very important to realize that photobook makers do not have to reinvent wheels that already exist. There are, of course, thousands of well-developed photobooks already in existence. Studying photobooks to see how they tell their stories is a good way to learn about developing a narrative. But it doesn't stop there. Stories are being told in many other forms of art. If you are a reader of fiction writing, you will know that it's filled with stories. If you love watching movies, you know they're filled with stories as well. Of course, the written word operates in very different ways than a collection of photographs, and the same is true for moving pictures that come with sound. But behind all those differences lie ideas that are shared in these different media. As its title makes clear Christopher Booker's book *The Seven Basic Plots: Why We Tell Stories* discusses very basic patterns used to tell stories.[2] Another book would be Ronald Tobias' *20 Master Plots: And How to Build Them.* The point here really is not to see whether there are seven or nine or 20 or however many different ways to tell a story. Instead, it is important to realize that there do exist very well-established patterns that stories can follow (think "rags to riches" or the standard Greek tragedy). As I said before, this does not mean that every photobook has to have a clear, obvious story. But neither do novels or even some movies. What is important for photobook makers to realize is that storytelling, however linear or elliptical or fragmented it might be, has a long history in the arts, and much can be learned from studying examples that do not necessarily have to come out of the world of photography.

3.6 Concept Revisited

Given the differences between the books *The Epilogue* and *Horizons* the questions at the end of section 3.3 can be rephrased. The challenge for a photobook maker is to find good answers to these following questions:

- What is the book supposed to do? What experience should the viewer have?
- What is the book going to tell its viewer? Note, again, that this can be a very specific story or a broad idea. This leads to:
- How is the book going to do that? Which leads to:
- What are the pictures telling the viewer? What does the way the book is put together tell the viewer?

If you have answers for all of these questions, you have the concept of your book. In other words, having a concept for a photobook amounts to having clarity about its most basic and most important properties.

Ultimately, these questions boil down to just a single one that lies at the heart of all photography: what does a particular body of work require? By this I mean that for each body of work to be fully resolved its maker needs to achieve absolute clarity of both what it is (in other words, what it speaks of) and how it has to be presented. In an obvious way, a photobook is a mode of presentation of a body of work—much like an exhibition is. As we saw in Chapter 1, these two modes of presentation are different. What unites them, however, is that the presentation should be driven by the photographs.

Each photographic body of work requires its own specific way of presentation. Of course, this does not mean that there is going to be a limitless number of different ways to, for example, hang an exhibition. An exhibition of a particular body of work might, in fact, look much like or maybe even exactly like that of a different artist's one. But the presentation in the exhibition has to be driven by the photographs in question first. In other words, presentation can be influenced by what other artists have done. But it has to make sense.

Photographers thus should pay careful attention to how their peers both present their work in exhibitions and in book form. Some of these presentations can serve as models or templates. A template is a good template if it applies, though, which is why it is so crucial to obtain full clarity concerning a body of work.

3.7 Concept: Sze Tsung Leong's *Horizons*

At this stage, it probably is worthwhile to discuss examples to see what these seemingly abstract considerations mean in practice. In Chapter 1, we already saw Sze Tsung Leong's *Horizons*, specifically the differences (and actually also similarities) between exhibitions and the book. Photographed in many different locations on this planet over the course of a decade, the series comprises a large number of landscapes (the book, which we will get to later, contains 144). Formally, the photographs are more or less identical (see Figure 3.1 for an example). In each picture, a location is photographed covering a fairly wide angle, with the sky on average making up two-thirds of each image and with the light and colors in every location being uniformly muted and neutral (not all locations provided a completely flat horizon, so there are occasional minor deviations).

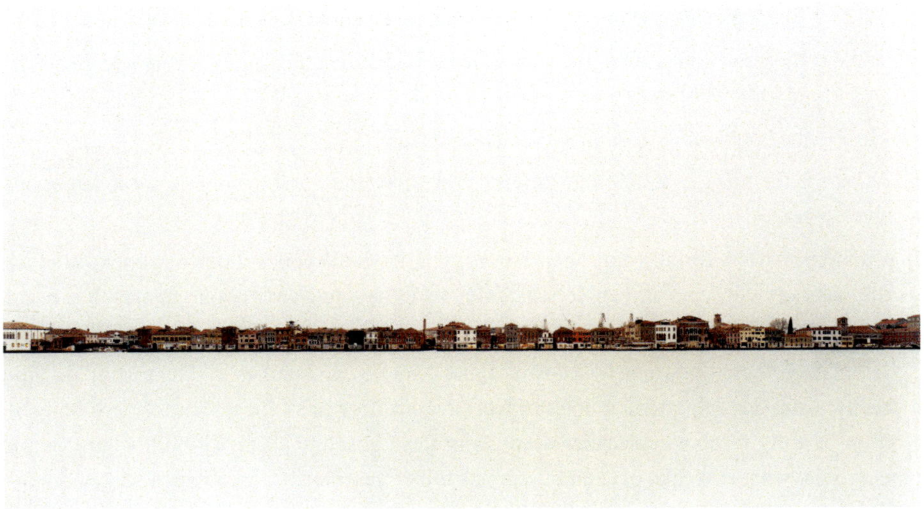

Figure 3.1 Sze Tsung Leong, from the series *Horizons, Canale della Giudecca I, Venezia*, 2007, Chromogenic Color Print
Image © Sze Tsung Leong, courtesy Yossi Milo Gallery, New York

Given the photograph's formal restrictions, placing them right next to each other, with the horizon lines aligned, offers itself as an obvious solution. This is, indeed, how the artist decided to exhibit them (see Figure 3.2). The prints, with small white borders around the images themselves, are displayed in simple white frames, and the frames are hung flush next to each other. That way, each of the locations is being kept distinctly different (each photographs lives in its own frame), but they are made to line up, inviting the viewer to make a connection between places that in reality are far apart. The photographs come in two sizes (14" × 24" with editions of 10 plus two artist's proofs and 28" × 48" with editions of five plus two artist's proofs), with the larger one being used in Figure 3.2.

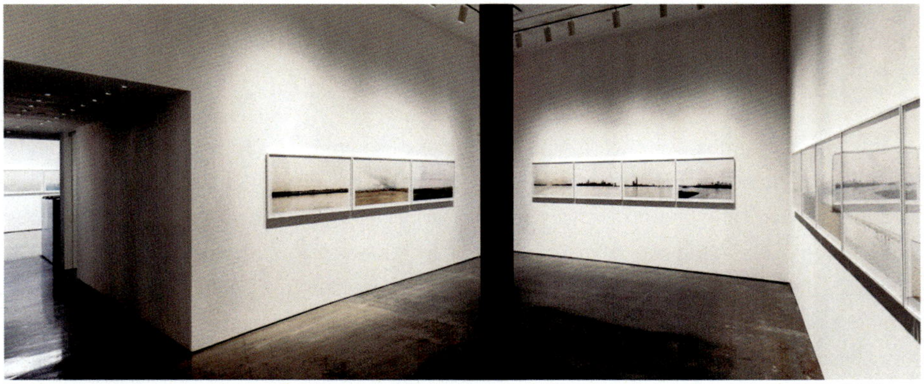

Figure 3.2 Installation view of Sze Tsung Leong's *Horizons* at Yossi Milo Gallery, New York City
Installation view courtesy Yossi Milo Gallery, © Thomas Seely

But this form of presentation is not only based on formal characteristics. The formal characteristics of this particular body of work are driven by the underlying concept, an attempt to make viewers consider this world in ways that deviate from the usual ideas of geographic differences. In other words, by creating a photographic form that is uniform for a large variety of different locations, the presentation actually is already inherent in the work's concept to begin with. The presentation is driven by the concept. Hanging these photographs differently, for example individually with a lot of space around each frame, or in a grid, would undermine some of the very ideas the work was based on.

Not every photographer will be in the somewhat lucky position that the presentation is driven that strongly by the work in question, of course. But an example like *Horizons* presents an obvious case that makes it very clear why and how a very specific presentation was chosen.

Given the fact that *Horizons* is shown in exhibitions as long lines of prints right next to one another, making a photobook from the work leads to an obvious solution. The possibly simplest and most obvious approach is to produce a book that shows pairs of photographs in every spread. The use of gatefolds might add additional images. To ask for more—to have a large number of photographs right next to each other—would result in too a wide a book. The medium photobook thus places restrictions on how *Horizons* can be shown, and the book itself does indeed follow the obvious approach (see Figure 3.3). At 13.7" × 10.9", the book has 176 pages, showing 144 photographs, with six additional double gatefolds, spreads in which a gatefold on the right and left can be unfolded to show a total of four photographs next to one another. Note that given the size of the book, unfolding these gatefolds requires a steady surface to place the book on.

The presentations of *Horizons* in exhibition and photobook form are thus very closely related, with the exhibition probably offering an experience closer to what the work might require. The artist himself certainly thinks so, based on what he said in an interview that can be found in the book. As discussed in Chapter 1, the differences in how viewers physically relate to the exhibitions and the book are unchanged: the act of walking around the exhibition

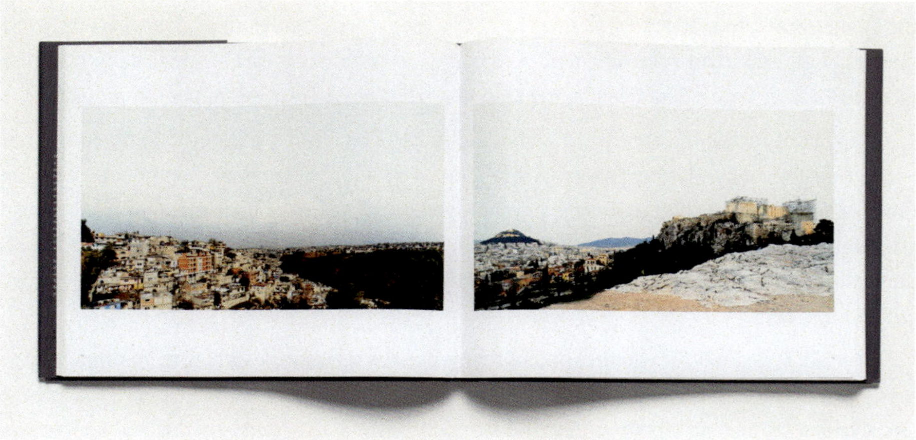

Figure 3.3 Spread from Sze Tsung Leong's *Horizons*, published by Hatje Cantz

becomes part of the engagement with the work (much like how we experience the world to a large extent by moving through it, whether on foot, by car, or however else). The differences in a viewer's physical engagement aside, the two forms of presentation are very similar. *Horizons* thus can serve as an example for work where this could be achieved. But note, it is the photographs themselves, the concept behind them, that drives the forms of presentation.

3.8 Concept: Laia Abril's *The Epilogue*

As already noted, *The Epilogue* deals with the tragic death of a young woman (Cammy Robinson) who had suffered from an eating disorder. Conceptually, it is a very different body of work than *Horizons*, and it thus required very different approaches in essentially every aspect, whether concerning the photography or the presentation in the form of a book or an exhibition. For Abril, the challenge was to, in her own words, "engage with and understand 26 years of someone's life from the point of view of over ten different people." Her solution included the use of not only her own photographs, but also of material provided by the young woman's family, in the form of family photographs and documents of all sorts, including diary excerpts, letters, medical records and more: "I realized that the focus of my work was no longer just the victim, but also the collateral victims—her family, her friends, her teachers, therapists; they had come to the fore. It was the first time I was going to tell the story of someone without hearing her voice: it would become a puzzle to explain who Cammy was through the memories of their loved ones." The basic concept of *The Epilogue* is thus grounded in a journalistic approach—as opposed to the purely artistic one used by Sze Tsung Leong in *Horizons*. Crucially, text is made to play an important role. Abril maintains that the book can in fact be understood without the text. A "goal was that the book would be able to be understood without reading of text; it has different levels of reading: the images, the quotes, interviews, documents, captions ... You can make a more visual read, or more superficial one, and you can even have your own story. Here I had to put a large amount of faith in the reader, deleting many captions that I thought were necessary but that hindered the freedom of the reader to imagine, to get to their own conclusions." But the text itself does play an important role. The text here comes in different forms, such as excerpts from interviews with family and friends, but also text from/in letters, newspaper clippings, etc.

The role of text in the context of a photobook has long been a source of confusion, if not contention for many photographers. Abril decided to adopt a pragmatic approach: "A long time ago I noticed that because of the psychological complexity of the stories, or just because I am not able to solve it with my own pictures, I always needed some kind of text." Beyond that, one might wonder whether it would actually be possible to fully tell *The Epilogue*'s story without any text.

After all, it is doubtful whether photography itself is a language, whether, in other words, it is possible to express in photographs what can be expressed with words (or vice versa). Discussions of that nature very clearly go much beyond the scope of this book. Readers interested in more details about the limitations of photography as a language or to what extent it can be translated into, say, writing might want to read, for example, Sol Worth's text *Pictures Can't Say Ain't*,[3] Larry Gross' *Modes of Communication and Acquisition of Symbolic Competence*,[4] or E.H. Gombrich's *The Visual Image*.[5] Everybody else might simply approach a similarly pragmatic approach as Abril, realizing that while photography is expressive in a very wide variety of ways, it still has its limits. Especially in the context of a photobook, text can help tell parts of a story that photographs, well, can't (the negation actually being one of the things that photographers often struggle with: you can show a photograph of someone or something, but how do you make a photograph that shows the absence of someone or something?).

"All photographs are ambiguous," writes John Berger.[6] "All photographs have been taken out of a continuity. If the event is a public event, the continuity is history; if it is personal, the continuity [...] is a life story. Even a pure landscape breaks a continuity: that of the light and the weather. Discontinuity always produces ambiguity." This is a marvelous observation that points to the core of photography's strength—and, indeed, its weakness. As we will see later when we look into sequencing, this particular ambiguity can be thought of as the main tool to use when dealing with photographic storytelling. But unfortunately, with his following statements, Berger simplifies things a tad too much: "Yet often this ambiguity is not obvious, for as soon as photographs are used with words, they produce together an effect of certainty, even of dogmatic assertion." This certainly is the risk once text is used alongside photographs, but it is not a given. It is not the automatic outcome of pictures used with text, as *The Epilogue* demonstrates.

The fact that photographs can't express everything words can (and vice versa) also has larger repercussions for how photographers might want to approach their medium. It has become customary to compare photographs with other modes of expression. From what I can tell, most commonly photographs are compared to poems. But photographs aren't poems, and poems aren't photographs, however similar their effects in many cases might be. In much the same fashion, even the most cinematic photography isn't cinema. However much one thinks photography has in common with poetry, cinema, or any other medium, at the end of the day, one needs to be very careful with such comparisons, given the differences between photography and poetry (or cinema or whatever else). The key ultimately always is to rely on what photographs can do and to then supplant this with possibly a little help from other media, which in the case of a photobook means the possible inclusion of text (in whatever form or way) and graphic design.

The Epilogue does just that: it tells a very complex story, narrated with the help of a dozen different voices—Abril's through her own photographs as much as the family's and friends', even Cammy's, and through their words (via interviews) and/or other modes of verbal expression (letters, diary excerpts etc.). Abril knew before traveling to the US to visit the Robinsons that the photobook would be the main vehicle to tell the story: "I went to Chattanooga knowing I was going to make a book." In terms of the way the story is told, she relied on some techniques usually used in cinema. "At the beginning of the book, at the present time, the characters are introduced and they speak about grieving, never about death in the present time. Then, there is a big flash forward, and everything is more chronological, so you grow with Cammy and you face all in 'real time,' sort of forgetting the end and hoping that it will end in a different time, just like it happens when you see a movie." In terms of narrative, *The Epilogue* is very clearly driven by the requirement to tell its story as forcefully as possible. While the story itself ultimately is complex, dealing with a young woman's eating disorder and death as much as with family members and friends reacting to and trying to come to terms with it (both before and after her death), there are parameters that cannot be changed, that are not subject to interpretation, such as the basic timeline.

At the risk of simplifying its structure, the book's construction is fairly straightforward. In a first section, surviving family members and friends are introduced, speaking about Cammy (Figure 3.4 shows a portrait of Ashley, Cammy's best friend, opposite a transcript of her description of their relationship). Very slowly, the story emerges, with details left vague. The second, much longer section follows the timeline of Cammy's life (Figure 3.5, which shows an archival photograph, a reproduction of Cammy's 1999 college grades, and a facsimile of a letter written to Cammy by her boyfriend). A last, very short section concludes the book, with the young woman dying from the second of two heart attacks (Figure 3.6, using an archival photograph from the family's albums, with a medical chart included in the form of a trifold). The structure of this narrative allows Abril to explore the many different aspects of the story, having multiple voices contribute (including her own, photographic, one). While this structure expands the story beyond that of the Cammy's death, it also offers a variety of ways in

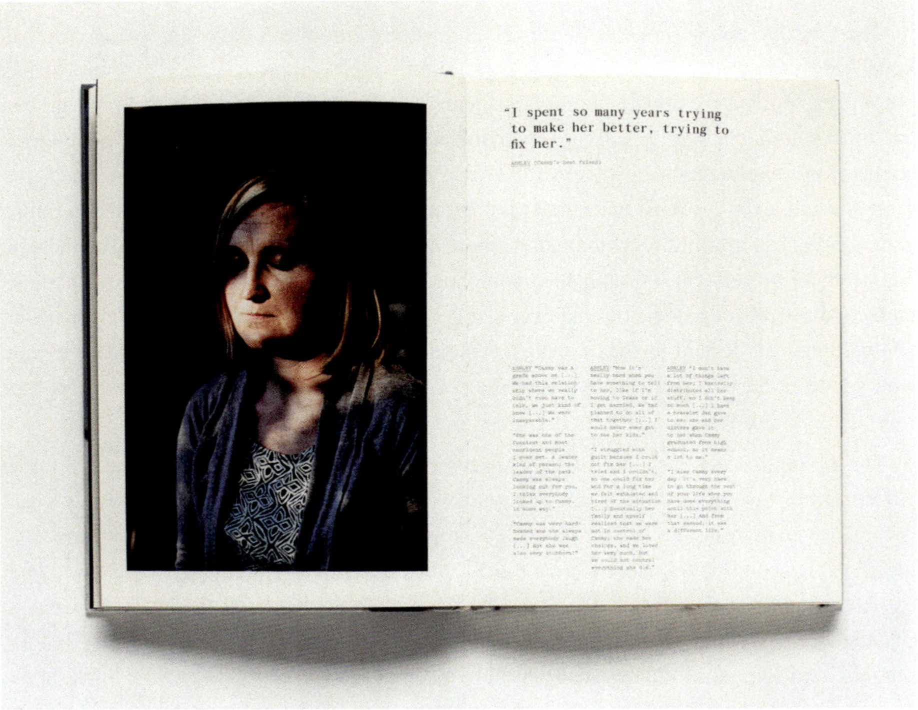

Figure 3.4 Spread from Laia Abril's *The Epilogue*, published by Dewi Lewis

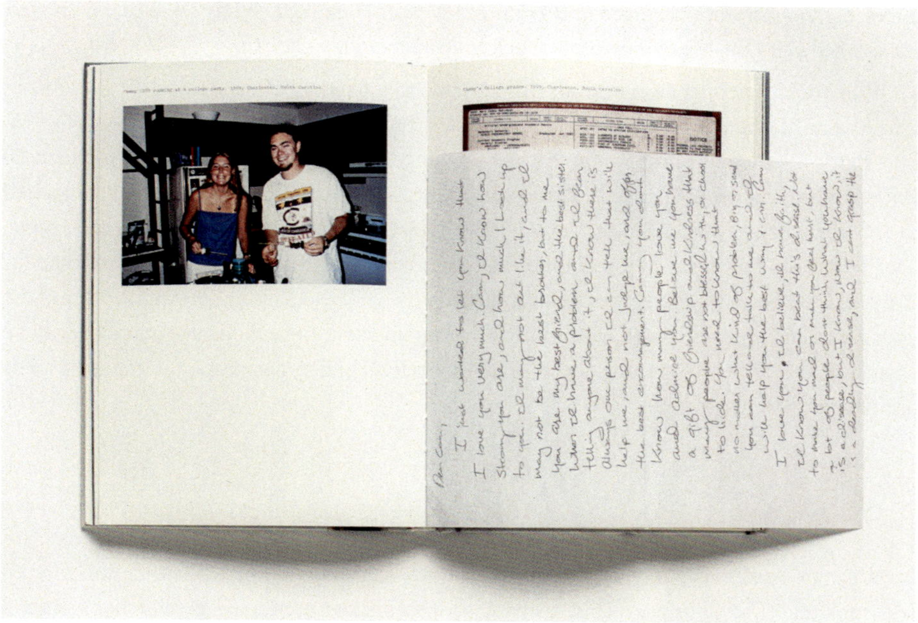

Figure 3.5 Spread from Laia Abril's *The Epilogue*, published by Dewi Lewis

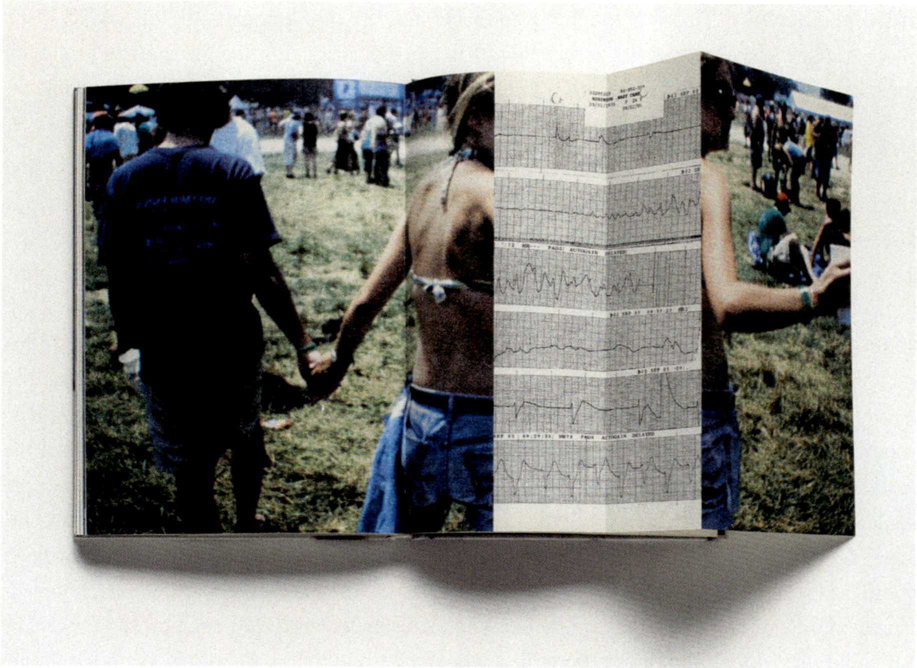

Figure 3.6 Spread from Laia Abril's *The Epilogue*, published by Dewi Lewis

which the viewer/reader is made to become emotionally involved. While the outcome is well established early on, the ending of the book is still incredibly shocking.

With books that operate against the background of a fixed timeline, a storyline going from a fixed A to B, the challenge usually is that it is very easy to construct a simple storyline. In fact, that construction does not have to do anything other than start with A and move to B. But it's quite another challenge to create something that will make the viewer feel compelled to revisit the book. After all, if the story is fully explored, there is no immediate need to come back to it. Seen this way, even seemingly simple narratives offer a considerable challenge for storytellers. *The Epilogue* solves this conundrum by vastly expanding the story beyond the young woman's life and death, essentially bringing up a lot of questions that cannot easily be answered, questions concerning social pressures behind eating disorders, the role of friends or relatives, and many more.

3.9 Concept: Donald Weber's *Interrogations*

In terms of narrative structure, most photobooks probably will lie somewhere between *Horizons* and *The Epilogue*. This, in part, is what makes producing a photobook such a difficult endeavor: how much should the potential viewer be guided through the book? Err on the side of caution, and an overly prescriptive book will not allow the viewer to explore the work's breadth, essentially suffocating her or his imagination. Err on the side of looseness, and the book will provide too little structure, leaving the viewer baffled as to what to make of the photography. This is a tough nut to crack, and the problem can only be solved if the photographer has explored the intricacies of her or his work in a lot of detail before even approaching the idea of a book, and if careful consideration is given to the eventual book.

Another insightful example of a very successful book is provided by Donald Weber's *Interrogations*. The underlying body of work comprises photographs taken in Russia and Ukraine over the course of a little more than half a decade. At its core, providing the obvious title, sit photographs taken in interrogation rooms of police stations. Framed rather tightly, these photographs depict only the subject of the various interrogations, the suspect, with parts of her or his immediate environment added, a chair, parts of a table (see Figures 3.7 and 3.8; there is a photograph without a suspect, showing just the chair plus part of a table, but this exception proves the rule). Occasionally, an interrogator's hand will enter the frame, and there are photographs of that person holding a gun to the suspect's head, whose terror is apparent (Figure 3.8). It is these later pictures that made the rounds on the internet when the work was first published, because clicks or "eyeballs" are the name of the game online: the flashier the photographs, the higher the chance an article will get shared widely by its audience. To briefly digress, this is more of a curse (or at least a burden) than a benefit for most photographers, given their work is usually reduced to the most extreme photographs, however representative of the whole they might be. And it clearly leaves a challenge for the makers of the book: how do you produce a book that will stand up to the expectations created by hype focusing on what are the most extreme photographs?

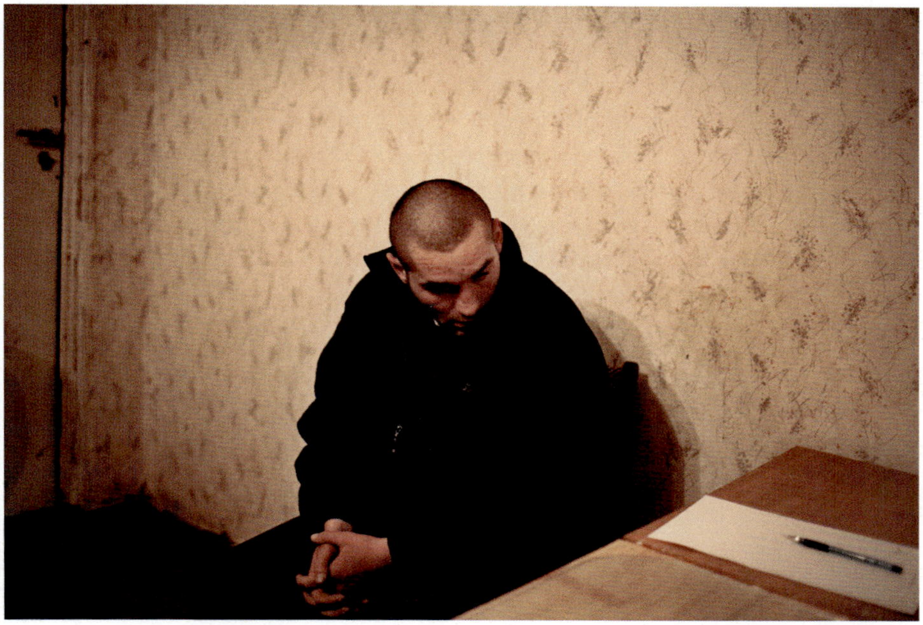

Figure 3.7 Donald Weber, Untitled, from the series *Interrogations*
Courtesy and © Donald Weber

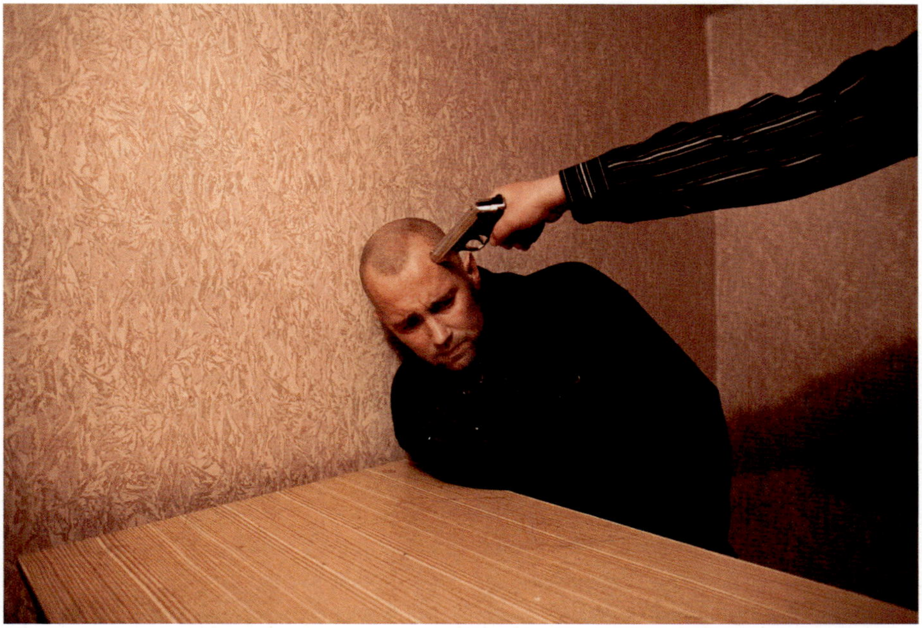

Figure 3.8 Donald Weber, Untitled, from the series *Interrogations*
Courtesy and © Donald Weber

What is more, on a surface level it's clear what the photographs are about, namely the often violent interrogations that happened—and one can surmise probably still happen—in post-Soviet Union countries. Framing the work in this well-defined context would be an obvious solution. However, the photographer opted to aim for more, given that state violence, physical and/or psychological, is not confined to the countries he photographed in. It has become universal. For this to work, the photographs in the book needed to be as country unspecific as they could be. In other words, anything that would openly give away the locations they were taken in needed to be removed. The photographs in the book might still hint at where they were taken, but they could have potentially been taken anywhere.[7]

Interrogations thus has a story of sorts, which is not quite as "fuzzy" as *Horizon*'s, but also not as clear cut as the life and eventual death of Cammy in *The Epilogue*. How would one show it in book form? For a start, the sequence of the interrogation photographs could roughly follow the course of how such an event might unfold. We are going to look into the various aspects of editing and sequencing in much more detail in the next chapter. But clearly, the concept stage already determines large parts of how to approach them. While the photographs in *Interrogations* show a variety of different people, an alert viewer will still pick up on an increasing intensity in the suspects' facial expressions. Seeing the very photos that online magazines picked to showcase the work would then lose at least part of their shock effect. At the same time, the viewer might try to come up with ideas in her or his head about what actually might have been said or what might have happened that resulted in the progression depicted in the sequence. And this is indeed how the photographs are presented in the book.

But a book solely with interrogation photographs still might fall quite short of what such a book should do. After all, interrogations do not happen without any sort of context. Establishing context always is a very important part of what photobook makers have to do. The key is to place the work, to create its framework, to allow the viewer to approach the photographs, while guiding her or him towards the intended goals. Given Weber photographed a lot of other subject matters during his time in Ukraine/Russia, the addition of some of these images helps establish a broader context. In the book, the non-interrogation photographs are included in a section entitled *Prologue*, which, as should be obvious, is placed before the interrogation photographs that come in their separate, eponymous section. An epilogue containing text by writer Larry Frolick and by Weber himself serves as the other bookend for the main part of the book, firmly establishing its mission.

The photographs used in the prologue establish the location in a more general sense, avoiding overt, clear specificity. The land that serves as a backdrop is depicted as rough, with harsh conditions for the mostly weathered faces of those depicted living there. Associations of the photographs with what one might expect from parts of the former Soviet Union (or maybe its satellite states) are probably unavoidable, but clear markers (such as, for example, flags or Lenin busts/statues) are absent. This land has seen better days, the prologue states, and the people living here are trying to get by as best as they can, given what is available. There are glimpses here and there of the aspirations shared by all humans, aspirations that might only too often get crushed by the larger world, the states or systems people find themselves living in. The prologue is thus specific enough to set a stage for what is to come, but it's not a stage that would easily allow a viewer to place the pictures in a very specific location, a location that might be quite different from her or his own. Seen this way, there is no need for a clear narrative in the prologue. Instead, it provides an extended establishing shot, to use a term from filmmaking. At the same time, the prologue also softens the blow of being exposed to the psychological and physical violence depicted in the interrogation photographs. The viewer is lured in, made to feel somewhat comfortable.

The overall form of *Interrogations* is driven by a simple idea. According to Donald Weber, "this was to be like a police dossier, a set of files, without being literal. That is why we ended up with the razor like edge of the book and put in a slipcase, in a subtle way, it resembles a dossier without sending a red flag up." Note how carefully the photographer describes the intent here. The book is supposed to resemble a police file, to feel like a police file, without very obviously looking like one. This is important: when making a photobook, subtlety will often—but not always—be better than the obvious. The obvious is easy to "get," losing a lot of its appeal relatively quickly. Subtle aspects, however, are often not being noticed consciously, yet impress themselves into the viewer's consciousness. We will come back to aspects such as this in the chapter on design.

3.10 Concept as a Basis for a Photobook

Despite the clear differences between *Horizons*, *The Epilogue*, and *Interrogations*, what unites these books is that their underlying concepts drive each and every one of the decisions that went into their making. In particular, these decisions concern:

- the basic—physical—form of the book (size, paper choices, etc.)
- the edit and sequence of the work in question
- the amount and use of the included text
- the layout/design of the material (photographs and text).

Unfortunately, photographers often approach the decisions regarding these very basic, yet incredibly important points as either independent of each other or, even worse, as secondary. As a consequence, often very little, if any attention is being paid to them, the unfortunately common result being that a photobook might contain good photographs, but suffer from all kinds of problems (bad edit, bad design, too much/few text, etc.) that ruin the viewer's experience. What makes these outcomes especially bad is that such problems can be easily avoided. The reality is that many photographers are not very good at editing and sequencing their own work, at writing about it, at working on the interaction between pictures and text, at knowing about even the most basic graphic design principle, or at any combination of these challenges. For this reason alone, it is extremely important for photographers to realize that making a photobook should be a collaborative effort that includes experts who can help with editing and sequencing, writing and/or editing, producing good graphic design, and making sure that the production of the materials works out OK.

As I already noted, the basic concept needs to be developed first, given it drives the decisions that underlie the book. Involving experts already in the early stages of the development of the concept usually is a good idea. For example, the design of a book is not completely independent from the edit or from the use of text. It is likely that any of the basic aspects of a photobook—edit/sequence, design, use of text, production—results in possible limitations, which should be incorporated into the concept. While ultimately the concept, the spirit of the underlying work, is king, it would be foolish for a photographer not to seek input from external experts even in the very early stages of working on a book.

When working with a publisher, such input often can be and will be provided. It is for this very reason that Dewi Lewis noted in Chapter 2: "Very few projects arrive as perfectly formed book dummies. And from my own perspective I am not that interested in projects in which I can't have a creative input. As a publisher who also designs a large percentage of our output, I see my role as working with the photographer at every stage of the process." While this input might result in obvious restrictions for the photographer, at the same time it will help address many of the issues most photographers struggle with.

However, there are publishers that do not offer much support for photographers or that offer support only when asked, publishers that will essentially allow a photographer to deliver the final product on their own, only to print and distribute it (often asking for considerable amounts of money). There is nothing wrong with such an approach per se, if—and only if—the photographer is either able to solve the various challenges on her or his own or is willing and able to enlist help from, for example, an editor, a designer, or whoever else might be needed. Self-publishers, of course, are completely on their own. Given the importance of these various aspects of photobook making, this book attempts to shed light on them in detail.

3.11 Developing a Photobook Concept

At this stage, it should have become obvious that a proper concept for a photobook is incredibly important and that its development includes a seemingly bewilderingly large number of factors, many of which are outside of the basic expertise of many photographers. At the same time, none of the problems that need to be solved amounts to rocket science, and their number is relatively small. So what is the best way to develop a photobook concept?

For a start, it is extremely important for photographers to look at their peers' books. While part of being in the loop is simply based on seeing the medium's general direction, other people's books offer the opportunity to look at solutions for a problem. Essentially, each photobook is the solution to a "simple" problem: how can these photographs be used to tell a story or to provide the viewer with a very specific experience? Not all of the solutions are equally good. Not all of the solutions make sense. Let's face it, there are a lot of very bad photobooks out there, just like there are numerous gems. The best and simplest way to learn more is to look at them. Hopefully, this has become clear from the look at the three photobooks discussed above.

Beyond studying photobooks in detail to see solutions for very specific problems, they can also serve as templates—or partial templates—for one's own work. It is this aspect alone that should make anyone interested in producing a photobook look at what already exists.

While using examples or even templates is useful, at the end of the day, each photobook ideally is produced around the requirements that result from the photographs at its core. I inserted the word "ideally" on purpose, since it is almost inevitable that there will have to be solutions that are not quite ideal, given constraints posed by, for example, a budget or by what can actually be printed. Before going into such details, I believe that anyone attempting to make a photobook needs to arrive at a solid, well-defined book concept first.

As I already briefly noted earlier, a photobook's concept is directly derived from the concept of the photographs in question. After all, a photobook is the translation of a body of work into book form. A completed body of work should be finished in the sense that it is consistent and makes sense: it has its own concept or however else a photographer might think of what the project is "about" (an expression of this usually—or maybe it would be better to say: ideally—is presented by the project statement). If there is no clarity concerning a body of work, translating it into book form or into an exhibition usually poses problems.

If there is clarity, the book concept is nothing other than the translation of the main concept into book form, taking the constraints posed by the physical medium book into consideration. Whatever a project might be about usually strongly drives all of the decisions required to make a book. We have seen how this plays out for the three books discussed earlier.

So the project's overall concept and the book concept are closely related, with the latter incorporating the fact that books have certain properties (which by now should be obvious): how can I tell this story, convey what I'm after in a book? Consequently, the edit of a book, the selection of the photographs inside, might differ from that of the overall project. Thus, the very first and possibly most important step in the process of making a book is translating the concept and edit of a body of work into the book concept and the book's edit. Figure 3.9 schematically illustrates this process. Note that concept and edit are interrelated: a body of work's concept (what it is about) is driven by the photographs; at the same time the concept itself determines the edit. This is one of the most important aspects of a finished photography project. I will revisit and discuss this aspect in detail in the following chapter.

It is probably impossible to define the role of text for each and every photobook. As we have seen already, some books do not require any text, while others rely on the combination of text plus images to tell a story. At this stage of the process, the role of text needs to be

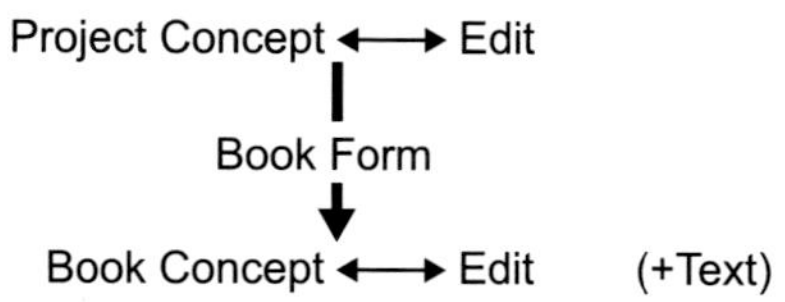

Figure 3.9 The form of the book results in a concept and edit that is related to the underlying body of work's concept and edit. Concept and edit are interrelated (see main text for details). What is more, the book might contain text, whose role should be defined at this stage

thought about carefully. Will text play a role, and if yes, what is that role? One needs to differentiate between accompanying essays—either at the beginning or end of a book—and text that interrelates with images. Essays will require some careful thinking: who might be (a) good person(s) to write the essay(s)? How can that (those) person(s) be contacted etc.? What is important about essays is that they usually do not play a role in the following process. In contrast, text that interrelates with images in the book requires more work. What kind of text should be used? How will it relate to the text? To use a very simple example, will there be captions? Extended captions? Will there be text blocks providing information the images don't or can't convey? These considerations are all strictly driven by the concept of the book.

For most bookmakers, creating an edit and a sequence goes hand in hand. So not including the sequence in Figure 3.9 almost feels a little artificial. Figure 3.10 provides a more complete picture, the next step of the process. I separated out the edit and the sequence, given that the sequence of the images can play very different roles, depending on the type of book. For example, in a book of typologies—a common type of photography project—the sequence often is created after the edit was produced, almost as an afterthought. In contrast, a book with a strong narrative structure needs to consider edit and sequence at the same time.

In Figure 3.10, the sequence is made to relate to layout. By layout I here only mean the way the images are placed on the individual spreads. This step can be done by photographers, as long as there is some input by a graphic designer who can help arranging things in a visually more pleasing way (unless they have training as graphic designers, photographers usually are fairly bad designers). In other words, by separating layout from design, my intent is to separate out the role the placement of images on a spread plays for the concept of the book from the role of their exact, designed placement to make sure the spread is visually pleasing, following the basic rules of professional graphic design.

For example, a photobook might simply consistently be blank on the left page and have an image on the right page—the well-known classic model of photobook making (used in Walker Evans' *American Photographs* and many other books). That layout is driven by the concept. And the sequence simply shows one photograph after the other. Now, how the photographs is placed on the page might require the input of a professional graphic designer, since even small differences in the margins often result in vastly different visual experiences: the placement of the images might feel clumsy or just right to a viewer.

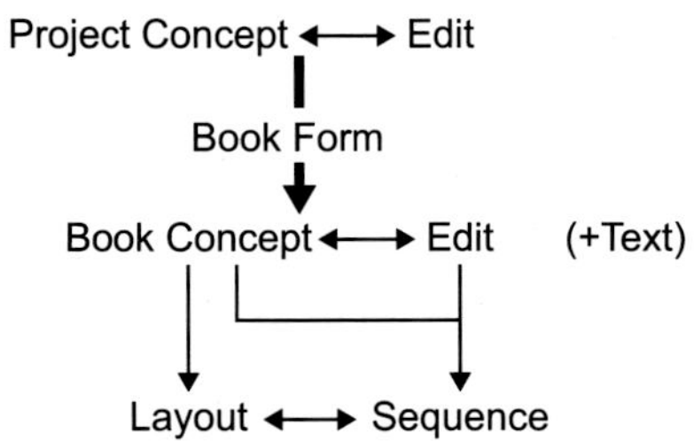

Figure 3.10 The next step in the process usually revolves around the sequence of the images plus their rough layout on the individual spreads

Ideally, the process of making a photobook is a collaboration between different people: the photographer, an editor, a designer, a production person … We will see more aspects of the contributions of the different actors in the following chapters. In light of what I am going to be talking about, the schematic description of the process discussed here is a bit simplistic. It might work very well for some people, whereas other people will collaborate with a team considering every aspect of the book right away. In my experience, photographers with little or no experience in making a photobook benefit from having the process broken down in a simple manner. It is for their benefit that I have produced the schematic breakdown of the process discussed here. As is always the case, the individual experiences of and preferences for making a photobook will be different for every photographer. Having followed this discussion and then having read the remainder of the book should allow every photographer to find their own process, whether it is following the process as outlined here or changing it up for a variant that involves the different aspects at slightly different stages.

With concept, edit/sequence and layout established, the object itself, the book should be considered. What size should it have? How many pages? Questions like these (and many others—we will visit these aspects in Chapter 6) should be addressed with the concept in mind. For example, if the concept centers on ideas of intimacy, a very large book might simply not feel right. But, and this often is a big but, at this stage the available budget often enters as well, providing restrictions in, say, the number of pages. There simply might not be the budget to produce a book with, let's say, 400 pages. So if the concept and edit/sequence revolve around a number of photographs that require that many pages, the edit (and, possibly, concept) will have to be revisited, in the form of reducing the overall number of photographs to accommodate what is financially feasible.

The budget itself might not even be the only limiting factor. For example, printing technologies limit the sizes of the pages that can be printed. Considerations like these will be discussed in much more detail in Chapter 6. An extreme example I have come across was provided by a photographer who was interested in a book with a very panoramic format. Getting the book printed commercially turned out to be very complicated, since many digital printing machines simply could not handle the required size: the sheets they use were too small. Problems like this one can be frustrating, but there always are ways to solve them, either by—as here—reducing the desired size of the final book, or by using other ways of printing. Offset machines can handle much larger sheets of paper, but in this case costs explode.

In most situations, the problems and/or restrictions will not be quite extreme, but they do exist. And it is very important for photographers to be able to adapt. In all likelihood, the perfect book simply cannot and will not be made, for a possible variety of reasons (budget, technology, etc.). But that doesn't mean that a book that contains a series of well-thought-through compromises cannot be made. Being able to make smart compromises is essential.

Figure 3.11 is an expanded version of Figure 3.10, which now includes the aspects of materials (page numbers and size of book) and budget, with the feedback loop back to the book edit. It is important to realize that that feedback loop might in fact not exist. Many books can be made with existing budget and materials. However, having to make some changes is

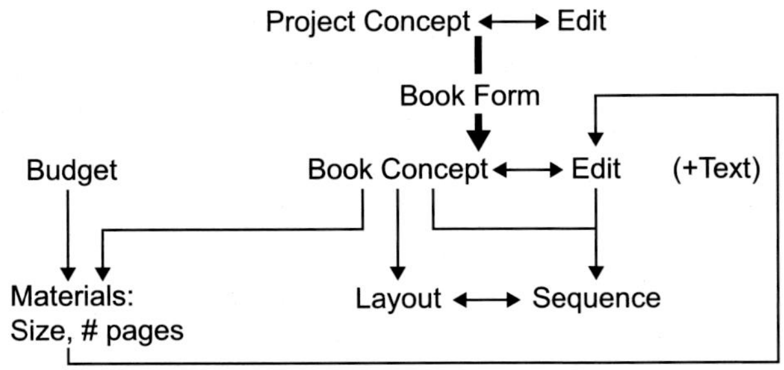

Figure 3.11 The physical properties of the book add another layer to consider, and they might require revisiting and changing the edit

very common (for example, a smaller book, or a book with fewer pages, or a book with a different number of pages).

Please note that considerations of the book's basic physical properties can happen at an earlier stage. In fact, it does not hurt to roughly know about the desired size of the book. However, in my experience aiming for a book with, let's say, 50 photographs or pages often is a bad idea: the extent of the book should first be driven by the concept, by what the work needs. Adjustments might then have to be made. But it is easier to adjust a relatively formed edit/sequence than to try to squeeze one into a container without knowing how well it might fit (after all, the edit might contain only 20 photographs to work perfectly—what to do then with the extra 30 pages?).

Figure 3.12 shows the aspects of design and of additional materials added. The concept drives design and layout. The design might be influenced by the materials (say, the choice of paper) and vice versa. The layout of the photographs is driven by the concept and the sequence. Again, I am using the words "design" and "layout" in a very specific way here. By "design," I mean all aspects of visual design (and typesetting)—that's where the input of a graphic designer usually is incredibly helpful (see Chapter 5 for more details). By "layout," I mean the principle of how the photographs are shown in individual spreads (also see Chapter 5 for a lot more details).

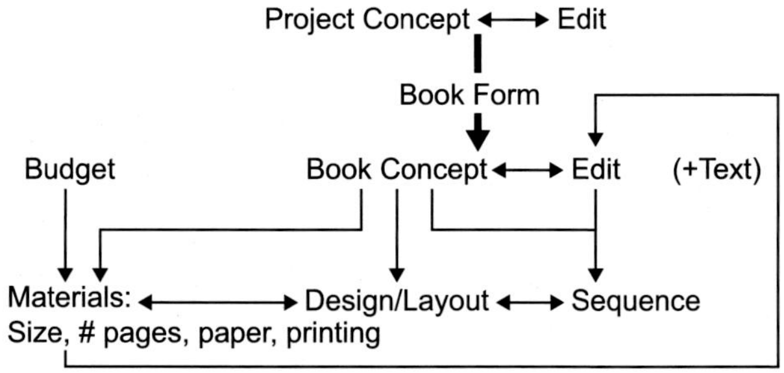

Figure 3.12 The full interrelation between the different aspects of photobook making. Details can be found in the main text

There are a lot more material aspects that ultimately need to be considered than are noted in Figure 3.12. We will revisit this aspect in Chapter 6. But briefly, once the overall shape of the book has been found (edit, sequence, layout, …), given the size and number of pages, production details such as the paper type, the type of printing, etc. should be considered.

Figure 3.12 might look bewildering, because it shows all aspects of photobook making in one diagram. In fact, the element of production is only implied. But the key point I have been trying to make is that while there are many different aspects that need to be considered, approaching them in a simple and relatively fixed order makes the whole process a lot easier. This order can be changed in a multitude of ways. The idea here is to give the reader an overview of all the aspects and a way in which they can be approached. Especially inexperienced photobook makers might want to stick to the suggested process, to then later, after having gained more experience, follow a possibly modified process that suits their own method of working better (or simply stick with the one I'm suggesting). In a sense, the process outlined here is a bit like a recipe for a meal: inexperienced chefs might want to stick to the recipe closely.

To summarize these steps that I discussed earlier, their order would play out as follows:

1 With the form and function of the medium book in mind, create a book concept out of the already existing project concept.

2 Create a book edit out of the project edit. Note that not all photographs might find their place in the book edit (much like in an exhibition not all photographs might be on the wall).

3 Using the book concept and edit, create a sequence and the rough layout of the spreads. If the sequence can't be made to work (which is not unusual) revisit point 2.

4 Consider basic materials such as the book's size and page numbers, with the overall concept, the existing edit/sequence/layout, and the budget in mind. If the edit/sequence/layout created earlier do not fit, go back to point 2.

5 Consider (or actually have a professional consider) design and other physical properties of the now fairly final book. This concerns what paper to print on, where and how to produce the book etc. Even at this stage, there might be changes required, which might need you to go back to point 2 (for example, your book might have 49 pages, but your desired production would require 48). But ideally, this will not be necessary.

Then again, the idea of "ideally" usually is very different from what actually happens during the process of making a book. The perfect book simply cannot be made. Something will require a compromise, whether it's the budget or the desired form of the book or production aspects, and photobook makers need to keep this in mind. You might not be able to print on that beautiful paper you found because it is not available or too expensive or unsuitable for your book. You might end up with more or fewer photographs in the book than you expected. Your book might end up being a little smaller because having a bigger one would not fit into your budget. The list of possible challenges is long. None of these challenges usually presents a major disaster for photobook makers other than those who are completely dogmatic and out of touch with how the photobook-production process works. So as long as you are flexible, while trying to stick as closely as is realistic to the book concept, you will be able to produce a good photobook.

In fact, at times technical challenges can result in changes to the book that enhance its appeal. During the process of working on a dummy (more on dummies in the next section), Donald Weber ran into a series of technical limitations concerning production. *Interrogations* consists of a single stack of folded folios. Weber: "This, however, caused a problem in binding, in that there was only one needle in Europe that could puncture this amount of paper in order to stitch the binding, and only a certain kind of paper could be used. It had to be a thick uncoated paper instead of coated to allow the needle to puncture. This was fine, because I wanted an uncoated, matte, textured paper anyway. The cover became textured paper with a wallpaper print printed on it as again, the presses could not handle real wallpaper which was another original idea from the dummy. So, everything was transformed, but it certainly made it better." Of course, there is no guarantee that things will always work out for the best, as it did in Weber's case. Challenges are there to be met, however. And challenges can arise from being overly confining with one's idea of what the book should be. "I was once an architect," says Weber, "and one thing I learned is how to not spread your ideas across the entire building, when it came to the materials and construction. You need to have a very solid foundation of ideas, of concept and vision, and from there, choose the key elements that need to be kept, everything else then is allowed to shift to support the ideas." It's thus important to keep the eye on the ball, allowing it to go towards its intended target, without trying to be overly deterministic. Restrictions or changes caused by simple production limitations might ultimately result in a greatly enhanced book.

3.12 The Dummy

While the process of making a photobook that I outlined earlier might appear to be bewildering and filled with traps and problems, the reality is that many of those traps and problems turn out to be a lot less problematic than one might think. One major reason why this is the case is that anyone attempting to make a photobook should work with dummies (or maquettes—I'm going to stick with the word "dummy" in the following). A dummy is a simplified version of the final book. In fact, a dummy can be very, very basic and raw, or it can be quite close to what the final book might actually look like. Usually, dummies evolve from very simple versions to increasingly more complex and finished looking ones—roughly following the outline of the photobook making process detailed above.

It might sound like too obvious an observation, but what makes dummies so useful is the fact that even if they're in the most rudimentary form the fact that they operate like a book vastly helps photobook makers see what a fully produced book might look and feel like. A lot of photographers now work on their books using computers and software like *InDesign*, creating what look like real books on a screen. But the physical act of turning a page is so vastly different from clicking a mouse to see the next "page" that using a computer to make a photobook almost always is a bad approach to the process. After all, the viewer will ultimately engage with a physical object and not a PDF, say, so a photobook maker needs to get as close to that final experience as possible.

Apart from their physicality, another advantage of making dummies is that they bring photographers closer to the actual process of book making. Dummies can end up being very elaborate productions. There are photographers who learn basic bookbinding techniques to make dummies. It's up to the photographer to decide how complex their dummies might be. It is probably obvious that the process of making physical dummies is more time consuming and expensive than working on a computer screen. But the investment in time is an investment in learning about the physical properties of the desired book. And the investment in money certainly in the very early stages can be very modest. In the photobook-making classes I have taught at art schools one of the biggest revelations for students has usually been to realize how vastly different dummies are from looking at a PDF. What is more, making dummies is a lot more fun than moving images around on a computer screen.

In the following chapter, I am going to discuss the process of editing and sequencing in more detail. Physical dummies play one of the biggest role in that part of the process. To edit and sequence a photobook, a dummy can be produced using a blank spiral-bound notebook, a set of small prints (which can be made cheaply), and removable double-sided tape. I am going to discuss how this works in the following chapter. Here, I just want to stress how something that is essentially a collection of very cheap materials, which might be quite far from the vastly more highly produced final product, is of immense utility. A notebook dummy with cheap prints still looks and feels like a book, and turning the pages will usually reveal problems in the sequence easily.

More advanced dummies go beyond the notebook stage and create something closer to the final book, incorporating the layout more closely, the final size of the book, possibly more complex production aspects such as gatefolds, etc. A fully realized dummy then essentially is a prototype of the (desired) final book. For most publishers I have spoken with it will make a vastly different impact than a PDF (which many publishers are not interested in seeing) or an on-demand book that might look somewhat professionally made (ditto). While some publishers might insist on bringing their own expertise to the book, suggesting all kinds of change, changes that might be based on considering the available budget or the need to improve the edit/sequence, layout/design, or materials, having a fully developed dummy (or a set of identical dummies—there needn't be only one) can only help a photographer approach publishers.

There is a variety of photography and/or photobook festivals that include a dummy component. What is more, groups of publishers now have dummy competitions. In both cases, the winner(s) will get their books produced by whichever publisher(s) is (are) involved. So the usefulness and importance of dummies has been widely accepted and established, and the process of developing a photobook must contain the making of a series of dummies.

3.13 From Concept to Editing and Sequencing

After the development of the book concept, an edit and sequence has to be produced. In the following chapter, I will discuss in detail how a photographer can go about it. As I discussed earlier (see Figure 3.9), the book concept and the book's edit/sequence are interrelated. This mimics the fact that the process of photographing for a project itself contains a very similar relationship between what a photographer thinks the project is about and what the photographs focus on: one must inform the other for the process to be fruitful. A photographer might start out with a very specific idea. But with time, the photographs often push the idea in a slightly, somewhat, or even very different direction. This aspect might be one of the toughest challenges for any photographer. Ultimately, the pictures need to drive the project, not what the photographer thinks the project is. After all, what is not in the pictures a viewer who is not familiar with the photographer's thought process will be unable to see.

In much the same way, a photobook concept should in part be driven by the best possible edit/sequence. But making a photobook usually is easier than working on a project, given that the process of making a book should start out from a finished project. It usually makes little sense trying to approach a book with an unfinished project. Occasionally, a photographer might realize that there are photographs needed for the book that aren't in the project, yet. That's fine. But if the gaps are vast, if, in other words, a very large number of photographs are missing to produce a book, the photographer needs to go back to photographing and finishing the project (now knowing about all the holes) before approaching the book again. This happened to Donald Weber, who showed an advanced dummy to photographer and photobook expert Martin Parr and designer Teun van der Heijden. Both pointed out the importance of the interrogation photographs, and Weber had to go back to take more of them, which delayed the release of the book by almost a year. Making that good photobook thus might occasionally require drastic decisions.

In the following chapters, I am going to assume that a fully realized photography project does, in fact, exist. We are going to start out with editing and sequencing, usually one of the biggest challenges photographers face.

Notes

1. See, for example, "Photobooks—affordable collectibles that are soaring in value," published in *The Guardian*, accessed July 22, 2011, at http://www.theguardian.com/money/2011/ jul/22/photobooks-affordable-collectibles-value.
2. Those who don't want to read the whole book might find the following article interesting: http://www.how-to-write-a-book-now.com/seven-basic-plots.html.
3. Sol Worth, "Pictures Can't Say Ain't," in *Film/Culture*, ed. Sari Thomas, Scarecrow Press, 1982, pp. 97–109.
4. Larry Gross, "Modes of Communication and the Acquisition of Symbolic Competence," in *Communications Technology and Social Policy*, ed. George Gerbner, Larry Gross, and Wiliam Melody, Wiley-Interscience, 1973, pp. 189–208.
5. E.H. Gombrich, "The visual image," *Scientific American*, 227, no. 3, 1972, pp. 82–96.
6. Quoted from "Appearances: The Ambiguity of the Photograph," in *Understanding a Photograph*, ed. Geoff Dyer, Penguin Books, 2013, p. 65.
7. In an interview with *Vice*, Weber outlined what made him come to this realization: "I kind of realized that I couldn't bring my American values of justice there [. . .] But then

another sort of major turning point is that in Canada there was this famous case about two years ago of an Air Force colonel, the prime minister's personal pilot, who was a serial rapist who murdered women. He would photograph them. He was caught, and they showed on television his interrogation because the news media were saying that this was like a classic interrogation—this is a perfect interrogation. And the techniques that these Canadian cops were using were exactly the same as the Ukrainian cops. Like the positioning of the chair, how they make the guy always sit, the cop is always standing. Of course there's no physical abuse, but the mental manipulation that these Canadian cops were imposing on the rapist were amazing. Because the rapist comes in as not a suspect, and within two hours he's confessed his crime. I just saw the parallels, like, 'Shit, it has nothing to do with a Ukrainian cop or a Russian or an American cop, it has everything to do with—you know, it's a power relationship'"; quoted from Donald Weber's Brutal Ukrainian Interrogation Photos (unsigned), April 18, 2013, accessed April 21, 2015, at http://www.vice.com/en_uk/read/donald-webers-interrogations-opens-tonight-at-the-foley-gallery.

B. In Focus

Awoiska van der Molen—*Sequester*

In the translation of a photography project into book form, there can be seemingly insurmountable challenges. The materiality of the printed photograph often is radically different for pictures on a wall and in a book. For example, a traditional silver gelatine print simply is not the same beast as a corresponding print using ink on paper. In addition, there is the issue of size. As (wall) print sizes have increased considerably over the past decades, book sizes have not. And if the decision is made to produce a large book, in all likelihood it will still be a lot smaller than the kinds of print now routinely found on the walls of galleries and museums. But these challenges are no reason for major concern, given that a photobook simply is no exhibition (or vice versa). The experiences they offer their viewers are very different. Thus, for a photographer little, if anything, is to be gained from dogmatism about an exhibition of a photobook and its corresponding book being as similar as possible in a superficial way.

A good case in point is provided by Awoiska van der Molen's work. This artist photographs landscapes in black and white, often at dawn or night. Prints are then made in the darkroom, with sizes of up to a few feet in width (or height—see Figure B.1 for an example of an exhibition). How could these photographs be translated into the form of a photobook? "With Awoiska's work," says designer and publisher Hans Gremmen, "the easy part was to instantly know which kind of book it should NOT be: a classical hardcover with perfectly printed images in it." Of course, such a book would probably be the most obvious solution for this work. Gremmen's approach was driven by prints on the wall: "My first encounter with her work was seeing it in an exhibition, in which she nailed a really large silver-gelatine hand-print in a very rough manner to the wall. Even the edges were not super-straight. This contrast between the border of the image and the image made the work even stronger. Seeing beauty in a perfect setting is boring, seeing beauty in a rougher setting is much more interesting." There is, then, the key to that translation: it's all about the experience.

Gremmen intended to translate the experience of seeing the work on the wall into the book, not the photographs as-is. To that end, the book, *Sequester* (published by his imprint Fw:Photography in 2014 and at the time of this writing in its second edition) employs a mix between the classical book—photographs printed on otherwise white spreads without any distractions—and a very unconventional one. The book begins and ends with a set of black pages, onto which details of individual photographs were printed using grey ink. There are two other such sections in the book, cutting up the conventional, classical part. "By showing details," notes Gremmen, "you get a bit of the sensation of being drawn into the work as in her originals print." The view thus alternates between the classical view and the very detailed, dark one, printed full bleed, which sucks the viewer in. "It changes your perspective every 16 pages," says Gremmen, "it gives you a break and the feeling that the book has chapters." Breaking up the classical book by immersing the viewer into selected photographs thus not only completely changes the overall experience, it also solves a problem often faced by classical landscape books: how to create a flow, possibly with chapters, without making it too obvious with text.

As can be expected, the making of the book entailed considerable challenges for the photographer. "Regarding the sizes," says Van der Molen, "I was concerned the images would look like 'illustrations' if appearing in smaller book form. For example I never liked the small silver gelatine prints I make for my portfolio box. These always seem too 'classical' and too sweet. My concern was how to let my experience of

Figure B.1 Exhibition view of Awoiska van der Molen's work at Kristof De Clercq Gallery, Ghent (Belgium), March 2013. All exhibited photographs are silver gelatine prints, sized 140 x 116cm
Photograph kindly provided by and © Awoiska van der Molen

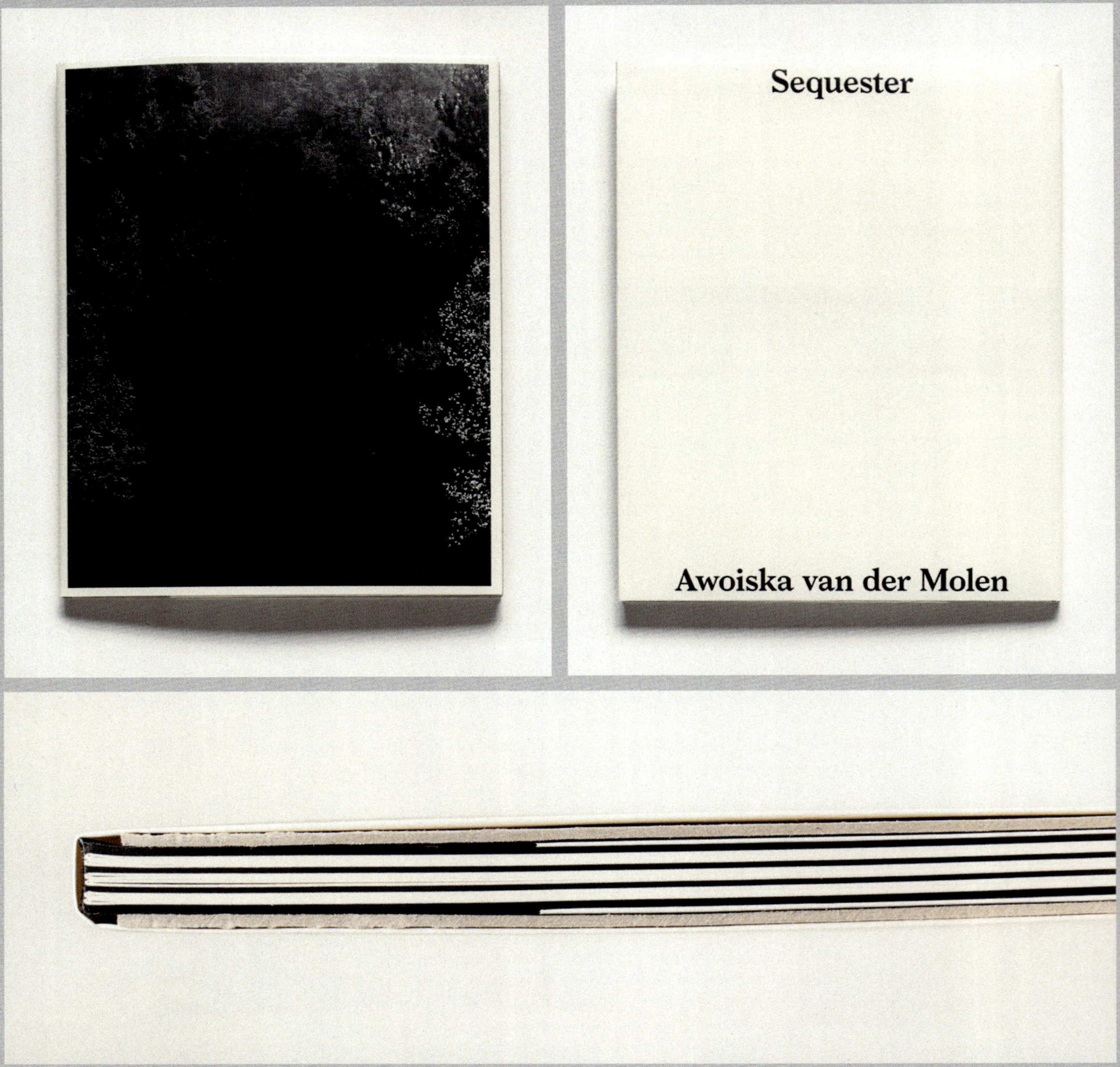

Figure B.2 Top left: front cover of Awoiska van der Molen—*Sequester* (Fw:Photography, 2014). Top right: back cover of the book. Bottom: view of the book from the head. Note how even unopened the basic structure of the book reveals itself, with four black sections and three white ones. Furthermore, the binding structure is clearly visible: untreated book boards are attached to the page block at the front and back, and there is a French-fold dust jacket for protection. In this case, the French-fold involves a dust jacket that has extra flaps at the top and bottom of the book. The use of these flaps results in a dust jacket that is thicker, with its edges and corners becoming less likely to tear. If you look carefully, you can see the flaps in the top-right image, where in the middle of the book, there is a section that is slightly darker, running from left to right. That is the section not covered by the flaps

being in the landscape come out strong in book form while not letting it become a 'landscape-plates book'." Obviously, such a mindset already provides a good starting point for a book, given that neither designer/publisher nor photographer wanted to get a classical book. What can be gained from a photographer understanding what a photobook actually is—in particular how it is printed—easily becomes obvious from another starting point for Van der Molen: "I was less concerned about the quality of printing than about the presentation using a smaller size. I understood I had to let go of the details of the silver gelatine prints that I knew so well and accept a different language of the offset printing. This was actually done very well in collaboration with the lithographer." And much like Gremmen, Van der Molen was driven by the intended experience for the viewer: "What I look for while photographing is to capture my experience when being in a landscape, at a given moment. I don't seem to perceive details consciously at that moment, being more focused on the whole. In the printed book details of my often dark images are slightly less obvious, and they therefore translate perfectly how I experienced the scene when I was there." Note how here the photographer not only thinks of the experience of the viewer when looking at the book, but she also relates it to her own experience while making the photographs. While this might not be possible, achievable, and/or desirable for every photographic body of work, finding such an approach must constitute one of the sweet spots of making a photobook.

As is the case with most photobooks, *Sequester* arose out of a series of dummies, with consecutive improvements (see Figure B.4). In the first dummy, Van der Molen says, "the first few pages showed zoomed in fragments of one of the landscapes printed on black paper. This immediately struck me: being sucked deep into an abstract space, being a bit lost, trying to comprehend where you are. It was a great find." And making the book also entailed going back to photographs that had not made it to the edit: "At one point we felt we needed certain images I had not provided in my first selection of images. It was exciting to go with them through my pile of contact sheets to see undiscovered images, and a few of these completed the final edit." While it seems obvious that such decisions make a lot of sense, this process also demonstrates not only that photobook making should be a collaboration. It also shows that photographers have much to gain from being flexible, from being willing to accept advice, even if it means going back to previously rejected photographs.

On its publication, the book was widely critically acclaimed. "*Sequester* is very volcanic," says critic and writer Colin Pantall, "and I like volcanoes. It's photographic. The black pages take you deeper into the night. It's murky, it's quite brave. In them, the mood becomes noisier. It's really night-timey, whereas the other pictures aren't quite that, their texture is more volcanic and geological." Note how Pantall's take on the dark pages puts a slightly different spin on them: "This is psychological. The purpose is to take you down to the depth of the volcano, to the underworld and the forest, to the foothills of these volcanoes, where you can get lost, and you do

Figure B.3 Spreads from Awoiska van der Molen—*Sequester* (Fw:Photography, 2014). Top left and right images: spreads from the "classical" part of the book, with b/w photographs printed on white paper

Bottom left and right images: spreads from the unconventional part of the book, where details of selected photographs are printed on black paper

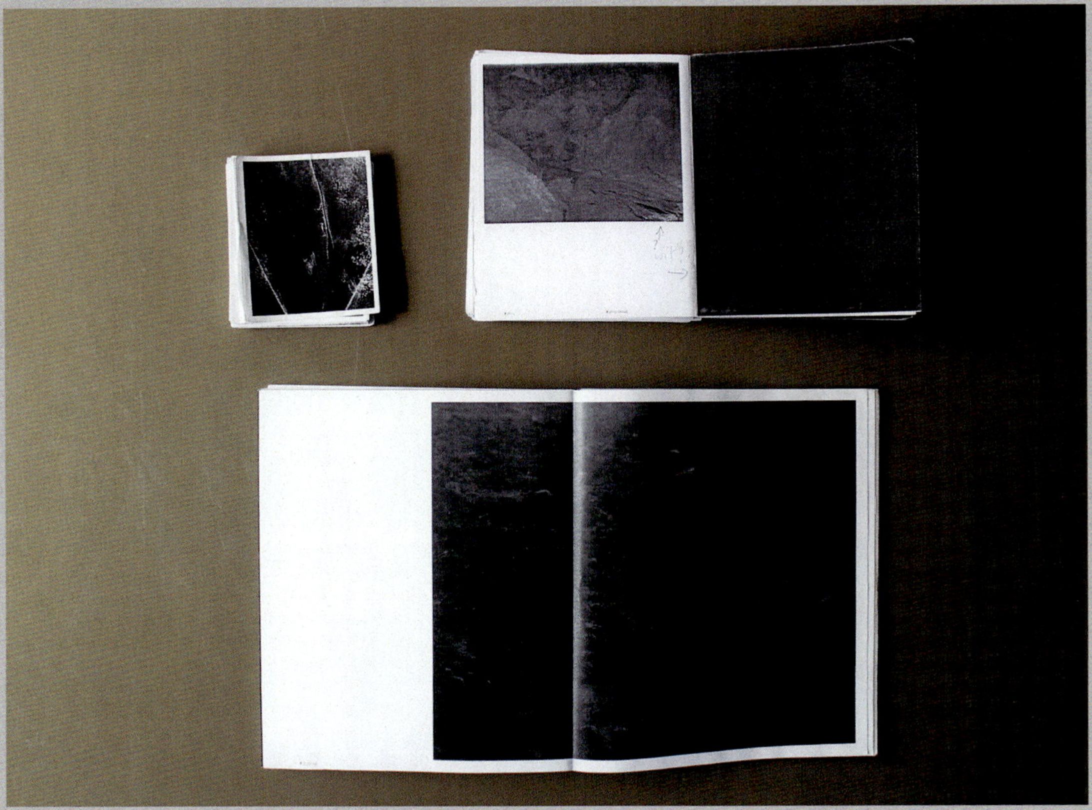

Figure B.4 Dummies for what ultimately became Awoiska van der Molen—*Sequester* (Fw:Photography, 2014). Each uses simply Xerox copies. The smallest one is the earliest one, produced roughly one year before the release of the book
Photograph kindly provided by and © Awoiska van der Molen

get lost." This ultimately is the best a book can hope for, that it succeeds on its own terms, while allowing for a variety of experiences that has its viewers come back to it frequently. Allowing for such experiences is a task photobook makers face, and it is usually achieved by not overdetermining the book's experience. Pantall: "As a photographer, you want to be leaving a gap for the viewer to get into. And that's what Van der Molen is doing here. These pictures are tying into major things. It's landscape and the psychology of that landscape." Critic and writer Adam Bell agrees with Pantall: "Although Van der Molen's work could have easily been given a more classical treatment, Gremmen's unconventional approach highlights the work's physiological edge that would have been lost with a more traditional design. Although the black matte pages place us in a dense thicket of darkness, the darkness prepares us for when we emerge into the equally dark landscapes that follow. Our eyes slowly adjust, the trees and rocks emerge, and we can see the sky, and we're alone in a vast desolate landscape—pauses before the next vista." For Bell, the book achieves this in part through its design and production: "From the superb printing to the mix of full-bleed matte images of close-up details and full frame glossy photos, the design is excellent and matches the content perfectly." But there is something else: "Thankfully, the book is also free of an annoying essay trying to explain the work. Nothing can kill a book faster than a self-important essay." Photobook makers might want to take note of Bell's last point.

CHAPTER 4

From Pictures to a Book: Editing and Sequencing

4.1 The Challenge of Editing

Imagine you are given a box with dozens, hundreds, or possibly thousands of puzzle pieces, knowing, or at least hoping, that they can be made to fit into a picture. Now also imagine that before you put it together, you don't quite know what the picture will actually look like. You might have a good idea, but a lot of details are vague. Then imagine you don't know how many of the puzzle pieces you will need to finish the task. This imaginary challenge is akin to the situation many photographers who need to edit and sequence their photographs for a book feel they are in.

But usually, things aren't nearly as bad as this. For a start, as I outlined in the previous chapter, making a photobook should start out with the book's concept. The concept provides a solid outline of the book, even as it might require to get modified itself in the process of editing the photographs. In addition, a book edit should be made from the project edit, a selection of photographs that encapsulate the core of the work. It is, of course, possible to work on a project and then attempt to make a book without creating the project edit first. But finding the project edit, which can then be used for a book and for exhibitions, is a good idea.

Things get even more complex given that some books can be edited much more easily than others. For example, an edit for a book containing typologies poses considerably fewer problems than making one for a well-defined story. A well-defined story, in turn, can be produced more easily than a book that centers on a vague, but still somewhat clear idea. In each of these cases, proper knowledge of the concept of the book, of what the book aims to achieve (and how) vastly helps during the process of editing. If you don't know what your book is going to be about, what kind of experience it is intended to give to a possible viewer, how can you make an edit?

But having a concept is one thing, translating it into an edit and sequence that do what they're intended to do is quite another. As a general rule, the vast majority of photobooks contain fewer photographs than were in the original sets their makers started out from. Consequently, decisions had to be made which pictures to include and which ones to omit. These decisions form the core of the process called editing. Editing the photographs in a project often is one of the hardest tasks a photographer has to face, a task many photographers simply dread. In principle, it need not be this way. Editing poses a tough challenge, but so does the taking of the pictures from which a final set is supposed to be culled.

"You have to look at every image that is possible for the book, absorb them in a subliminal way," says Alice Rose George, an independent editor, adviser, and curator, who has authored and/or edited a large number of photobooks. "Slowly, you begin to see a beginning, a possible end, a way to move from one image to the other, how to move within to make rhythms, to make visual phrases. As the pieces begin to come together, one move will create the necessity for another." Ultimately, she notes, "intuition plays a big role in the editing and sequencing of a book." This does not mean, however, that there aren't some basic things to be considered.

4.2 Approaching Editing—Basic Rules

While it might seem like almost magic to see an experienced editor very quickly pick photographs out of a larger group, creating a smaller, much more coherent set, in reality a large part of the process relies on experience. This experience can be gained by learning some basic rules that apply to editing.

One of the most important rules is to always run the edits by at least one other pair of eyeballs. Ideally, that other person should be someone who has knowledge of and understands photography and who is going to provide the honesty needed to refine problematic edits. This rules out significant others or loved ones, who might simply be too personally close to offer critical advice. One common mistake photographers make is to assume they will be able to produce an edit without any input by someone else.

Another mistake that is commonly made is to consult a large number of other people about an edit. Editing by committee never works. With too many chefs in the kitchen the edit runs the risk of becoming shapeless and generic. In the worst case, the photographer will end up with a "best of" set of photographs—the photographs everybody can agree on, instead of that focused set the process of editing should produce.

There is a simple reason for involving another person when editing. For a photographer, good editing must start with the process of disassociating what is in the pictures from whatever background knowledge exists about them. The other person might simply neither have the access to the background knowledge, nor might it play much of a role for them.

In late 2014, I spent time with a photographer's contact sheets that showed work done 35 years earlier. After retiring from teaching, the photographer felt she finally wanted to give the work shape in the form of a book. There were stories for almost all of the pictures. This man, I was told, had been briefly accused of murder. That woman, one of whose portraits I had picked, was the photographer's sister.

All I could see, however, were the pictures. I was picking photographs for the first, rough edit based on their form and content. It didn't matter to me, for example, that the blond woman in one of the pictures had been a German citizen who had married a GI, moved to the US and learned English from watching sitcoms. Of course, that's a great story, but it didn't make the pictures that failed to make the cut any better. In much the same way, it didn't matter to me whether the picture of the sister I had picked was the most flattering. I chose the one that photographically looked strongest, the one where content—a woman looking at herself in a bathroom mirror—and form excelled, where the gestures, the position of her body and especially her arms and head (including the reflection of her face in the mirror), filled the frame the best. For me, this was easy, given that I had no emotional attachment to the person whose photographs I looked at. I had no memory of working with her to make the picture.

At some stage the photographer remarked that when reacting to some of my choices, she was not following the advice she had been giving her own students for 35 years: study the pictures, and try to forget all the stories you know about them. It's hard, very hard, to do that, especially if the stories are good, or if the emotions behind the pictures are strong. This is why so many photographers struggle when having to edit. It's easy to become attached to photographs, either through stories behind them or emotional attachments to whatever is being depicted.

At the same time, over the course of their making, many (maybe most) projects evolve. The evolution often results in some early photographs not fitting in any longer later. That great picture that early on defined so much what the project was going to be all about—it might just have to go. Letting go of "important" photographs that simply do not fit into an edit is one of the hardest struggles. It is important to realize that no step during the editing process really needs to be irreversible, except for the very last one: agreeing that these pictures here really are the final edit. This means that if a picture gets cut, there is no reason why it cannot come back in later, provided adding it back in makes sense. Photographers often are very apprehensive about removing a picture from an edit, in particular if they are attached to it, often for reasons that have nothing to do with the image. But if a picture doesn't fit it has to go. If during the process it turns out that it might fit in after all, it can come back in. And even if a picture gets permanently discarded from a book, it might instead find use in a different project or context. Some photographs that do not fit into a book edit might work very well in an exhibition, in much the same way as many photographs that are needed in a book might look terrible when hanging in a frame on a wall.

Even if there is another person involved in the process of editing, the reality is that every photographer has to learn the skills to be able to edit her or his own work, provided she or he is serious about photography. Editing, the selection of one picture over another (or a few others) lies at the very core of the medium. In fact, conceptually speaking the act of editing is only an extension of the process of photographing, of making a decision to take a picture of this–versus that, to take a photograph of this particular part of the landscape instead of the part right next to it etc. Photography is editing, editing is photography.

Of course, there are differences between taking a photograph and editing. But there are important similarities that photographers need to bear in mind. For example, one of the technically most deliberate ways to take a photograph is to use a view camera. A photographer operating a view camera will compose the photograph in possibly the most deliberate way, with the camera sitting on a tripod, and every one of the camera's movements requiring separate, deliberate attention. What is in front of the camera is visible on the ground glass, upside down, the sides reversed. In effect, the photographer is almost looking at the photograph she or he is going to take. Decisions have to be made about the framing, about what to exclude and include, etc.

Generally speaking, the more cumbersome a photographic process, the more deliberate the decisions that go into the framing are. There is no guarantee, however, that the resulting picture will be a keeper. Even for view-camera photographers, there still is that dreaded aspect of editing. But view-camera photographers do what every photographer needs to be doing already when taking a picture.

Being able to edit one's photographs comes down to being able to see them for what they are in a photographic sense. It means being able to study their form and content, and to identify those pictures where form and content work best. This ability really lies at the core of editing. There is no reason for any photographer to say "I'm really bad at editing"—just as there is no actual reason for anyone to say "I'm bad at math." Research has proved that only a very tiny fraction of the population is actually unable to perform the basic math operations required for our everyday life. The vast majority of us are perfectly capable of doing math—to, for example, learn how to calculate a 15 per cent tip on a restaurant bill. But most of us prefer to tell themselves "I'm bad at math" instead of figuring it out. "I'm really bad at editing" is the photographer's equivalent.

Studying form and content is not rocket science. Apart from the resistance I just discussed, what makes it seem hard commonly is an inability to separate out form and content from what one knows about the picture. It's like the photographer I mentioned earlier who would see the GI's German wife instead of a woman with long blond hair. But separating one's knowledge from form and content is also a straightforward process. Form and content are available to anyone who is looking at a photograph. They are what we all see, however conscious we are of what our brains are doing. Form and content are what a stranger will see. That same stranger, however, is very unlikely to possess the same kind of background knowledge as the photographer.

So when studying form and content, the most basic and at the same time most important question should always be: is information I have in my head actually in the picture? In other words, is there anything in the picture that clearly conveys a particular piece of information. That GI's German wife, for example, was not wearing a t-shirt that said "I'm a GI's German wife." There was nothing in the pictures that would indicate her background. Given that the information was not given in the picture, it simply didn't exist.

And this is exactly the point where photographers who are happy to learn about form and content start to baulk. It's one thing to separate one's knowledge from what is in a picture. But it turns out to be much harder to accept that what is not in the picture cannot be taken as existing photographically, however important it might be. In other words, if something that is important is not in a picture, then the photographer either has to take another picture to make sure it is included (take a portrait of the blond woman with a German flag, holding her marriage certificate), or she or he needs to see whether that piece of information is in any of the other pictures. Given we're interested in the medium of the photobook, of course, there are other options to include vital information, be it in the form of text or in other ways (aka indirectly).

4.3 Very Basic Editing

The process of editing begins at the stage where two or more photographs of the same scene are to be considered. With very few—usually conceptual—exceptions, only one of the photographs will make the cut to the next stage. Those conceptual exceptions (think Paul Graham)[1] aside, the moment a photographer looks at a set of frames on a contact sheet or in any of the various programs used these days to organize photography (*Lightroom*, *Aperture*, or whatever else) a decision will have to be made which frame to pick over all the other ones.

Basic editing usually starts with the elimination of anything that technically has problems. Any frame that suffers from technical problems that cannot possibly be fixed will have to go. Of course, that's very obvious, but it's important to realize the different aspects of editing. What is more, when discussing work with students I often come across the case where a frame really is the best one, the one that is needed, even though it suffers from technical problems that cannot be fixed. But the reality of photography is that if you didn't get your picture perfectly then, well, you will have to try again. Eliminating photographs with technical problems usually reduces the task of editing somewhat, in particular in the case of digital photography where there are often countless variants of an image.

At the same stage, photographs with obvious photographic problems will have to be removed. For example, unless you really want and need that portrait where the subject happens to have their eyes closed, it will have to go (you better have a very good reason for it that works inside the framework of the project in question). In much the same fashion, all versions that suffer from similar problems need to be discarded (again, unless you can come up with a very good justification for not doing it, given the parameters of the project—and not your own back story).

Thus editing should always start out with pictures that photographically and technically are sound, given the parameters of the project. I'm mentioning the project parameters on purpose here. Your project might be that exception that uses portraits of people with their eyes closed, or underexposed photographs, or whatever else ordinarily would be eliminated. If that is the case, you will have to make decisions which pictures to exclude using slightly relaxed basic considerations. But for the vast majority of photography projects pictures that are problematic need to be removed.

4.4 Basic Editing

Once we're beyond very basic editing we're at the stage where decisions have to be made about variants of the same frame. It now might be best to discuss the following steps using examples.[2] Figures 4.1 to 4.4 show four frames from Richard Renaldis' *Touching Strangers* (in the following, I'm going to refer to the photographs in Figures 4.1, 4.2, 4.3, and 4.4 as *Nathan and Robyn 1*, *Nathan and Robyn 2*, *Nathan and Robyn 3*, and *Nathan and Robyn 4*, respectively). A series of photographic portraits, for *Touching Strangers* the photographer found pairs or groups of people who did not know one another, waiting with his camera at

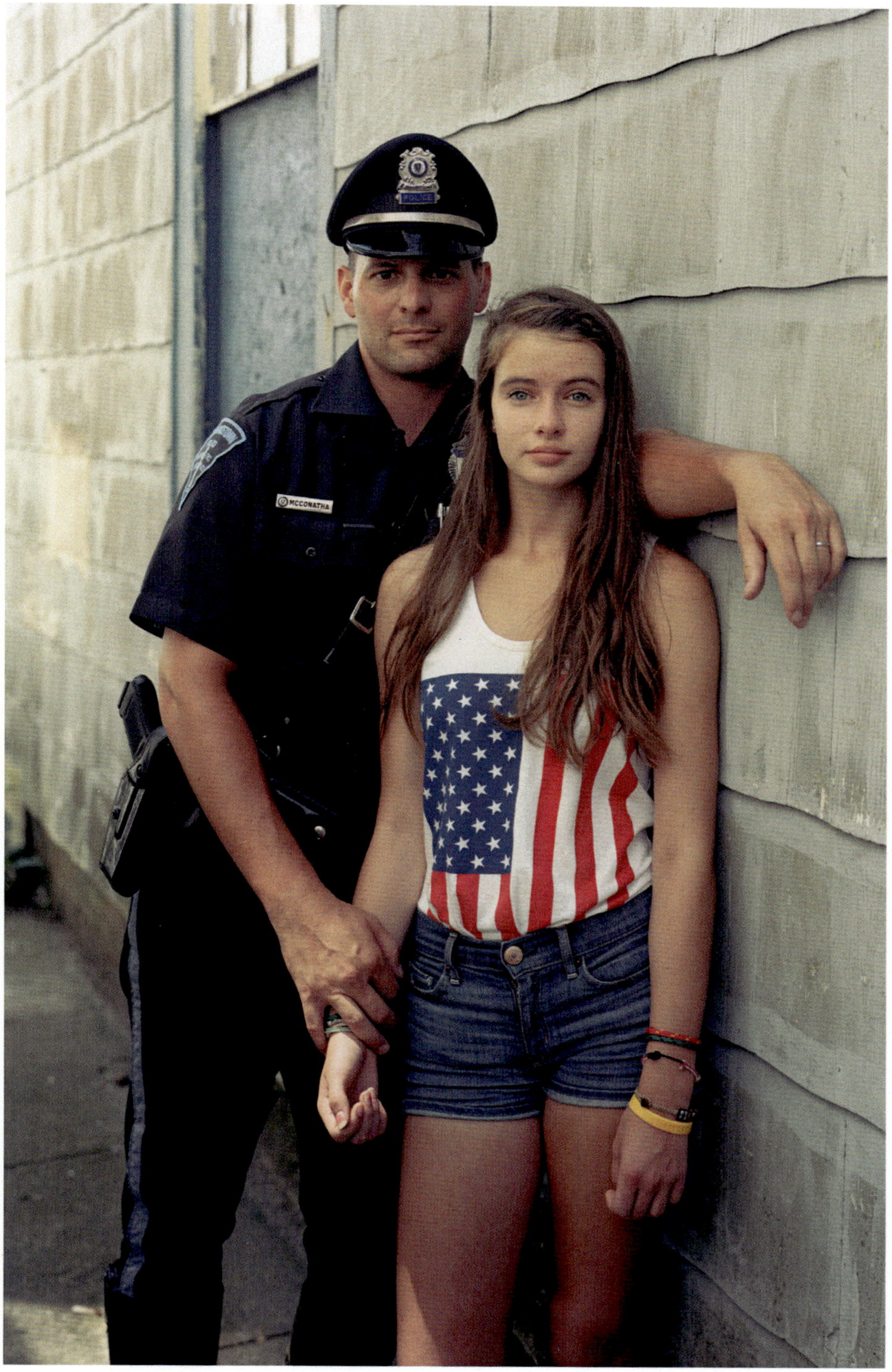

Figure 4.1 Richard Renaldi—*Nathan and Robyn, 2012*
Photograph courtesy and © Richard Renaldi

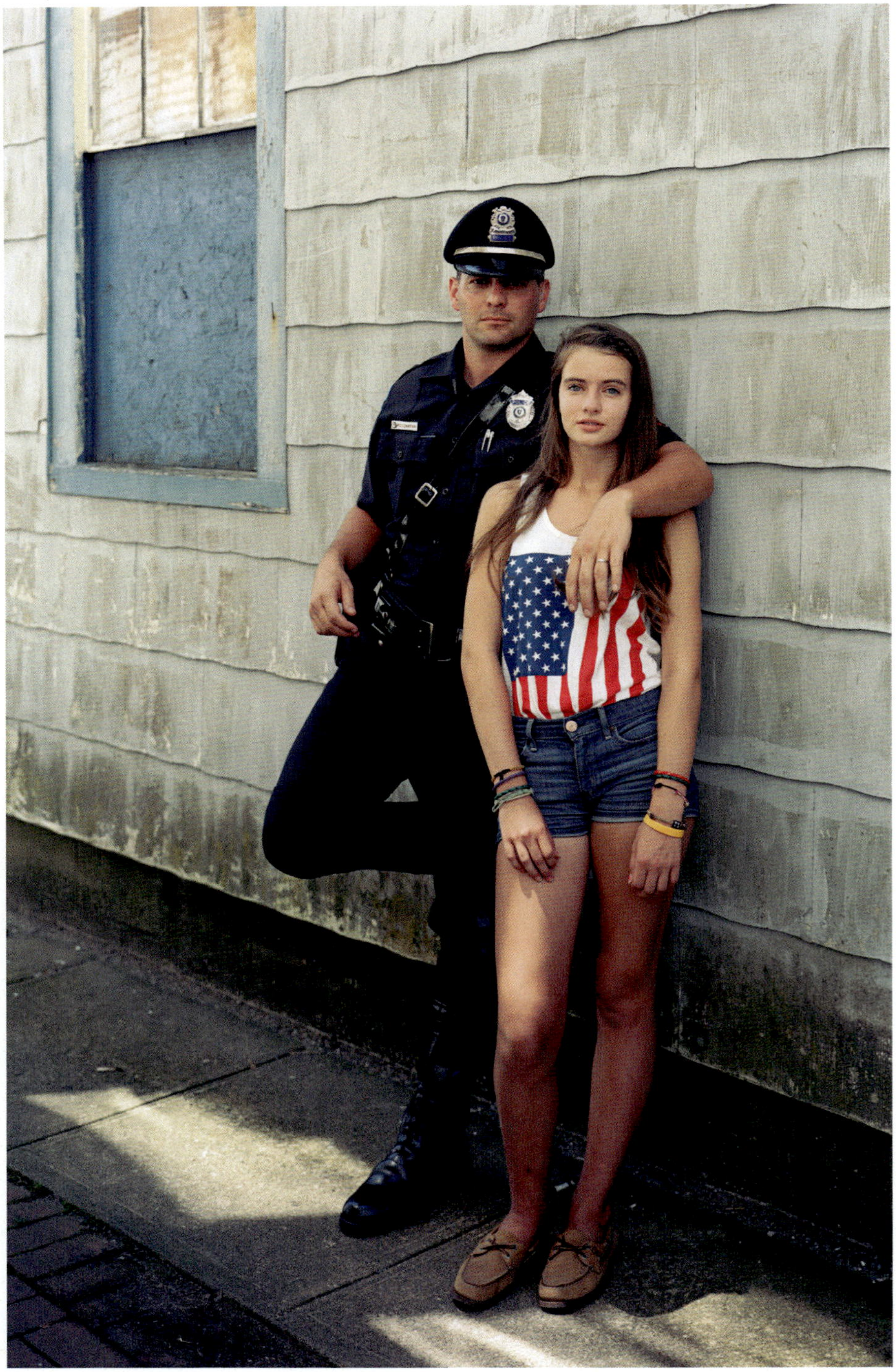

Figure 4.2 Richard Renaldi—*Nathan and Robyn, 2012*
Photograph courtesy and © Richard Renaldi

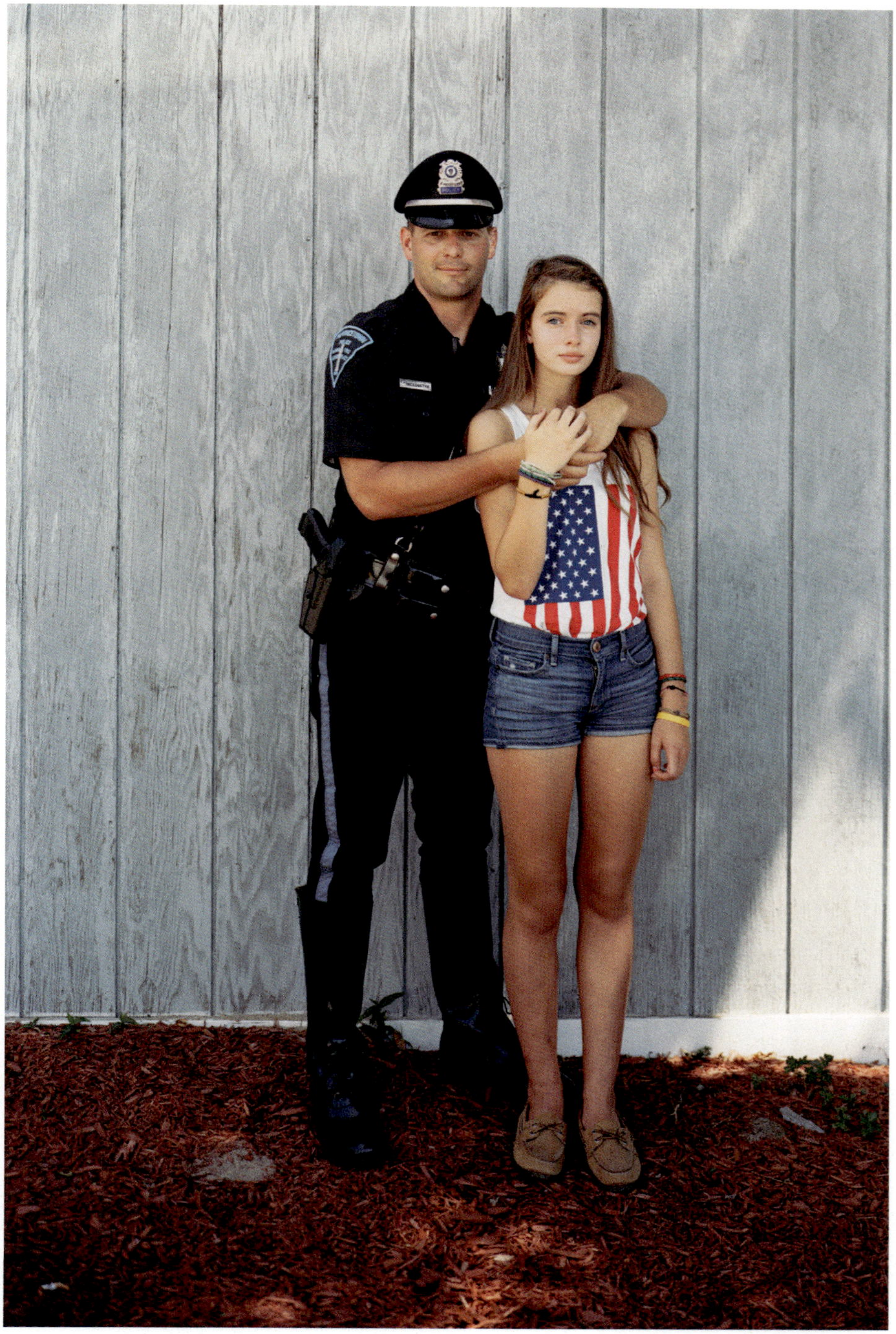

Figure 4.3 Richard Renaldi—*Nathan and Robyn, 2012*
Photograph courtesy and © Richard Renaldi

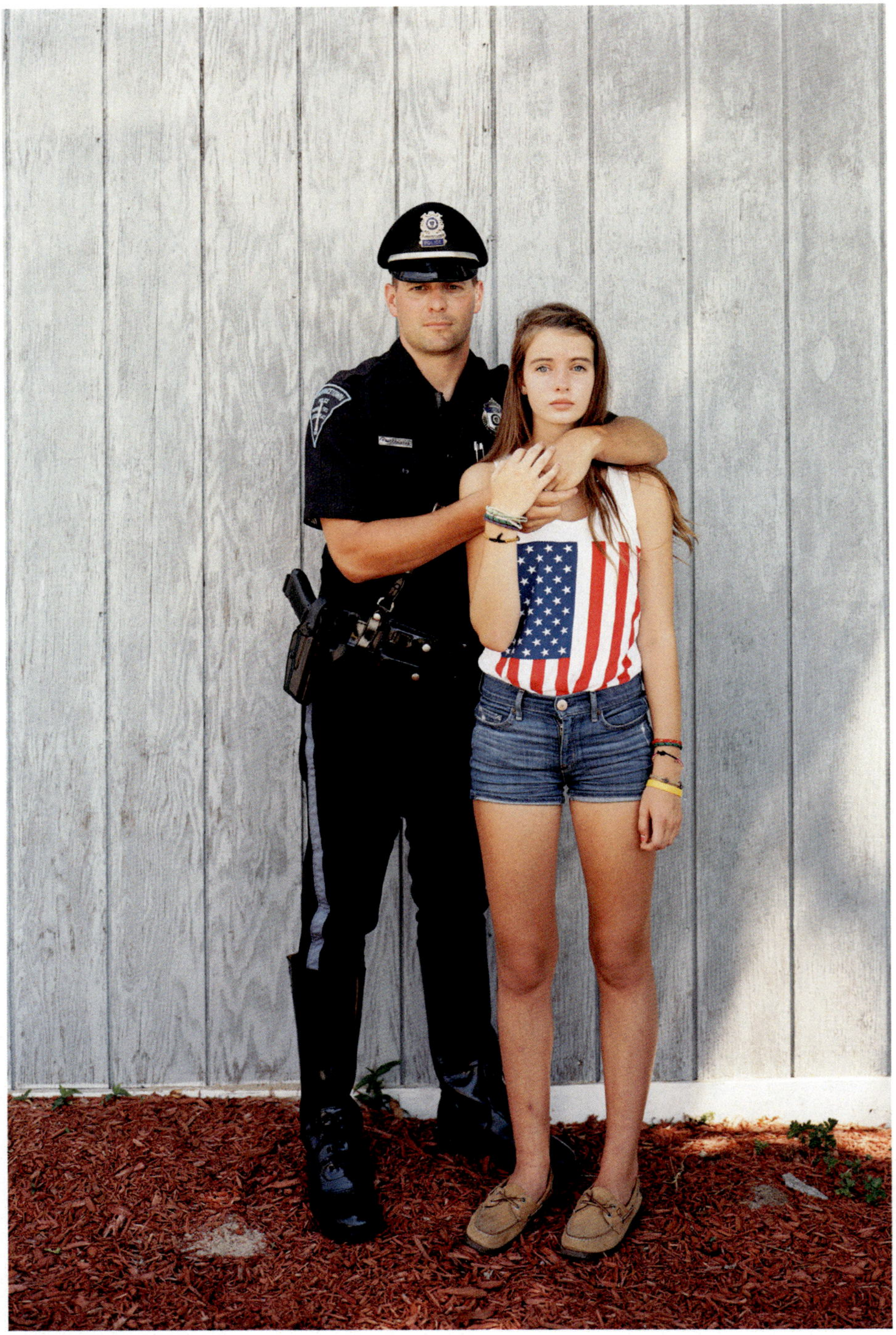

Figure 4.4 Richard Renaldi—*Nathan and Robyn, 2012*
Photograph courtesy and © Richard Renaldi

selected locations. He then asked his willing subjects to pose for a portrait, the condition being that they would have some form of physical contact with one another. In the United States, strangers will not easily touch each other, with all kinds of minor variation caused by differences in gender, age, etc.

The four photographs in question here show the pairing of a police officer, Nathan, and a young woman, Robyn. In general form, the portraits are similar. They each show Nathan and Robyn standing close to and touching each other, against the backdrop of nondescript buildings with blueish grey sidings. Both look straight at the camera. These general similarities aside, the four pictures differ in a lot of details, however. *Nathan and Robyn 1* and *2* appear to have been photographed in the same spot, with the building angling towards the camera (and thus viewer): the building's farther end is slightly outside the depth of field. In contrast, in *Nathan and Robyn 3* and *4* the building has changed, and it is now photographed straight on. What is more, in contrast to the other two exposures where there is a sidewalk, Nathan and Robyn now stand on what looks like dry mulch. Even though *Nathan and Robyn 1* and *2* were photographed in the same spot, the pictures differ in the way they are framed. *Nathan and Robyn 1* shows the two roughly from their knees up, while *2* (just as *3* and *4*) provides a view of their full bodies.

But there are more differences, given that the subjects' poses are not identical, and neither are the ways they are in physical contact with each other. In *Nathan and Robyn 1*, the officer is leaning a little bit stiffly against the siding of the house, his left arm extended across the young woman's shoulder (while not touching it), his right hand holding her wrist in the loosest possible way (his pinkie wraps around the wrist, while his thumb is aligned with the rest of that hand's fingers). The two look somewhat comfortable with each other, yet at the same time, they clearly look like the strangers they are. We might also add that near the left edge of the frame, there are weeds visible that, while they are out of focus, still provide a green note that is somewhat distracting. What is more, one of the boarded-up windows of the building looks like it's coming straight out of the officer's right shoulder, which creates a slight distraction.

Nathan and Robyn 2 clearly is an improvement, given that the weeds are gone, and the window is far enough away from the couple. Here, the officer is also leaning against the building, albeit with his back now, his right foot placed against the wall. Nathan has now placed his left arm on Robyn's shoulder, his left hand hanging loose in front of her chest, while his right arm rests on top of his gun holster. Just as in *1*, the young woman stands in front of the officer, her hip cocked, and her arms hanging loosely in front of her body. Here, however, Robyn's facial expression seems to indicate that she feels a little bit more comfortable.

Much like the background itself, *Nathan and Robyn 3* and *4* include a few important changes compared with *2*. Just as in the previous image, the officer has his left arm resting on the young woman's shoulder, but with his right hand touching his left one, there now exists an embrace of sorts. Unlike in the previous two images, Robyn here acknowledges the embrace, touching the officer's hands with her own right one. Her relatively comfortable posture has now given way to one where there is equal body weight on both legs, while there appears to be a bit of unease in her face. But *Nathan and Robyn 3* and *4*, while so similar, also offer subtle differences. The slight deviation in framing aside, these differences concern both the young woman's posture, and the couple's facial expressions. In *Nathan and Robyn 3*, it looks as if she has her body turned slightly away from the man standing next to her. Her feet are pointing at the camera, yet her right shoulder is turned towards the camera. In contrast, in *4*, Robyn's feet are now slightly turning towards the police officer, while her body confronts the camera squarely. In addition, there are subtle, yet important differences in their facial expressions. In *3*, there is a very slight smile on the officer's face, as is on the young woman's (at least that is how her facial expression comes across). In *Nathan and Robyn 4*, however, both subjects' facial expressions are much more neutral, with a hint of maybe unease in the young woman's face. The third photograph looks like a pleasant enough photograph of two strangers touching each other and posing for the camera. But the fourth one removes whatever pleasantness there is, to add elements of something being possibly wrong, for reasons that aren't quite clear. To use Roland Barthes' notion, there is a *punctum* in *Nathan and Robyn 4*, but not in 3.[3]

In light of the preceding, *Nathan and Robyn 4* appears to be the most interesting of these four photographs. Compositionally, it is strongest, and it also carries most tension concerning the aspect of two strangers touching. This tension is actually amplified by the juxtaposition of the two characters. The police officer's role is to protect citizens such as Robyn. With her looks and outfit—shorts and a top that features the American flag—the young woman can serve perfectly as a stand-in for the "all-American girl." But something in the juxtaposition of the young woman and police officer, in particular in *4*, is off. The man is not old enough to be her father, and their contact does not look close enough to be a relative's. Seemingly protective at first, the officer's arms around the young woman look a little bit too restrictive, a fact supported by the slight discomfort in Robyn's face. Something is a little (or maybe even more than a little) off in *Nathan and Robyn 4.* The photograph invites speculation, certainly interpretation, in the way it uses its symbolism. These are not just any two strangers touching each other. The tension in this photograph is absent in the other three. So based on all of these observations, it might not come as a surprise to the reader that photograph *4* is the one known as *Nathan and Robyn, 2012* in Renaldi's *Touching Strangers*, with the other three being outtakes. In fact, this particular photograph ended up on the cover of the widely acclaimed, eponymous 2014 Aperture book.

The discussion of these four photographs should have made it clear why and how it is extremely important during the process of editing to consider each and every detail. Note that in order to decide on which photograph to select we did not have to rely on background knowledge of what took place during the photography session. As noted before, editing must rely on what is in the pictures and only what is in the pictures. Not more, not less. The photographer had this to say about these photographs: "I think all [...] are actually interesting to look at and if I never made the image in front of the vertical wooden siding that is now the cover of *Touching Strangers* I likely would have included one of the other [ones] in the book. Perhaps the outtakes feel a little more casual and familiar than the chosen image but I think the sentiment isn't that far apart between the [...] images. I am drawn to the image

I chose because it has a pleasing formalism, it is a strongly graphic image, and has an elegance that might be missing from the other two."[4] Renaldi's comments make it clear how hard editing can be when the individual candidate pictures are all very strong. But they also show a photographer at the top of his game, selecting the picture with ultimately the most power.

4.5 Pictures Next to Pictures

As has become clear in the preceding section, every photograph in an edit should be the strongest of its possible variants. Whether or not there actually are going to be variants depends on the photographer's preferred mode of working. While it is advisable for a photographer to have more than one candidate for a photograph, in reality that might not always be the case, either because of the nature of the work in question or because of the photographer's approach. If there are variants, selecting the strongest pictures comes first.

Given an edit is a group of pictures, it is very important to understand the relationships photographs can have with each other. An accomplished edit will feel like a unified body of work, where each of its members performs just the right task and operates in a very specific way next to all the other ones. Beyond picking the strongest variants for any picture, the next and very important step is to understand how two pictures relate to each other. Even if the resulting photobook might never show two pictures right next to each other, the relationships between photographs will still be easily apparent to its viewers.

As it turns out, for many photographers there is a lot to be learned from placing two photographs next to each other. There will inevitably be a dialogue between the two pictures, even though that dialogue could easily be dissonant. But whatever it is, the dialogue is based on each photograph's form and/or content.

I want to discuss what the relationship between two photographs means, and how there is a dialogue between them, using a few examples. The very first, trivial, example would be to place the same photograph next to another copy of it. While there might be cases where this could possibly be interesting (I can't remember seeing one, however), things get a lot more instructive when there are two different photographs.

Figure 4.5 shows two photographs from Sjoerd Knibbeler's *Paper Planes* (Fw:Photography, 2015). Both in terms of form (the way these photographs are organized) and content (what they show) *P-139B* and *Tu-2000* are very similar. Yet they are also different. Let's pretend we know absolutely nothing about these pictures, not even their titles or what body of work they are from. What do we actually see? For a start, both photographs are black and white. Furthermore, they both center on an object that is suspended through the use of two thin wires. These objects are shaped like planes, and there are various indications that they are made from paper. Of course, we would have known this from the title of the project. But as I noted before, in photography, we need to strictly work with what is in the pictures, ignoring additional information.[5] These are photographed against a nondescript, uniform background,

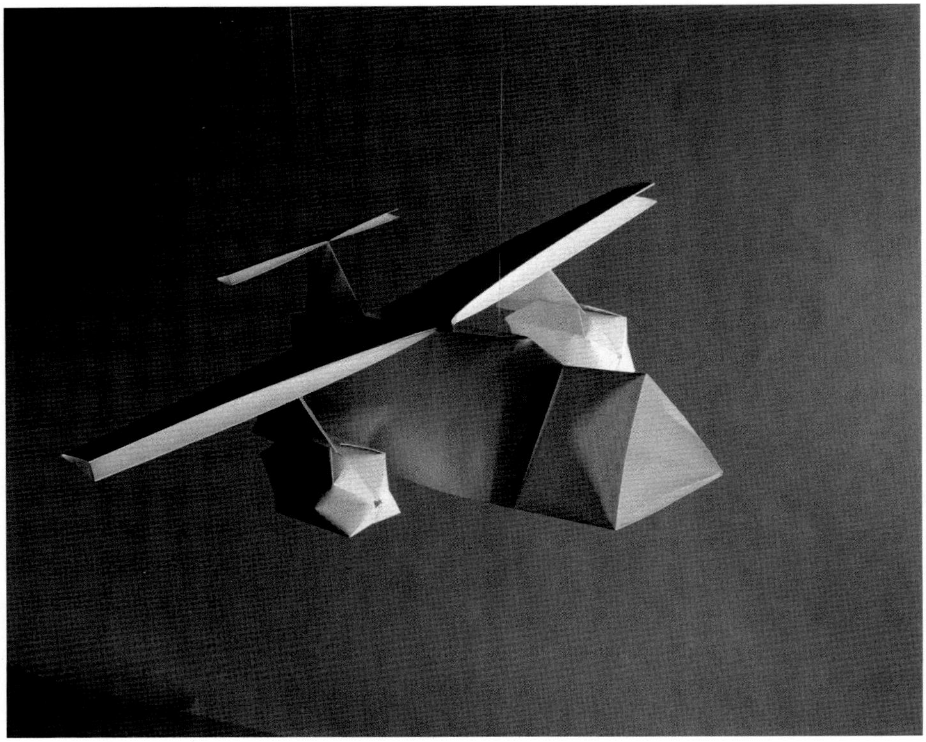

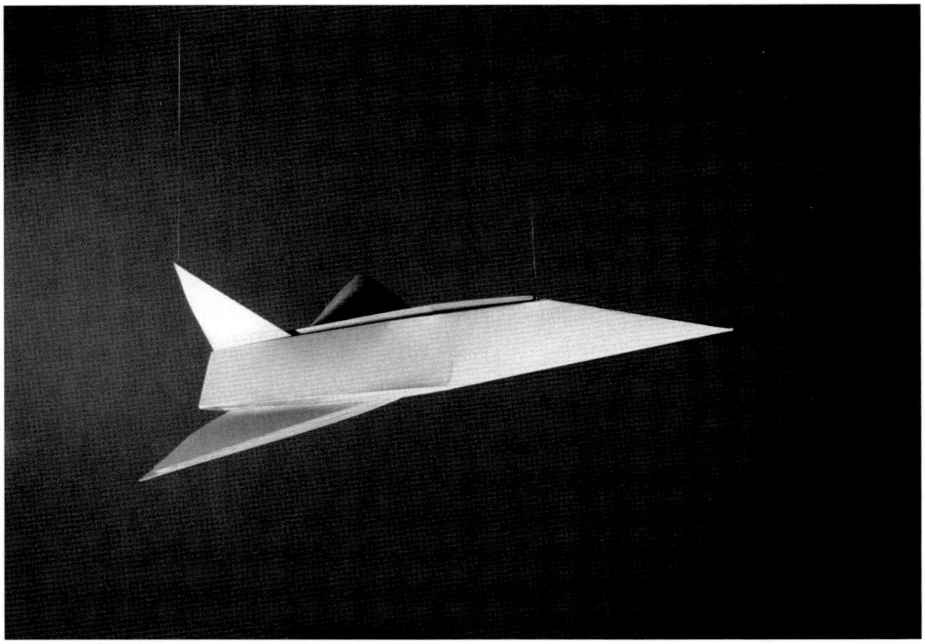

Figure 4.5 *P-139B* (top) and *Tu-2000* (bottom), from Sjoerd Knibbeler's *Paper Planes*
Photographs courtesy and © Sjoerd Knibbeler

which, due to the way the scenes are lit, contains graduations in grey tonalities. Although we have no way of knowing this from the pictures, we can assume that the lighting was based on the planes themselves, to make sure that each plane's structure would be seen most clearly. So the photographs are kind of the same—each is a picture of a paper plane (in the broadest sense, their form and content are identical). But they're not the same picture. Start to look more carefully, and you'll note differences in both form and, crucially, content. They're different, and the more we look at them, the more differences we see. We obviously see that the planes' shapes are different. Given that that's almost all we have got to play with, we focus on it. There is a type of photography that uses this kind of mechanism to make the viewer engage with specific objects, all of which essentially are the same, but look different, the typology. The most well-known example of typologies is provided by Bernd and Hilla Becher's work on industrial structures.

Photography history and theory aside, what I'm interested in here is not so much the idea of a typology. Instead, I'm interested in what happens when we look at two pictures from a typology side by side: given that the pictures inevitably will be very similar, the differences in the content will be magnified (usually, a typology is done in such a way that there are no formal differences whatsoever). In other words, when we look at two pictures next to each other that are very similar, yet slightly different, the dialogue in our heads focuses around these differences. Questions possibly arise, such as what those differences might mean. Needless to say, this dialogue is not necessarily a given. A viewer might well lack the willingness and/or focus to engage with the photographs to the degree needed for this to happen. But whatever willingness and/or focus a viewer will be able to bring to the work is more or less uncontrollable. It needn't concern us.

For an artist working with typologies or other work where there are very strict formal similarities (think, for example, Richard Avedon's *In the American West*—a series of portraits, all shot against the same nondescript white background; also see the discussion of the very similar portraits in the preceding section), it is extremely important to be aware of what exactly these small differences between the pictures do. Will they point at whatever she or he is interested in? If not, then one of the pictures will have to go. If they do, another, third, picture can be added in, and the process can be expanded.

For photographers not working along those veins, it is possible that this preceding discussion really might be a variant of what I discussed in section 4.4. I'm using the phrase "might be" on purpose, because it could also be the case that the two photographs might, in fact, play their slightly separate roles in the edit. Again, the main question centers on whether the two pictures will point at something the photographer is interested in. If not, it's quite likely one of the photographs will have to go (in this case, the discussion from section 4.4 can be used to determine which one). If they do, then they both stay, and another picture needs to be considered.

Before discussing expanded edits, I want to continue looking at pairs of pictures. Figure 4.5 provided a relatively simple example. Let's look at two pictures that are not so obviously similar. Figure 4.6 shows a pair of untitled photographs from Tamara Shopsin and Jason Fulford's children's book *This Equals That* (Aperture, 2014). While billed as

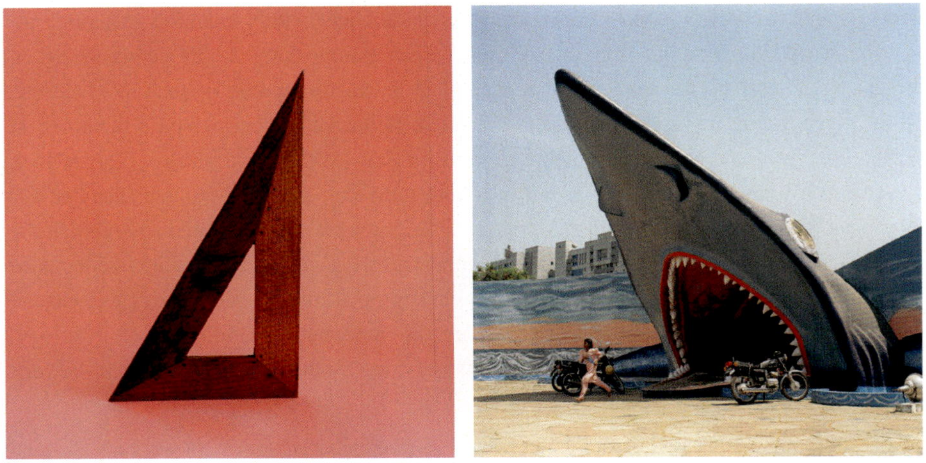

Figure 4.6 Pair of untitled photographs from Tamara Shopsin and Jason Fulford's children's book *This Equals That* (Aperture, 2014)
Photographs courtesy and © Tamara Shopsin and Jason Fulford

aiming "at children aged five and up,"[6] the book offers invaluable lessons for any photographer interested in understanding the relationships between pairs of pictures, in particular those struggling to get to a closer understanding of them. In a very literal sense, the photograph on the left-hand side of Figure 4.6 does not "equal" the one on the right. A wooden triangle tool is not the entrance of what might be an amusement park that happens to look like a shark's open mouth. Looking at the photographs this way, however, causes a few problems. For a start, one needs to be careful with confusing the photographs with what they depict. A photograph of a wooden triangle tool is not a wooden triangle tool. This might sound incredibly obvious, but surprisingly enough many photographers will still talk about a photograph's subject matter when they need to be talking about the photograph itself. In other words, while form and content are both important, content often is being solely considered while form is ignored. But what is it in Figure 4.6 that makes one think that this photograph on the left indeed equals (in some way) the one of the right? Given how I set this up, it's obvious that form needs to be considered. The wooden triangle tool's shape can indeed be found in multiple ways in the photograph on the right. For a start, the scale of the tool and the shark's mouth are roughly the same in the two photographs. They're also very similar in their shapes. And the more the viewer looks at the photograph on the right, the more elements of the left one appear. There are many triangles, including the shark's teeth. On top of that, the overall shade of red from the picture on the left can be found in the other picture as well, such as in the shark's mouth, but also as two bands of color that run towards it from both sides. What is more, the blue tones in the image on the right (the sky plus the blue and grey-blue of the structures) work as complementary colors to the red tones in the picture on the left (which, as we just noted, can also be found in small parts in the picture on the right—note that even the girl running from the shark's mouth is wearing something mostly red with a blue stripe in it).

Thus, a photograph's form centers on a variety of aspects, all of which, here, point to this picture on the left indeed being equal to that picture on the right. Similarities concern the dominant shape used in the pictures (the triangle), the relative scales (the largest triangles in both pictures are very close in size), and color (here both the direct correspondence as well as the aspect of complementary color tones). Of course, there always is the photographs' content, which clearly differs. A viewer is unlikely to be made to think that a wooden triangle tool somehow is the same as that shark-shaped building. But the correspondence in formal elements brings the two pictures into a dialogue. Specifically, once the viewer realizes the formal similarities, she or he will establish a relationship between the pictures. That aspect of recognition in a viewer's mind is of utmost importance for the process of editing and sequencing, since it can also work when two similar pictures are not seen next to each other. A very dominant shape or color in a picture can be mirrored by a very dominant shape or color in another picture, in all likelihood triggering this very sort of recognition in a viewer's mind. Obviously, the same is true for elements of content. Typically, though, finding such patterns poses a tough challenge for most photographers. What is crucial here is the fact that even young children—the audience Shopsin and Fulford's book is aimed at—are already good at spotting such patterns. Humans are visually very adept animals. What this means is that editing and sequencing can indeed be learned, provided careful attention is paid to form and content.

Figure 4.7 presents another example of a pair from Shopsin and Fulford's *This Equals That*. Much as in Figure 4.6, the pair has a photograph featuring geometrical shapes versus one that a lot more obviously is what we could call a "straight photograph." But unlike earlier, here, the dominant shapes—diamonds versus circles—don't match up. Formal similarities are reduced to the simple use of colors—the individual diamonds on the left, and the flowers on

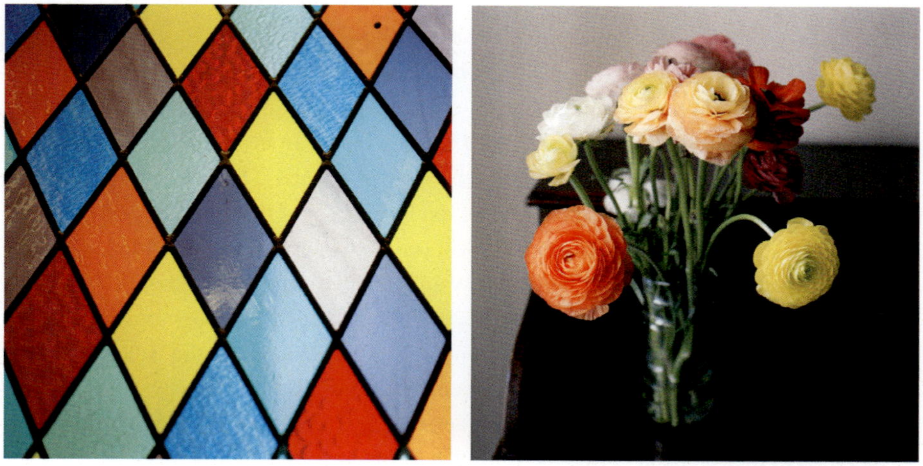

Figure 4.7 Another pair of untitled photographs from Tamara Shopsin and Jason Fulford's children's book *This Equals That* (Aperture, 2014)

the right. But on the left, the colors dominate, filing the entire frame. On the right, the colors are embedded in an almost monochromatic-grey background. So it seems clear that the juxtaposition of the two photographs in Figure 4.6 provides a much closer formal match than the one in Figure 4.7. Mind you, the two images don't clash. But what dialogue they invite pales in comparison to the one seen earlier.

4.6 The Kuleshov Effect

To understand and/or explain what two photographs might do when seen right next to or after each other, the Kuleshov effect is often invoked. It is named after Russian filmmaker and theorist Lev Kuleshov, who in the early twentieth century attempted to understand the then new medium of film.[7] In a nutshell, the Kuleshov effect is the outcome of showing two short shots right after each other. In the original 1918 version, Kuleshov used a short clip of silent movie actor Ivan Mozzhukhin. In it, Mozzhukhin simply stared at the camera. Kuleshov combined this short clip with other, seemingly unrelated ones such as a short clip showing a bowl of soup or a dead child. What he found was that the audience would interpret the actor's emotion based on the juxtaposition of the two clips (Mozzhukhin plus a bowl of soup would indicate hunger etc.). Sergei Eisenstein, a student of Kuleshov, later surmised that these kinds of juxtaposition, known as montage, were what made film *work*.

It is true that in films, such montage techniques are often used, and they work. But, of course, one needs to be a bit careful when applying montage ideas to photography. In a very simple sense, placing two photographs next to each other, to use the dialogue created between them, is a basic montage technique. It still has to be made to work, however, and this might be a bit different than what an audience would see in a film. For a start, a film carefully controls the viewer's exposure. In particular, the element of time enters movies in ways that are absent from photography. In a photobook, a viewer can decide to look at a single image for any amount of time. She or he can go back and forth between the images, regardless of whether they are placed next to one another or follow each other on consecutive pages, once or as often as might be needed to grasp things. In filmmaking, these possibilities of engagement are if not entirely absent then vastly reduced. The director will take that decision away from a viewer. Two images are rarely, if ever, seen next to each other. And a sequence of a shot followed by another shot, will last a fixed, predetermined amount of time, after which the film will continue moving forward. Another way to describe the difference between a photobook and a film would be to say that a photobook, through its form, allows for a kind of analysis that in films is not intended.[8] So, when applying the Kuleshov effect to photography, it needs to be considered against the possibility of analysis. Analysis will not necessarily undermine what two photographs do next to each other (or right after one another). What they do derives from their form and content, but only to a very small amount from the way the images are placed. And note, this doesn't even take into account that in filmmaking, sound also plays an important role now, something that, of course, is entirely absent from photobooks.

4.7 Sequencing a Photobook

Editing and sequencing a body of work for a photobook are not necessarily two completely independent activities. Part of the reason why I am discussing them separately is due to their complex interactions. What is more, there are aspects of both that can be separated out. In reality, however, editing and sequencing often go hand in hand, with, for example, a set of photographs on a table getting arranged and rearranged in many ways. Photographs might be taken from the table or added (back in). Photographs might be placed next to, or moved apart from one another. Little sequences might form, or they might be broken up. Larger sequences might be formed from smaller ones. And then pictures might be brought back to fill gaps in a sequence, or they might be taken out because the sequence doesn't work. That said, the basic properties of editing discussed earlier always hold true. Without knowing about how to look at photographs and how to see how they relate to each other, editing (let alone sequencing) is impossible. In fact, one might argue that every pair of photographs that work together already contains the nucleus of a small sequence: you could simply show one photograph and then the next one.

But sequencing itself does not solely rely on the various aspects of editing I discussed earlier. There are other and/or additional ones. In the most basic sense, putting a set of photographs into a sequence by showing one after the other creates a flow from a beginning to an end.[9] This is a completely trivial observation, but it's extremely important at the same time: a book has a beginning and an end.[10] The task of the sequence, of the order in which the photographs are presented in the book, is to take the viewer from the beginning to the end in a way that makes sense. There has to be a logic to the sequence, however we want to define this logic, that allows the viewer to understand how one gets from the beginning to the end. If not, the book won't make sense to the viewer. "You have to guide the viewer to see what you and the photographer have seen." says Alice Rose George, describing the sequencing in terms of a flow: "A book goes between a front and back cover. You know you have to have movement within. That movement can be linear, narrative, or a more chaotic structure, maybe using color or shapes or subjects or any other thing!" The idea of movement is crucial, and a great way to approach thinking about sequencing. The book "can't just sit there with images that don't go anywhere, whether it's a 'story' progressing from a to b or a symphonic type elaboration of themes and moods. Without movement one would have a catalogue." Finding a sequence amounts to finding that logic, that way of making these individual steps from one picture to the next and then to the next etc. that will allow the viewer to understand what is going on. If talk of a logic sounds too abstract or theoretical, thinking about a trail of breadcrumbs that can be followed might help. In a gallery talk at Blue Sky Gallery in Portland, Oregon, in October 2015, Christopher Rauschenberg used this picture speaking to students of mine about photography projects. There would have to be such a trail of breadcrumbs, he said, for viewers to be able to follow the photographer's ideas and intentions.

Note that the inclusion of text does not change this game in the least. If there are snippets or sections of text that are included in the sequence, they also have to follow the very basic logic. Usually (or maybe often), text is added simply because the pictures alone fail to carry the viewer/reader from the beginning to the end. Please note that when I say "fail" I don't mean this in a negative way. Some things simply cannot be shown with pictures. Some books require text (remember the discussion of Laia Abril's *The Epilogue*). That said, this does not mean that if a sequence can't be made to work without text adding text necessarily solves the problem. As we saw in the previous chapter, everything needs to firmly be embedded in the book's *concept*.

Let's ignore text now. Let's assume we're dealing with a photobook in which the pictures alone carry the burden of taking a viewer from a beginning to an end. How can this be done? It is tempting to look at other media, in which an audience is taken from a beginning to an end. Given it is also a visual medium, as we already saw cinema is often brought up. I will have to admit that while there is nothing wrong per se with comparing two different types of medium, such comparisons only make sense as long as one keeps their differences in mind. A movie has a beginning and an end, and the viewer will typically get there by watching it at the pace its creator(s) intended.[11] A photobook, in contrast, is being looked through at the viewer's pace. So as a photobook maker, you do not have the same tricks at your disposal that you can use as a filmmaker. You cannot show an image for just a split second. What is more, cinema usually does not use still photographs, but short segments, each of which contains moving images. Those segments differ from still photographs. Plus, cinema employs sound. So one really needs to be careful when comparing photobooks and movies. In particular, one must be careful when trying to take something used by filmmakers, to apply it to photography (in much the same fashion as comparing photography and poetry, say, is also problematic).

But films, whether fictional or not, do go from a beginning to an end, just as photobooks do, and there are some things photobook makers can learn from filmmakers. Much like you are unlikely to continue watching a movie that simply doesn't appear to make any sense, you will put aside a photobook that you cannot understand. So establishing whatever a photobook centers on is one of the first and most important aspects of creating a sequence. Needless to say, given that there is a huge variety of possibilities for photobooks, there is no recipe for how to do that. But the beginning of a photobook has to provide an entry point, a relatively small number of pictures that give the viewer the feeling that she or he will be taken on a tour with a probably as-of-yet unknown destination and that that tour will make sense. In other words, a viewer puts her or his trust into a photobook's maker(s), and that trust must not be betrayed. That is extremely important. The moment the viewer loses faith, she or he will put the book aside, often to never look at it again. "I get angry when I look at a book and am not taken where the book promised to take me," says Alice Rose George. So a sequence has to make sense, there has to be a logic of sorts (even if that logic is entirely poetic), and the very beginning needs to provide the basis for that logic. There could be, for example, "establishing shots"— photographs that introduce, let's say, a location, or a person, or a group of people. The relevance of establishing context in a photobook varies with the type of work, but context is extremely important, because it allows the viewers to understand what is going on. For example, as described in the previous chapter, Laia Abril's *The Epilogue* has a very clear first section, in which the very basis of the whole book is laid out: these are the people who matter throughout the course of the book, this is what we're dealing with here.

Of course, *The Epilogue* is a book based on a very specific idea of storytelling. In general, the closer a book adheres to the idea of telling a story, the more specific the introduction has to become. In other words, if you go from an A to a B, from a clear beginning to a clear end, you will have to make sure the viewer understands what that A is and how things move from there so that the viewer understands that the book works towards some B. The most obvious examples would be provided by a trip where someone is traveling from one place to another place. There, the sequence could be very obvious, starting at the first location and ending at, well, the final location. At the same time, however, the viewer would need to be made to understand that it's a trip. In a very similar fashion, instead of traveling in space, one could travel in time, from some earlier point in time to a later one. While these examples are very simple, they still are instructive. Once the viewer understands she or he is taken on a trip, she or he will be happy to come along. As a matter of fact, while the photographs could have been taken in a completely different order, in the sequence the viewer has to be convinced that the order in which they are presented makes sense. If the sequence makes sense to a viewer, the job is done.[12]

Sze Tsung Leong described the sequence of his book *Horizons* as follows:[13] "I started the book with relatively empty images populated with people to establish both how the horizon line marks space, and our relationship to viewing our surroundings. The visual field then gradually becomes more filled. The end of the book returns to that relative emptiness, a cycle of sorts." Sequencing a book following such formal considerations can make perfect sense, provided it suits the work, as is clearly the case for this particular book. Needless to say, what sounds like a fairly simple and straightforward description of the sequence might only have been arrived at after considerable effort. As is often the case in photography (actually indeed, in life in general), in hindsight, solutions for problems are easy to describe.

As we already saw, thinking of a sequence as taking a viewer from a beginning to an end is an obvious approach. A book, after all, will go from a beginning (the front of the book) to the end (its back). That said, one needs to be careful and not only think of a sequence as something that goes from one picture to the next, to the next, to the next, and so on, in strictly logical ways. There are a lot of books in which this happens, and there is absolutely nothing wrong with it. But relationships between pictures might also go beyond those of close pairs. Describing a book by Nathan Lyons, Keith A. Smith says the photographer not only takes the photographs, "but *modifies* these by placing each picture in context not only to the adjacent one, but to every picture in the book. [...] This permits speaking between the pictures, to speaking on many levels."[14] In fact, in his *Structure of the Visual Book*, from which the preceding quote was taken, Smith separates between series and sequences: "A series is structured so that the relationship of terms is such, that each successive term, is derived from the one preceding it by the application of a specific principle. A sequence is structured by allowing one image to follow another by an order of presentation which is not apparently thematic or systematic."[15] While I can see where Smith is coming from, I personally don't find this distinction too useful, because as many books demonstrate, even if constructed as a series in the Smith sense, his definition of sequence might apply at the same time. But his description of what a sequence does is very apt: "Each picture in a sequence exists in context to not only the facing page, the following page, but to *every* picture in the book. A picture many pages distant can completely alter the meaning of an earlier image. Displaying the first image isolated is like speaking part of a sentence—it may have some meaning, but is incomplete and must be qualified by the total statement. Each word in a sentence suggests some meaning, but each is qualified by context of the total statement."[16] This is what makes creating a working sequence often so hard: you have to build something that will take the viewer from a beginning to an end, and it will all have to make sense as a whole. But thinking of individual photographs as units of a larger whole, as fragments of something bigger, might also be liberating for photobook makers, provided they are able to reorient their view from the pictures to the whole. That might just be one of the toughest challenges, since photography, in terms of the making and even viewing, usually comes down to these individual units, the photographs. Once you have a rough edit, they all seem to be equally important, much like one's children, say. One would be a bad parent preferring one over another. But when making a photobook, a photographer must move away from treating her or his photographs this way. As I noted earlier, some photographs might simply not be included, simply because in the end, it's about the book itself, that larger unit, that object that ultimately is more than the sum of its parts. Lazlo Moholy-Nagy spoke of a book (and similar collections of photographs) and the pictures it contains as follows: "Here the single picture loses its separate identity and becomes a structural element of the related whole which is the thing itself."[17] So how can this be done?

Some sequences can be made in a very simple and obvious manner. Figures 4.8 to 4.10 show the first three photographs from Gerry Johansson's *Deutschland* (MACK, 2012). Ostensibly a book about Germany, but in reality containing the photographer's specific vision of the country, the photographs in *Deutschland* are sequenced in the alphabetical order of the cities' names they were taken in, here Alt Horsbüll, Altenlingen, and Altheim for Figures 4.8, 4.9, and 4.10, respectively. Of course, this is a completely obvious way to sequence a book about a country. But at the same time, it still has to work in terms of the overall book's experience. In Johansson's case, it does. In fact, he used the same strategy in his books covering the US (*Amerika*) and Sweden (*Sverige*). In the cases of these books covering geographical regions, the photographs each are completely self-contained little entities (here reproduced in exactly the same size as in the original book, which itself is 7" by 9 ¾"). They're really not about the cities they were taken in at all. Instead, they're each incredibly well executed formal exercises, often involving surprising amounts of visual games. Johansson loves nothing more than to relate and/or arrange things in pictures that one wouldn't see that way in the actual locations at all. In other words, there is no need for the book to contain an additional voyage, say from the coast to the mountains or whatever else there might be. As a viewer, you can open *Deutschland* on any page and still arrive at essentially the same experience. *Deutschland* is the visual organization of seemingly random spots in a number of places that happen to be in the same country. As someone who was born and grew up in Germany, I found that *Deutschland* does not tell me much I already knew. Instead, the way it is organized mimics the photographer's own approach to organizing pictures, a mixture of being extremely methodical and inventive at the same time.

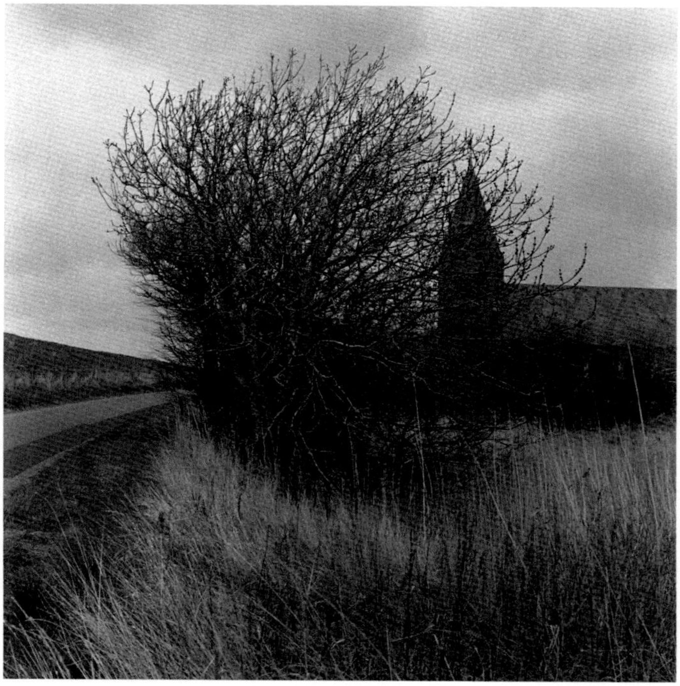

Figure 4.8 Gerry Johansson—*Alt Horsbüll*, from the photographer's book *Deutschland* (MACK, 2012)
Photograph courtesy and © Gerry Johansson

In much the same fashion, sequencing a book in such a simple, strict order, be it alphabetical, geographical or based on time, can work for a book, provided that such an organization is in concordance with what the photographs require. For example, a book about someone's life might show the pictures in the order in which they were taken, especially if the element of time provides a flow through the book (by means of form and, probably more importantly, content). In much the same fashion, a book about a road trip could follow the physical trip through the order of the pictures.

It might also be conceivable to abandon the idea of a sequence completely and to present photographs in a random order. In fact, Miguel Ángel Tornero's *The Random Series* (RM, 2015) is organized—or maybe *not* organized?— that way. The randomness includes every element of the book, including its (internal) title page and the various essay pages. While conceptually, this arrangement might be easily defendable—the photographs in question were created in part through some computer randomness, it is hard to see what is actually being gained from pushing this concept to its logical conclusion. While I do possess considerable patience with photobooks, the book's form ultimately ends up being too confusing, and the quality of the work doesn't appear to justify the considerable amount of work one would have to engage in to find the essay pages in the right order etc. This then points at something I will discuss in a lot more detail below: a book's concept clearly is incredibly important. And even following the concept properly is important as well. But the end result,

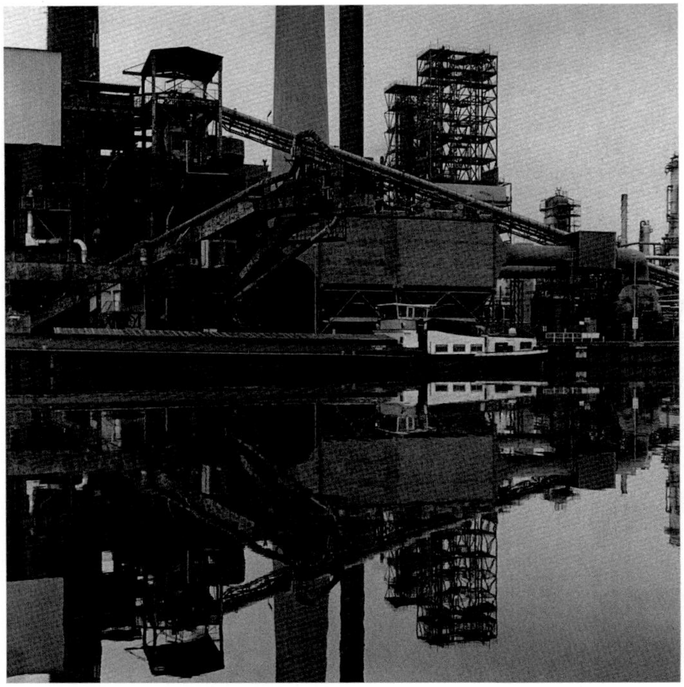

Figure 4.9 Gerry Johansson—*Altenlingen*, from the photographer's book *Deutschland* (MACK, 2012)
Photograph courtesy and © Gerry Johansson

the book cannot, no, *must not* exist for the sake of a clever concept alone. Instead, the book has to invite the reader to be engaged with, and that's where *The Random Series* fails: it is trying too hard to be clever, a problem that, unfortunately, a lot of contemporary photobooks suffer from.

To continue the discussion of sequencing, I would now like to discuss more examples. Needless to say, each book requires its own careful sequence—how simple or complex it might end up being. The best way to learn about sequencing is to look at examples. Given that I cannot possibly discuss a large number of books in detail, the reader is urged to carefully study well-known photobooks such as, especially, Walker Evans' *American Photographs* and Robert Frank's *The Americans*. When going through these books, the reader needs to figure out how their sequences work, how one gets from one picture to the next and what larger threads might possibly get used. Anyone attempting to produce a photobook needs to carefully study these two widely acclaimed photobooks, given they are done so well.

Figure 4.11 shows a photograph entitled *In Cold Spring* from Joshua Lutz's *Hesitating Beauty* (Schilt, 2012), which in the book comes towards the end.[18] By that stage, the book's narrative has unfolded, and the viewer is firmly embedded in the world created by the artist. In the following, I am going to follow a short sequence that starts with this photograph and see how there are connections made. Inevitably, this short sequence, taken out of the full context

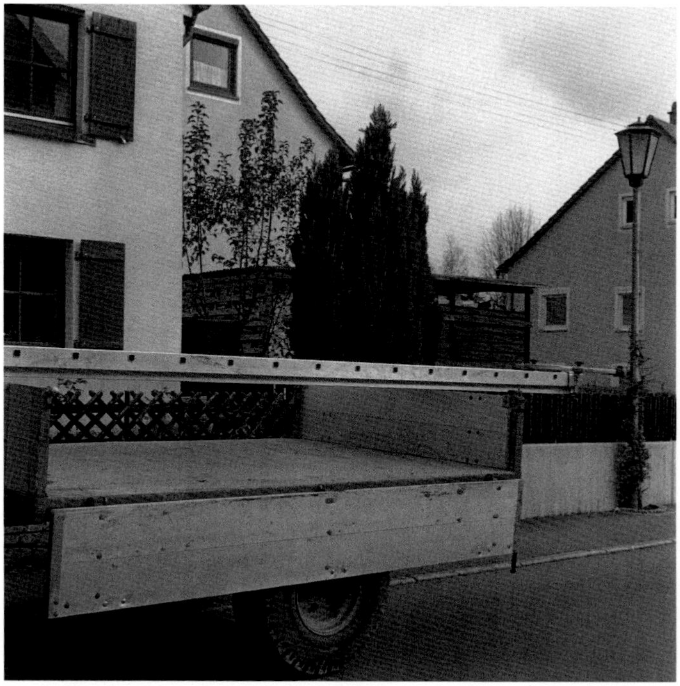

Figure 4.10 Gerry Johansson—*Altheim*, from the photographer's book *Deutschland* (MACK, 2012)
Photograph courtesy and © Gerry Johansson

of the book, only alludes to part of the story. But the discussion will allow me to analyze how this particular segment of the book's overall sequence works, going from one picture to the next.

In Cold Spring is a photograph of a man sitting in a rocky area. The man is looking at the camera, his hands buried in the pockets of his coat. There are traces of snow on the ground, which makes the man's choice of wearing shorts a bit curious. But the snow might explain at least part of the man's discomfort.[19]

Once the viewer turns the page, she or he will see the photograph shown in Figure 4.12, *M.I.C.K.E.Y.* Here, we see a woman sitting on a box or container of sorts, of which there are quite a few other ones right behind her (three of them featuring the label "fresh seafood"). The woman has wrapped a crocheted blanket around her shoulders, and she is looking at a piece of paper, which might or might not be a photograph. The fact that both the man in Figure 4.11 and the woman in Fig 4.12 appear to be a bit cold provides a first visual clue that there is a connection between them. What is more, we are made to see the woman after the man, so there has got to be some relevance to this fact. After all, if there were no connection between them, why would we be made to see them one after the other like this?[20] This then is part of what sequencing, of placing one image after another image, will do: it will make connections between photographs in such a way that a viewer who trusts the book to make sense will understand the eventual story.

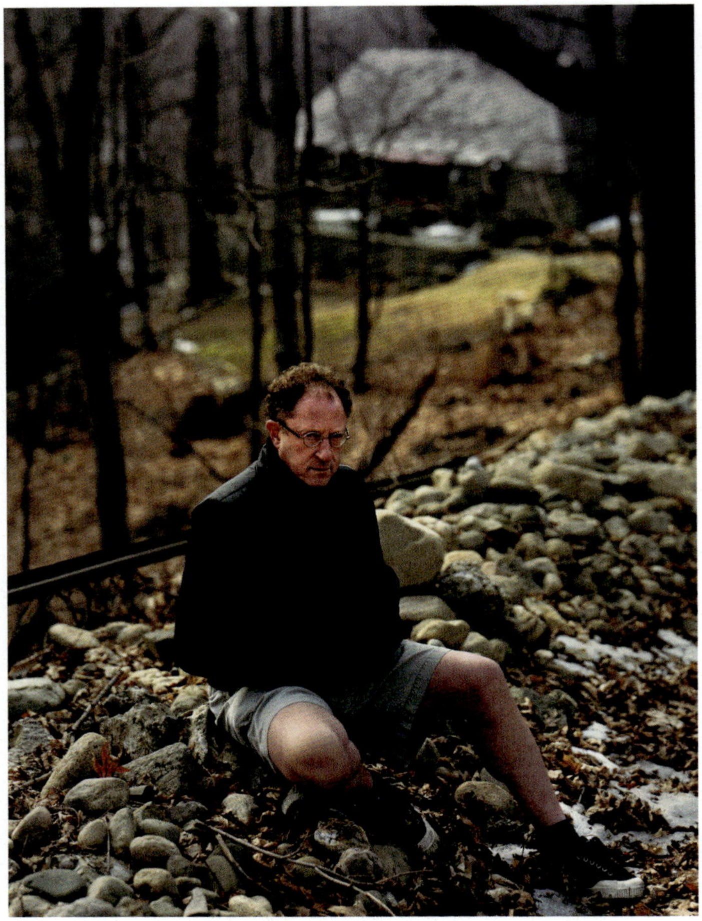

Figure 4.11 Joshua Lutz—*In Cold Spring*, from the photographer's book *Hesitating Beauty* (Schilt, 2012)
Photograph courtesy and © Joshua Lutz

The next photograph in this short sequence, *Potentially Grateful*, is shown in Figure 4.13. It shows part of what was visible in Figure 4.12, in particular the woman's thighs, part of the blanket, and her right hand. In this hand, there is a photograph placed. We remember from Figure 4.12 that the woman was looking at a small piece of paper, so now we get to see that our suspicion—it is a photograph—was, in fact, correct. The b/w photograph the woman is holding in her hand shows a couple, the man smoking, with his left arm around the smiling, happy looking woman's shoulder who is sitting right next to him. If we look carefully, we see that the man in this b/w photograph bears a resemblance to the man from Figure 4.11. Now, this could just be a coincidence. But clearly, if you sequence things this way, these kinds of visual connection matter: if they don't matter, what is the viewer supposed to make of the sequence?

So we have a lone man in some discomfort, a woman in a somewhat similar situation looking at a photograph, and that photograph shows what looks like the man at an earlier

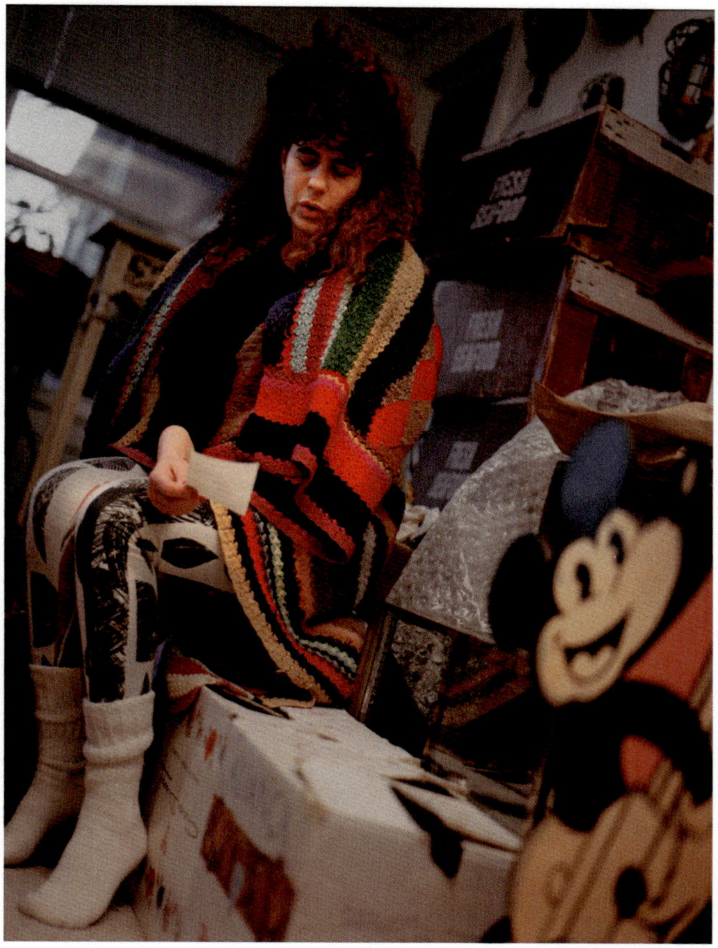

Figure 4.12 Joshua Lutz—*M.I.C.K.E.Y,* from the photographer's book *Hesitating Beauty* (Schilt, 2012)
Photograph courtesy and © Joshua Lutz

age in the company of a woman. The three photographs in Figures 4.11, 4.12, and 4.13 have started to tell a little story, which revolves around a man and a woman, and it has to do with the past as well.

Turning the page, the viewer will find *Hometown Hero*, shown in Figure 4.14, next. In it, a man is depicted smoking a cigarette, his left arm resting on a woman's shoulder. The woman is smiling, holding a glass of wine in her left hand. Clearly, *Hometown Hero* visually echoes the b/w photograph contained in *Potentially Grateful* (Figure 4.13). They're not the same people, but the situation and gestures are very similar. Look carefully, and you will find that the man in *Hometown Hero* sports the same hairline as both the man in the b/w photograph and the man in *In Cold Spring* (Figure 4.11). Again, this obviously cannot be coincidental. Instead, we are led to believe that this particular young man is the other man's son, finding himself in, well, the same situation as his father years ago, enjoying family life with a happy partner.

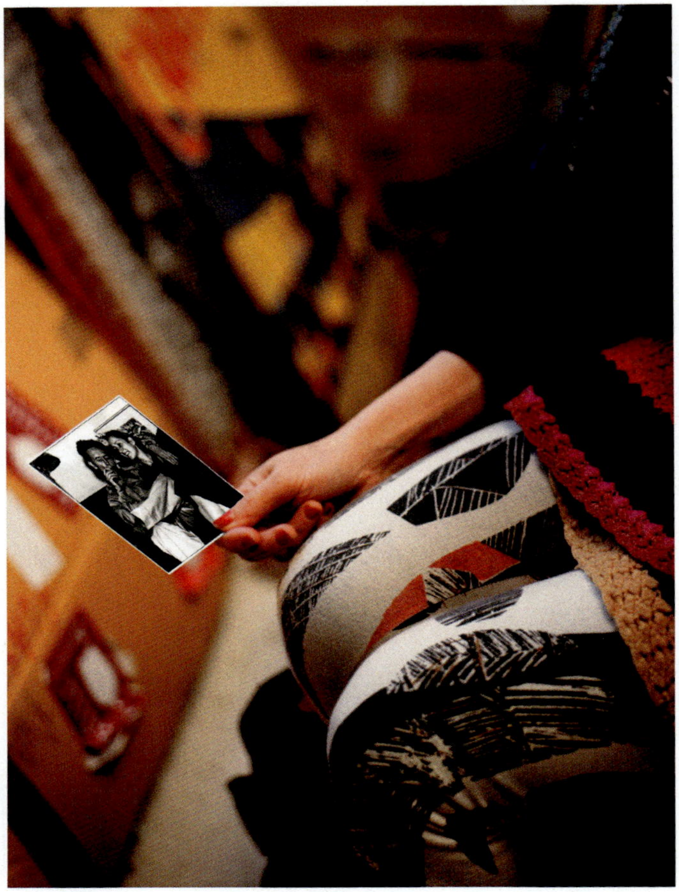

Figure 4.13 Joshua Lutz—*Potentially Grateful*, from the photographer's book *Hesitating Beauty* (Schilt, 2012)
Photograph courtesy and © Joshua Lutz

So it is visual clues that have unfolded more and more of a story from Figures 4.11 to 4.14. It would be conceivable to continue the sequence in this particular way, making visual connections from one photograph to the next. But good sequences need not operate along these lines only. Figure 4.15 shows the photograph the viewer will find turning the page after seeing the happy couple, *Wall Collapsing*. There do not appear to be any visual traces of what came before. Instead, it is a photograph of a wall of bricks that is slowly being pushed out from the inside, seemingly getting ready to burst, to collapse. Seeing this image after the one of the happy couple (Figure 4.14) is jarring, and that is the idea.

As a book, *Hesitating Beauty* deals with the effects of mental illness on a family. Using archival photographs as well as his own, Joshua Lutz tries to come to terms with his mother's illness and the consequences for his own life. While the aspects of mental illness are absent from the photographs discussed earlier, the sense of a family, and of something being amiss are clearly present. In the full context of the book, the sequence works just as it does when

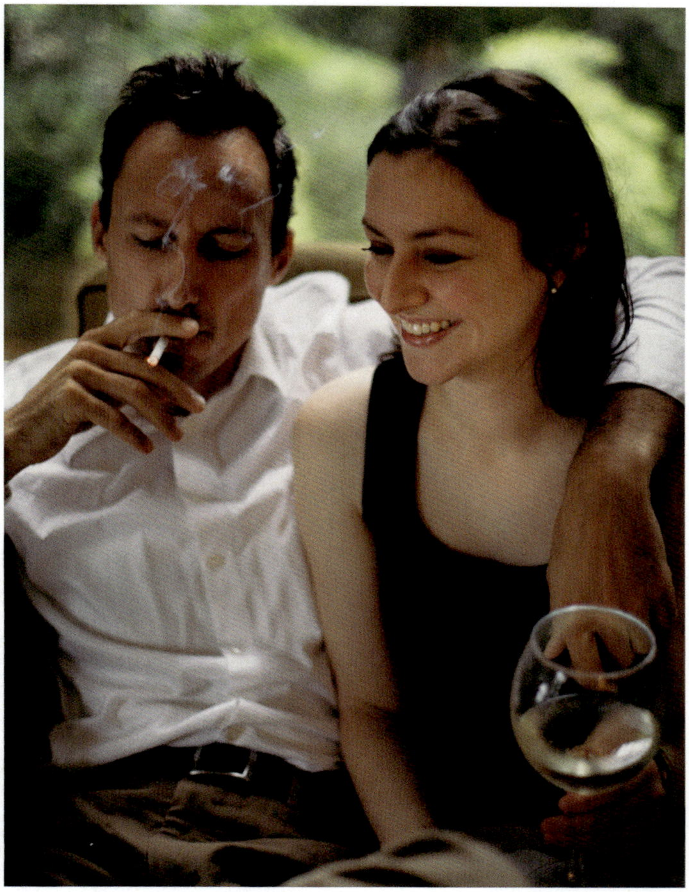

Figure 4.14 Joshua Lutz—*Hometown Hero*, from the photographer's book *Hesitating Beauty* (Schilt, 2012)
Photograph courtesy and © Joshua Lutz

taken in isolation. Of course, there is a plethora of additional information the viewer is given, so the people in the photographs are already familiar. But even seen in the relative isolation I presented them in here, the short sequence in Figures 4.11 to 4.15—five photographs—very powerfully tell an important part of the larger story.

Like Laia Abril's *The Epilogue* and Joshua Lutz's *Hesitating Beauty*, *In the Shadow of Things* by Léonie Hampton (Contrasto, 2011) deals with mental illness, in this case the photographer's mother's struggle with a form of obsessive-compulsive disorder (OCD). Unlike the other two books, *In the Shadow of Things* keeps photographs and text separate, however. The book moves through over 70 spreads of images, before it presents a block of pages (on a different paper stock) that is densely filled with text in the form of transcribed recordings done at the family's house. As might be obvious, establishing the core of the book without the help of text is a considerable challenge, especially right at the beginning. In the following, I want to look at how this is being done.

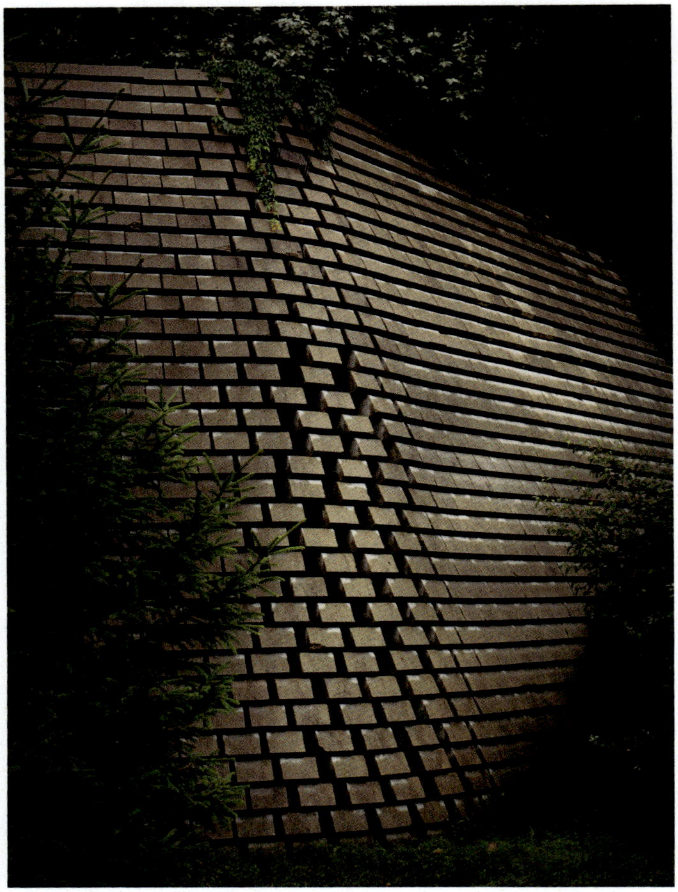

Figure 4.15 Joshua Lutz—*Wall Collapsing*, from the photographer's book *Hesitating Beauty* (Schilt, 2012)
Photograph courtesy and © Joshua Lutz

Figure 4.16 shows the first photograph in Hampton's book, entitled *Two Shoes*.[21] It is probably fair to say that this is a strange photograph, showing a rather skinny woman posing somewhat awkwardly for the camera. Her jacket appears to be a size or two too small maybe, her pant legs are pulled up, and there is a second pair of shoes between her feet, in addition to the shoes she is wearing. We can, actually we must surmise that this woman is going to play an important role in the following, even though we don't really know, yet. But for this to be the first photograph we encounter, showing a portrait of someone who plays no important role in the book would be an odd choice.

Having turned the page, the viewer next comes across *Daphne's Sun Chair* (Figure 4.17), a rather moody and dark photograph, in which the only object that can be made out clearly is an empty lawn chair. At this stage, we have no knowledge of the title of the picture (given it is listed in the very back of the book). Even if we did, we would not know who Daphne is. That aside, we are left with another somewhat strange impression. Much like *Two*

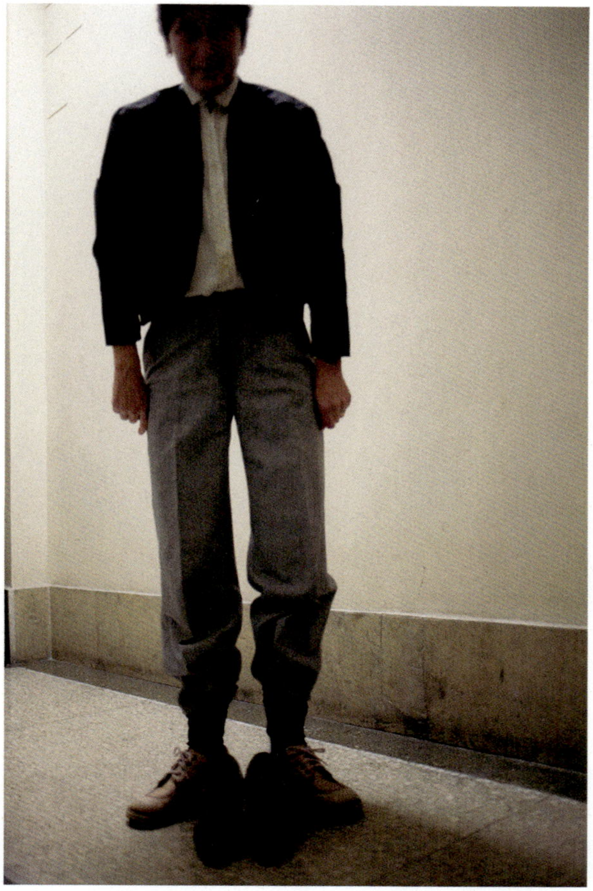

Figure 4.16 Léonie Hampton—*Two Shoes*, from the photographer's book *In the Shadow of Things* (Contrasto, 2011)
Photograph courtesy and © Léonie Hampton

Shoes, *Daphne's Sun Chair* looks and feels foreboding. Something is not quite right here, but we don't quite know what it is. Unlike in the case of the sequence from Lutz's book, in which visual clues tied one photograph to the next, here no such clues are given. This is a valid strategy for establishing a story in a photobook. Elements of the story can be introduced without seemingly being related, to make sense later. Of course, eventually things will start to relate to what was seen before, otherwise, the sequence would be little more than a disorganized mess.

David and Jake #1 (Figure 4.18) comes next. The photograph is dominated by the figure of an adolescent, frozen in mid-air, having just jumped or possibly stumbled. There is another person visible, the head of an older man in the window behind the adolescent, even though that figure is very easy to miss. There is a house, a one-story brick building, and there is a rather uninviting looking backyard, where the adolescent is photographed. Again, the connection between this photograph and the two that came before it is not based on formal

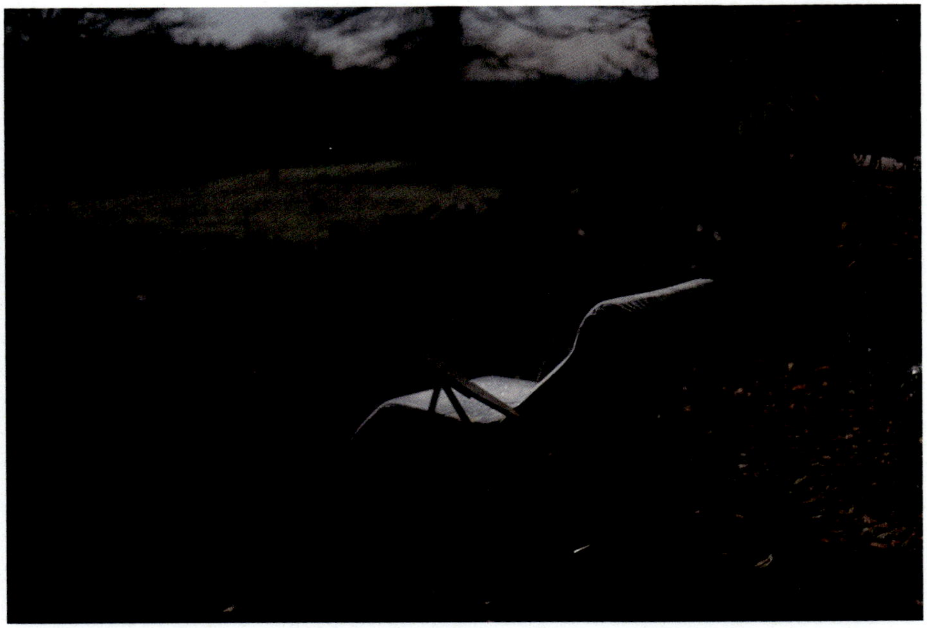

Figure 4.17 Léonie Hampton—*Daphne's Sun Chair*, from the photographer's book *In the Shadow of Things* (Contrasto, 2011)
Photograph courtesy and © Léonie Hampton

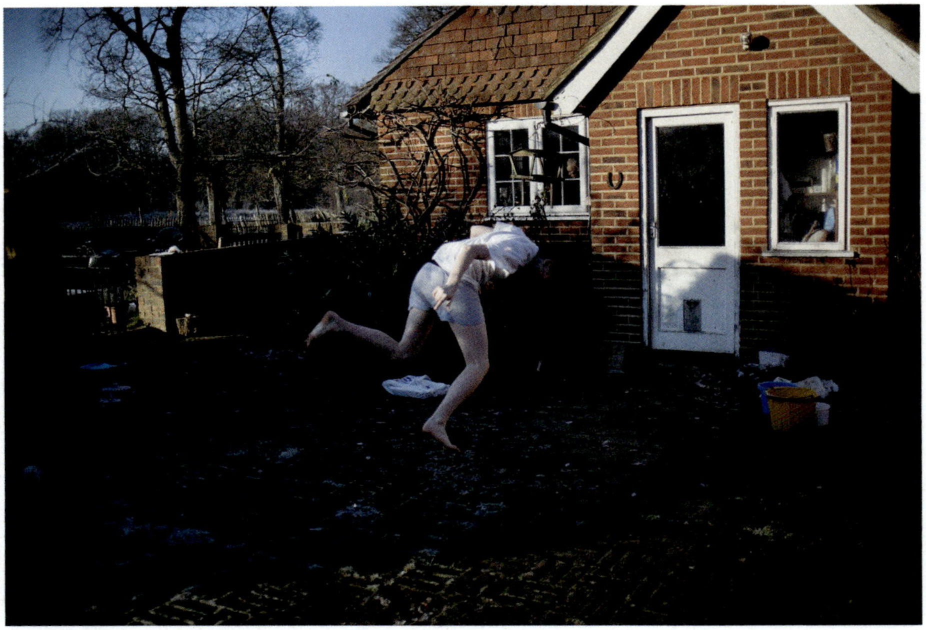

Figure 4.18 Léonie Hampton—*David and Jake #1*, from the photographer's book *In the Shadow of Things* (Contrasto, 2011)
Photograph courtesy and © Léonie Hampton

criteria at all. But a feeling of unease is very clearly established now. We must assume that the adolescent and the woman from *Two Shoes* have something to do with each other (again, otherwise why include these pictures this way in the sequence?). We thus have a woman who could be—but we don't know—the adolescent's mother or some form of relative, and we got a house, where the adolescent might live, given his clothes and behavior (people don't usually jump or stumble in other people's backyards, especially not if there is a man inside the house who isn't concerned with the presence of the young man at all).

The following picture, *Two Spoons* (Figure 4.19), takes us into the house. Now, given the absence of textual confirmation that we are actually inside the house from Figure 4.18, we have no way of knowing that it is the same house. It could be a completely different house. But the book is trying to establish a story, and for that story to work, the connections between the pictures and what they show cannot be completely random. Seen that way, sequencing photographs does not "only" consist of establishing visual connections (which, admittedly, often is hard enough). It also means establishing connections between photographic facts. What I mean by this is that presented in this order, from Figures 4.16 to 4.19, the viewer will assume that what can be seen in the pictures does in fact set the stage for a story. These people, this house, this backyard—they are connected. They are facets that matter in the following, because—yet again—if they don't matter together at all why show them this way?

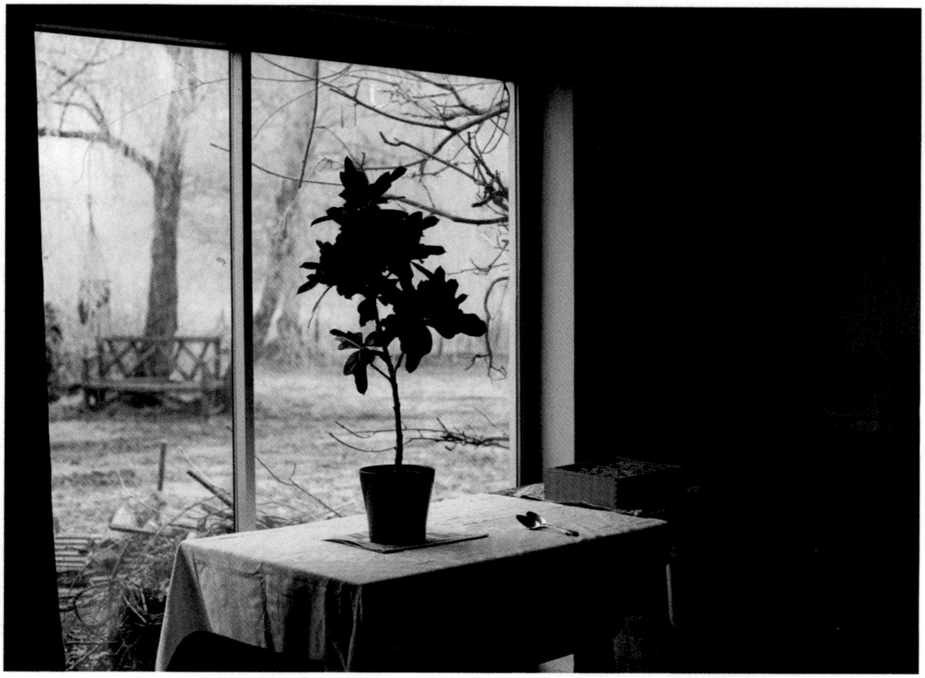

Figure 4.19 Léonie Hampton—*Two Spoons*, from the photographer's book *In the Shadow of Things* (Contrasto, 2011)

Photograph courtesy and © Léonie Hampton

In other words, the overall story gives the photographer some freedom how to approach it in the sequence, as long as she or he carefully picks some details that will be relevant in the following. The story can be allowed to unfold itself on its own, because the viewer will trust the photographer to do a good job guiding her or him into it. If the woman in Figure 4.16 is indeed going to play an important role in the book (which she is, but the viewer finds out only later), then showing her first provides a very strong clue for this. The same is true for the boy, for the house …

So Figure 4.19 now has the viewer inside the house, which spite of the fact that there is a plant with a flower sitting on a table near a window looks and feels just as drab as the exterior in Figure 4.17, the picture of the empty lawn chair. There is an interesting detail in the form of two spoons lying very closely next to each other on the table on which the plant is standing. Given the titles of the photographs are only given at the end, the connection between *Two Shoes* and *Two Spoons* is purely visual, to be picked up by an attentive viewer. But we see, connections between photographs are being established. As I have already noted, connections between photographs allow the viewer not only to see more details of the story, but they also provide comfort: there is indeed a form of logic to the presentation of the photographs, even though the full extent of what's going on might only fully reveal itself later.

Bron Sorting #1 follows next (Figure 4.20). This photograph shows a skinny woman in a bikini on her knees, looking through an assortment of boxes and plastic and trash bags in what looks like a garden. The tonality of the photograph matches the one already established. And

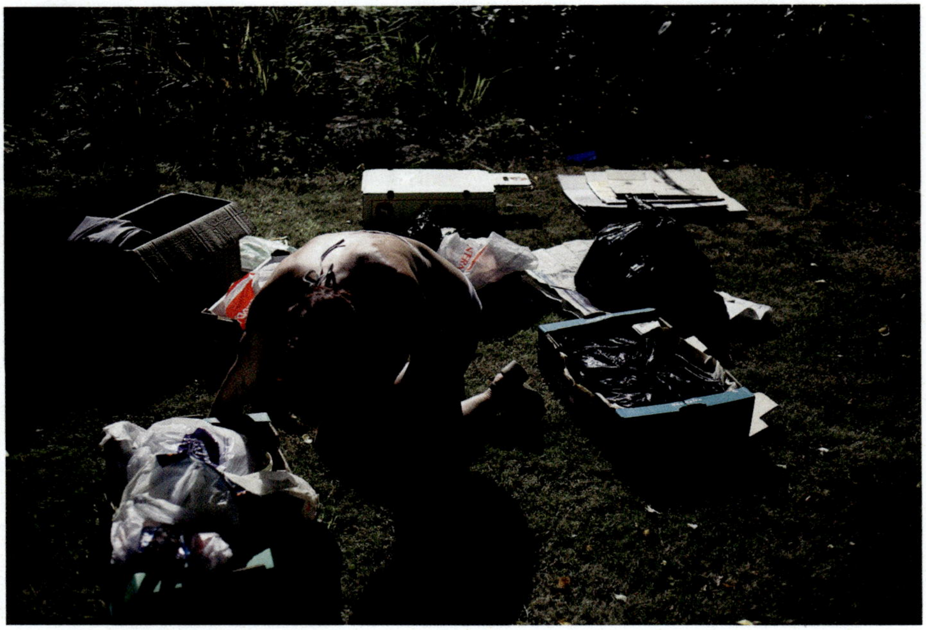

Figure 4.20 Léonie Hampton—*Bron Sorting #1*, from the photographer's book *In the Shadow of Things* (Contrasto, 2011)
Photograph courtesy and © Léonie Hampton

even though we do not get to see her face, this must be the woman the viewer encountered in the very first photograph in the book (Figure 4.16). Little care seems to have been taken with the materials in the boxes and plastic and trash bags on the lawn, yet whatever it is inside them the woman is still taking some form of care of them. Why would she do that? We don't know (yet). But the atmosphere of something being awry is becoming intensified. Something clearly is not right.

What is off kilter is then made visible in the following photograph entitled *The Yellow Room* (Figure 4.21). The photograph shows a room literally filled to the brim with stuff in bags piling up against the walls. The ceiling lamp barely manages to illuminate things in the center, the boxes and bags, plus a shirt hanging in front of some piece of furniture (that cannot be fully made out, given there is so much stuff in front of it). This is a hoarder's house, and the woman encountered just before, on her knees looking through stuff in boxes and plastic bags, must be the person collecting all these materials. There is the story, or rather the background of the story, fully established.

Now, the real complication for any sequence usually is not to work out how to establish important facts. Instead, it is what to do right after they have been established. How do you go from *The Yellow Room* to something else, whatever that "something else" might be? Sequencing here becomes a bit similar to a rock concert, where there needs to be a progression of fast songs and slower ones. As a photobook maker, you probably do not want to try to organize a photobook like a punk concert, throwing intense snippets of stuff at viewers.

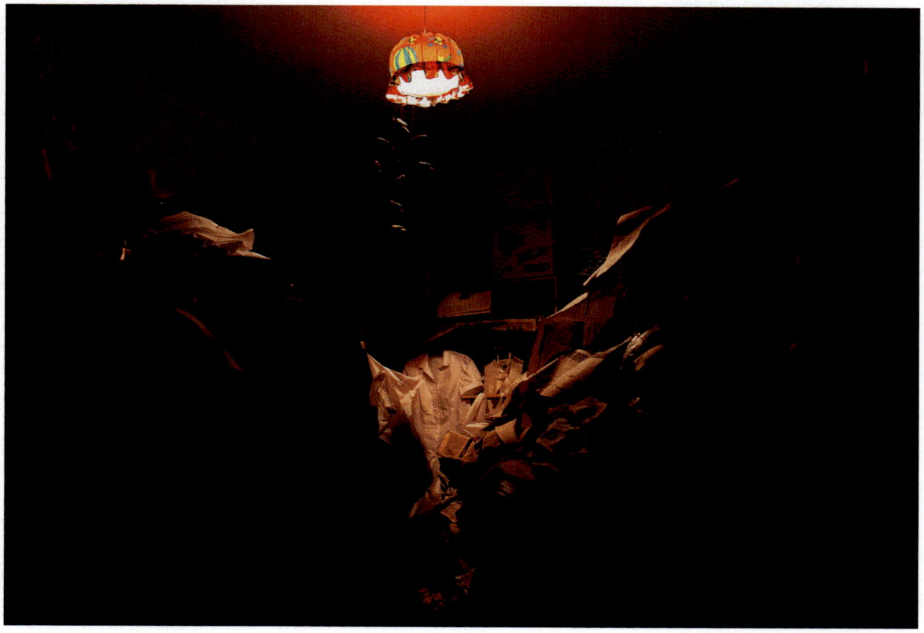

Figure 4.21 Léonie Hampton—*The Yellow Room*, from the photographer's book *In the Shadow of Things* (Contrasto, 2011)
Photograph courtesy and © Léonie Hampton

Instead, you have to establish a rhythm. There will have to be pauses or breaks. *The Yellow Room* leaves the viewer not quite in the right space for a break, yet. To do that would be akin to a strategy well known from horror movies where the most intense shock ends a scene, and things then continue elsewhere. This is doable in a photobook, but it might not necessarily be the best strategy, especially here.

Thus, *Our Home* (Figure 4.22) is presented after *The Yellow Room* as the picture providing the break. *Our Home* serves multiple purposes. For a start, after the overwhelming fact of seeing a hoarder's room, the exterior of the house, photographed at night, some of its windows lit, provides a visual relief for the viewer. This is a comforting picture. What is more, it also is an important picture, given that it speaks of the fact that while this house has seen its fair share of troubles, it is someone's home, the woman's, the boy's, the man's … In other words, *Our Home* rounds off the very first section of the book, the introduction of the story. The book carries this point home by following up on *Our Home* with a collection of photographs from the family's archive, before continuing to explore the main story further.

Unlike the short sequence from Lutz's *Hesitating Beauty* (Figures 4.11 to 4.15), which comes fairly late, the introductory sequence from Hampton's book has to establish the main pillars of the overall story. It does so not by creating strong visual connections from one picture to the next, but instead by showing aspects of the story here and there, and by then connecting them. While Keith Smith's discussion of a serial set of pictures versus a sequential

Figure 4.22 Léonie Hampton—*Our Home*, from the photographer's book *In the Shadow of Things* (Contrasto, 2011)
Photograph courtesy and © Léonie Hampton

one ends up being a bit too dogmatic and narrow, we could say that Lutz's sequence is more serial, whereas Hampton's is more sequential in Smith's sense. One, however, is not better than the other. It's simply a difference in working with sequences.

What this means is that sequencing a book cannot follow any recipe. A purely visual connection from one picture to the next might work for one book, while another one might require a broader interweaving of elements that reference each other across multiple pages. That said, usually the project in question will if not dictate then at least strongly suggest an approach. So provided there is clarity over the aspects of the book discussed in Chapter 3, a photographer who has properly worked out a book's concept should at the very least have a rough idea of what strategy to follow concerning the sequencing. As I noted (and outlined) earlier, much can be learned from existing photobooks. There really is no need necessarily to reinvent the wheel. That said, of course, there still is ample room to expand existing narrative photobook structures. Whether or not a book might in fact be in need of such expansion will reveal itself easiest by first adopting a simple sequencing strategy, possibly based on similar work. Only if such simple strategies don't work might it be necessary to expand. One of the shortcomings of many photobooks is that their authors are too ambitious, trying to cram too many tricks, too many bells and whistles into them (this is particularly true once we look at design, but even here). This usually is not a good idea. In the natural sciences, one of the main and most important pillars of modern research states that if there is more than one theory explaining something, the simplest one is the one to be preferred. And the same is true for photobooks: concerning every aspect of a book, the simplest approach usually is the best ("simple" here being seen in the context of the particular book—compared with others, things might be more complicated).

As we thus saw, editing and sequencing are complex tasks that require a lot of careful attention to detail. Therefore, it is important to keep them as simple as possible, employing just the right tools for them. Given digital technologies appear to have made large parts of photography a lot easier and more convenient, avoiding those kinds of tool, however, is very important for anyone making a book as I will outline in the following section.

4.8 Tools of the Trade

Image-management software such as, for example, Adobe's *Lightroom* has become a common tool for most photographers. How else to keep track of the many photographs on one's computer, especially if digital capture is being employed? But while organizing the content of one's hard drive(s) is one thing, organizing and handling photographs from a project one currently is working on, in particular editing, is quite another. Just like I advise my students (and readers of this book) to use physical dummies when working on a photobook (more details on this a little later), using actual, physical prints is supremely important during the process of editing.

This assertion might sound oddly old fashioned. Why should one have to make prints of all those pictures when they can be so easily be looked at on a computer screen, when they can get so easily organized in seemingly endless ways electronically? There are two main reasons for this, both of which are equally important.

For a start, as a photographer, you will want to live with the photographs you are currently working on, meaning you will have to have the opportunity to see them at any given time during the day, even when you're not focusing on them. While having a dedicated studio space is, of course, the ideal for a photographer, even someone who does not have one should at least have access to a decently sized wall that can hold prints. Make (or get) prints of your photographs and pin them up on that wall so that you can see the pictures even when your computer is switched off, or when you're on your computer writing email, or whatever else you might be doing. The human brain is enormously adept at processing visual information that is available (aka in view), even when the mind seemingly is focused on something completely different. You will not get this mechanism working with pictures only on your computer. The old saying "out of sight, out of mind" truly applies here.

So that wall of photographs should be in a location where you can see it easily. It's great if you have a little studio space in your basement, but if you hardly ever spend time there, the pictures on a wall there aren't that different from the pictures on your computer that you don't get to see. It is important to realize that there need not be any anxiety over the exact content of the wall. Editing is a process that will require time, so when starting out, producing the perfect edit on the wall is not the idea. Instead, maybe even start with random pictures. Hang them up, step back, and see what you make of it. If there's nothing wrong with what you see, that's fine. Get back to it the next day, or the day after. In all likelihood, you will start to realize that a picture, or maybe more than one, will not fit with the rest. Take it (them) down, and replace it (them) with something else from your pile of pictures. As long as you have regular access to the wall, both actively as in standing in front of it and consciously focusing on it or passively as in walking by holding, let's say, a plate with a sandwich on it, your mind will be processing the information, and the project's pictures will start to create connections between each other.

Figure 4.23 shows a partial view of Peter Puklus' studio in Budapest, Hungary. At the time when the photograph was taken, the artist was working on a project entitled *The Epic Love Story of a Warrior*. As can be seen, the walls are covered with small work prints, hung in groupings that include variations of the same idea. As is obvious from Figure 4.23, one of the important aspects of having photographs on a wall is that you will be able to see a larger number of them at the same time. You can look at one and then another one, there will be pairings, some of which will work, others won't. You cannot easily replicate this effect on your computer screen at all, especially since just like in an exhibition space you will be able to physically move forward and back, focusing in on one picture and seeing more than one. In contrast, you're likely to always be at the same distance from your computer. If you open many pictures on your screen, they each become quite small. If you click from one picture to the next, you'll just see one. The convenience of being able to switch out pictures, of walking back and forth, of easily comparing pictures on a wall cannot easily be replicated on a computer.

When working with physical prints, you will have to take care of two aspects. First, the print quality should be at the level of good or very good work prints. In other words, the

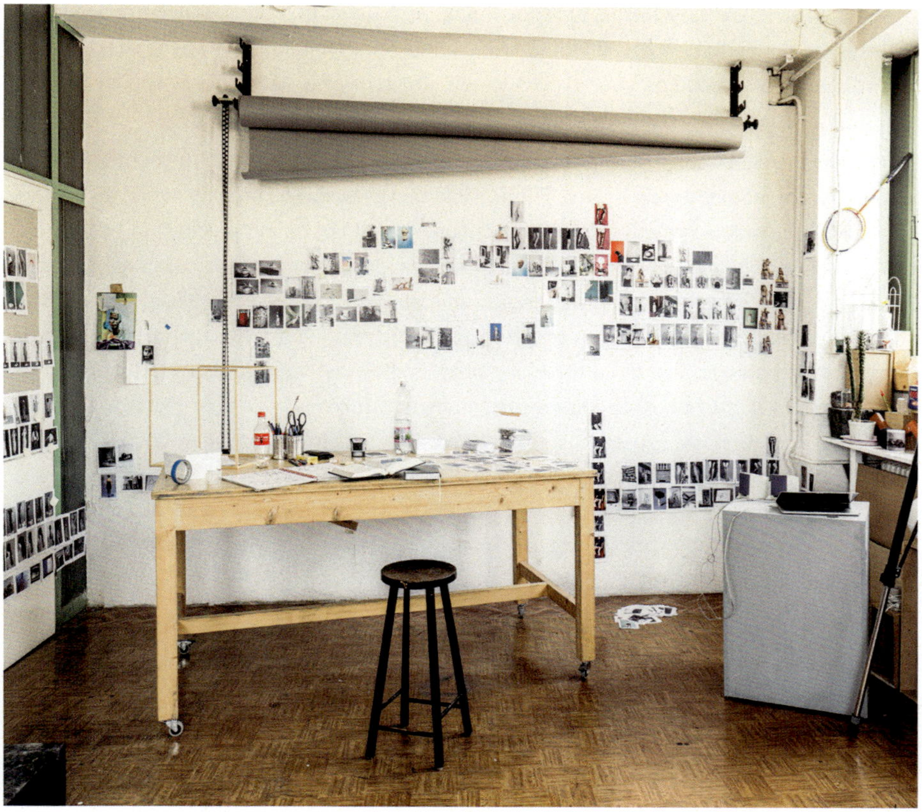

Figure 4.23 Partial view of Peter Puklus' studio. Note the large number of small work prints on the walls
Photograph courtesy and © Peter Puklus

images should be fairly close to their final form. While there is no need to work with exhibition-quality prints, it's important to work with prints that are properly color calibrated, cropped, and whatever other work you usually do with your photographs. I occasionally encounter students who will tell me that they only fix up a picture if they really know that it is a keeper. Aspects of sheer laziness and commitment aside, that's simply no way to work. The making of art requires a tremendous amount of work, some of which seemingly will be "wasted" on things that ultimately will never see the light of day. To pretend that there is a way around that is simply foolish. So even if you're in doubt about a picture, fix it up first, and treat it carefully, before rejecting it. It is not uncommon at all for photographs that initially were almost discarded by their makers to acquire often considerable importance. This is also part of the editing process: while the real star images often are obvious right away, a lot of the material will reveal itself with time.

In terms of sizes, the prints on your wall should be of a size that makes looking at and handling them easy. Small prints, of course, can be handled easily, but if they're too small, having them on a wall is like looking at a stamp collection (unless you get really close). Large prints, of course, are easy to see, but they might be so large that they reduce the number of pictures you put up too much. Anything around letter size (roughly 8" by 10"; of course, the exact dimensions depend on your chosen image format) works very well. If you have a very large wall available, you can go a little larger.

The advantage of using work prints is that you can push a pin through the borders without having to worry about ruining a print. This is important as well. The prints you will be working with during the process of editing and sequencing should not be too precious to be handled! You will have to be unafraid to handle your pictures, to pile them up, to risk them falling to the ground … Why a work print that might ultimately just get rejected should be precious I have never understood. Often, in crits at art schools, I am surprised how careful students are with their photographs. Even the worst photographs that were roundly rejected will get carefully put back into a box. If you feel that amount of reverence for your pictures, try to get away from it as quickly as possible. I'm not advocating you treat your photographs like junk. What I *am* advocating, however, is that you will get to a place where you can clearly see that many pictures in your project simply won't fit. They will not make the cut. You will have to let them go. Approaching your raw material as too precious will produce a tremendous mental block during the process of editing.

While a wall is a great tool to get exposure to a project and to make slower edits (changing out pictures one by one), a large table (or even the floor) is a much better tool once you approach the stage of sequencing. I would always start out with pictures on a wall. Once you feel comfortable enough with a raw edit on a wall, move to a table. You might need slightly smaller prints (in other words, a second set of work prints) depending on the size of your table (I'm not opposed to working on the floor, even though I personally find using a table a lot easier). On a wall, prints will be fixed in whatever way (pins, magnets, maybe even tape). On a table, you don't need to fix the prints (as long as your table is level enough). A table offers you a great opportunity to move prints around very easily. You can create groupings, you can even line up pictures to produce a sequence. Again, this is not something that you can do easily on a computer. Seeing picture after picture after picture on a computer screen is not the same at all as seeing a line of pictures on a table.

In other words, when working on a photobook, physical objects always matter—even before you make a physical dummy. No computer program will be an adequate substitute for prints on your wall, or prints on your table, or physical dummies that behave like the photobook you are hoping to make.

4.9 Working with Dummies

As indicated previously, for me dummies play an indispensable role during the process of working on a photobook. When working on an edit to which then a sequence (and a basic layout) will be added, a physical dummy should be produced. By "dummy" I here mean any physical object that looks and behaves like a book, regardless of whether its quality is even remotely close to what the final book might look like. Much like the book itself will evolve from a concept to a set of pictures to an edited set of pictures with a sequence, etc., a dummy should also evolve from something very simple and basic (that still does its job) to something that ultimately might even be sent to a publisher or to any of the many photobook-dummy awards and/or competitions. Let's face it, the moment you have a first edit and an idea of a sequence, you could print out those photographs, take the resulting stack of paper and staple it together at their left edge to get something that looks and feels like a book, even as it might not even remotely be what the final book is supposed to look like.

While you could certainly make a very simple dummy that way, in the earliest stages, I would advise against using a method that produces something you cannot change easily. Granted, you could remove the staples from the aforementioned dummy, change the sequence (based on your realization that the first didn't work), and re-staple the pages. But ultimately, it would be much easier to start out with a set of prints, some removable double-sided tape, and a blank spiral-bound notebook. By construction, the blank notebook gives you a book. Using spiral binding might not be what you will want to do, but the point of using such a notebook is not the type of binding, it's simply the flexibility it allows for. So assuming you have an edit plus a sequence and a basic idea for a layout, you can stick the prints into the notebook using removable tape. With this type of tape, taking out pictures to put them somewhere else is straightforward. The notebook is likely to have more pages than your final book, but all you have to do is to ignore the blank, unused pages at the end. In the usually unlikely case that you run out of empty pages, simply get a blank notebook with more pages. Given the spiral binding, the pages will separate neatly, without creating the kind of bulging book you would get with a notebook that is bound in a different way. Not that there's necessarily anything wrong with a dummy being a bit bulging, but a spiral-bound notebook also allows you to easily turn pages, because the individual pages are quite loose. And if a page really doesn't fit even though everything else works perfectly, then tearing out that page is simple. Off it goes. So a spiral-bound notebook also allows you to remove pages at a stage where larger sections might already be working, and you don't want to move dozens of photographs. In fact, you can even insert pages, by tearing some out at the end and then sticking them in. Those added pages will end up being a bit loose, but it will do. No other type of notebook allows for this much flexibility—at, essentially, very low cost.

Your very first dummy will thus look pretty cheap. But it will also look and especially feel like a real book. There are pages to be turned, even as those pages consist of pages onto which pictures are stuck. If you think about the world of music, an early dummy would be akin to a demo take—something recorded in, say, someone's house with very basic equipment. If you have ever bought an album (especially a reissue) that features demos, you know what I'm talking about: it sounds like a real song, but its form isn't fully there. Yet still, provided it's a good song, you get a very good idea of the song.

Adobe's *Lightroom* software, unfortunately, contains a book-making module that, from what I can tell, is widely used, even by photographers who should know better. I have made it abundantly clear that in order to work on a photobook you need to be using physical objects, but you might decide to work on a computer anyway. It's up to you, of course. A lot of my students create their very first dummies in the form of PDFs on a computer. Fine, I get it. Now, the only thing that is absolutely crucial is to print out the PDF "dummy" and create an actual book by gluing or taping or stapling together the pages thus created. However much you're wedded to the computer, you will have to produce an actual book eventually. Starting early is extremely important. And the earlier you can break your possible habit of producing another PDF and then another PDF and another PDF etc. ad infinitum, the better. I yet have to encounter a single student who will not tell me how surprised they were that that great PDF they thought they had in actual book form not only looked and felt very differently, but that, in fact, it also didn't work, something they would have never seen on the computer screen. Problems usually range from the edit and/or sequence not working, to layout problems (the most common problem I run into is the mix of too many different layouts and image sizes for different spreads), to the whole thing not working at all. Thankfully, the last is quite rare, while the first two are very common.

So the process of editing and sequencing should involve the production of a physical dummy at any given stage. Once you are confident that your first dummy is in a good state, create a second, slightly more elaborate one, one that is more polished (print out the pages properly) and that involves more of the bells and whistles you hope your final book might have. And then you work towards your final dummy (and eventual book) by adding things to it. One of the main reasons why I advocate doing this tiered process is simply that as we have seen in the last chapter making a photobook involves a lot of decisions that are waiting to be made. There is no reason why those decisions cannot be made incrementally instead of trying to figure everything out in one step. Photographers commonly create a "book" on the computer, get a copy produced by companies such as Blurb, and then they have a dummy that looks like a somewhat well-produced book, but it has problems everywhere: the edit/sequence are off, the layout doesn't work, it's too big or too small, the paper really doesn't work (it's too glossy, not glossy enough, or whatever other problem there might be), and all the pictures have a slight magenta (or green or blue) cast. If you end up in that situation, you certainly have to go back to the beginning. But why try to tackle all the problems at once? As I advocated, start with the edit and sequence and simple layout with a very basic dummy and then take it from there. Thing is, photographers often spend a lot of money on an on-demand dummy, only to get a pretty lousy product (and it's mostly lousy because it's their own fault, production problems notwithstanding). There is no need for that.

Figures 4.24 and 4.25 show selected spreads from two dummies Donald Weber produced during the process of working on *Interrogations*. Figure 4.24 shows an earlier one, which still is very far from the eventual book. A spiral-bound date book serves as the backbone—wherever date information is visible, it's simply ignored. Photographs have been pasted in, using cheap inkjet prints, whose sizes often don't quite match the size restrictions of the date book. Where photographs are supposed to cross the gutter (see top right panel), they're fixed only on one side. This early dummy is quite far from the eventual book, given it includes photographs taken during arrests (top panels), and some of the images that ended

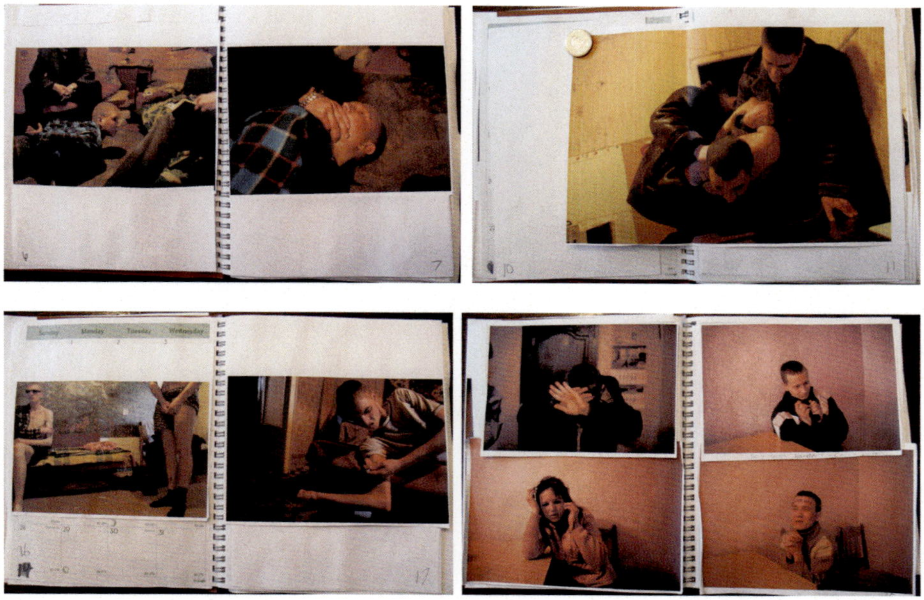

Figure 4.24 Photographs of selected spreads from an early dummy of Donald Weber's *Interrogations*. As is clearly visible in the bottom-left panel, the photographer used a spiral-bound date book, into which he pasted what look like inkjet prints
Photographs courtesy and © Donald Weber

up providing the bulks of the final book are presented in a grid (bottom right panel). A dummy like the one shown in Figure 4.24 clearly violates the sensibilities of all those who like things neat and proper. But the idea of a dummy isn't really to have a neat and proper book. Instead, it's a work in progress, the only and most basic condition for which is that it works like a book and that it conveys the ideas and (here) possible layout of the final product. Those who prefer their work to look neat and proper might find making such dummies oddly liberating.

Figure 4.25 shows selected spreads from a more advanced dummy of *Interrogations*. The date book from Figure 4.24 has been replaced with what looks like a fairly well-printed photobook. Pictures are now not pasted in any longer. Parts of the earlier dummy (Figure 4.24) remain, such as the photographs during arrests (bottom left panel). There are also inserts, which didn't make it into the final book (bottom right panel). As a working dummy, this book has a variety of PostIt notes attached to it that serve as bookmarks for improvements. One could imagine that a dummy like this one (without the PostIt bookmarks) could be used to approach publishers or to submit to dummy competitions.

It would appear that with a concept for a book fully developed, and an edit and sequence made, the bulk of work required for making a photobook is done. Unfortunately, that is not the case at all, as I will discuss in the following two chapters. Before talking about aspects of production, the next chapter will deal with design, often just seen as an

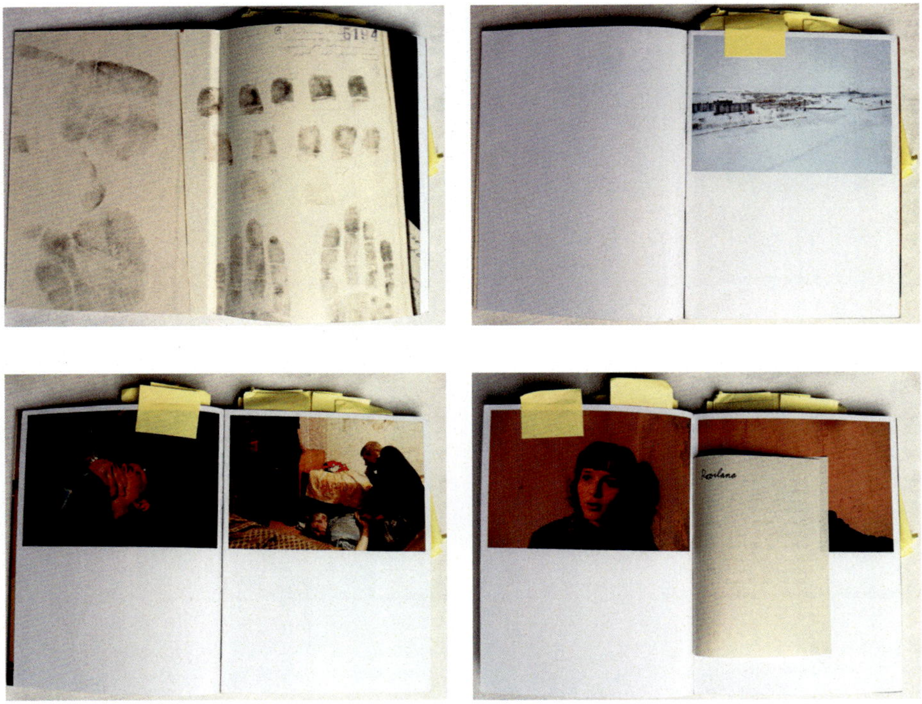

Figure 4.25 Photographs of selected spreads from an early dummy of Donald Weber's *Interrogations*. This dummy has a higher production value than the earlier one in Fig. 4.25, but just like most dummies, it is subject to all kinds of possible modifications, with PostIt notes added as simple, removable book marks

Photographs courtesy and © Donald Weber

afterthought by many photographers (many of whom foolishly think they can just do it themselves).

Notes

1. In his widely acclaimed *a shimmer of possibility* (SteidlMACK, 2007/2009) and *The Present* (MACK, 2012), British photographer Paul Graham has explored moving beyond the single photograph, taken at a given moment, to pairs or short groups of often very similar photographs centered on specific, albeit somewhat generic events or circumstances. This approach moves beyond ideas such as the decisive moment—the single, well-composed photograph—to one where the group of pictures encapsulates the moment.
2. The following discussion of editing employs the simplest approach, aiming to make the task of those struggling with editing easier. Once a photographer has moved to a stage where s/he feels more confident about editing, some of the ideas expressed in this chapter can probably be somewhat relaxed.

3. French philosopher Roland Barthes introduced the idea of the *punctum* in his seminal book about photography, *Camera Lucida*. Therein, he distinguishes between the *studium* and the *punctum*. "The *studium*," Barthes writes, "is that very wide field of unconcerned desire, of various interests, of inconsequential taste." In contrast, the *punctum* is the "second element which will disturb the *studium*": "A photograph's *punctum* is that accident which pricks me (but also bruises me, is poignant to me)" (quoted from Roland Barthes, *Camera Lucida*, Hill and Wang, 2010, p. 27).
4. Quoted from website: accessed September, 2, 2015, at http://www.fototazo.com/2014/04/ outtakes-richard-renaldi.html.
5. I will admit, of course, that in this particular case, ignoring the title of the project and then inferring it from the pictures seems like a pretty dumb idea. OK, point taken. But in many, if not most cases, which aren't quite so simple, there is a lot to be gained from doing that.
6. Per the publisher's website: accessed July16, 2015, at http://aperture.org/shop/this-equals-that.
7. See, for example, http://www.openculture.com/2012/05/alfred_hitchcock_on_the_essential_filmmakers_tool_the_great_kuleshov_effect.html for a very brief introduction.
8. The internet and at-home film watching have enabled "rewinding," of course. But in terms of watching a film, this almost amounts to cheating. In a movie theater or on TV, these options are absent; and films are made with a continuous, uninterrupted viewing in mind.
9. Please note that merely for reasons of simplicity I am talking about one photo after another. There can, of course, be pairs etc.
10. Of course, one could imagine books that don't have a beginning and an end, but as before, I'm trying to keep things simple right now.
11. Of course, you can fast forward or go back to an earlier scene if you're watching a movie at home. But that's not how directors envision their movies to be watched. If you go to the cinema, those options are absent.
12. Photographers often baulk at "cheating" in the form of showing pictures that were not actually taken after each other as that or showing pictures from a different location elsewhere. While there are cases in which factual truth actually matters—think a strict photojournalistic or documentary environment—in most cases a photobook is a piece of fiction (much like all photography is fiction—at least to some extent).
13. In an interview with Stanley Wolukau-Wanambwa, accessed October 2, 2015, at http://www.thegreatleapsideways.com/?ha_exhibit=horizons-a-conversation-with-sze-tsung-leong.
14. Keith A. Smith, *Structure of the Visual Book*, 4th edition, Keith Smith Books, 2003, p. 29.
15. Ibid., p. 30.
16. Ibid., p. 233.
17. As quoted by Keith A. Smith in *Structure of the Visual Book*, p. 219.

18. Please note that in the book, the titles are not given next to or near the photographs. Instead, there is a separate list with page numbers at the end.
19. In the book, there is text facing *In Cold Spring*, and at this stage, the viewer is familiar with the story. I'm going to ignore all the extra information, given that a part of a good sequence should work regardless of where it was taken from (assuming, of course, it's not just some random part, which this one clearly is not).
20. Of course, the woman could have appeared earlier, and her position at this particular spot might refer to something entirely different. If you're that skeptical a reader, please simply bear with me. I have picked this particular sequence for a reason; it is self-contained enough to make sense on its own.
21. Just like in the case of Lutz's *Hesitating Beauty*, the titles of the photographs are provided only at the very end of the book in its List of Plates.

C. In Focus

Mariela Sancari—*Moisés*

Photographs cannot show what could have been or what might be, only what was. How then can an artist go about showing what might be? "*Moisés*", says Mariela Sancari, "is a typology of portraits of men in their 70s, the age of my father if he were alive today." Her father committed suicide in 1980, disappearing forever from her life. With the help of a newspaper ad, Sancari found men of the right age who looked what her father might look like if he were still around. She made them wear his father's clothes, and she photographed them, using a variety of angles for their portraits, and she also captured details of their faces. Ultimately, the photographs are more about a search that can never lead to its conclusion than about anything else. The father will never show up in the pictures. Instead, the photographs all are what-ifs, down to the ones in which Sancari had a man comb her hair. A book would thus need to translate this futile search into an experience for its viewers. This is what *Moisés* (La Fabrica, 2015) does.

It's no ordinary book. Instead, it combines two separate, saddle-stitched booklets that interleave to have the viewer go through it, having to turn a page to the left, then one to the right, etc. "I wanted the book to resemble this impossible search," says Sancari. "Turning the pages, one from the right, one from the left and so on, creates a certain rhythm and the feeling that you are looking for something (someone). At the same time you are unfolding the story." The book thus provides an experience that cannot be had in any other presentation of its photographs. It is one of the books in which the viewer's interaction with the physical object, the having to turn pages, makes her or him be an active participant of the search represented by the photographs. Sancari makes her thinking behind the book very clear: "The structure of the book achieves two things I was very interested in. First, to be able to present the diptychs and triptychs of the series representing insistence through repetition (symbolizing the obsessive search of my father). Second, to slow the viewer's pace by having to unfold the pages, searching, discovering and finding as I was, and to force him/her to look at

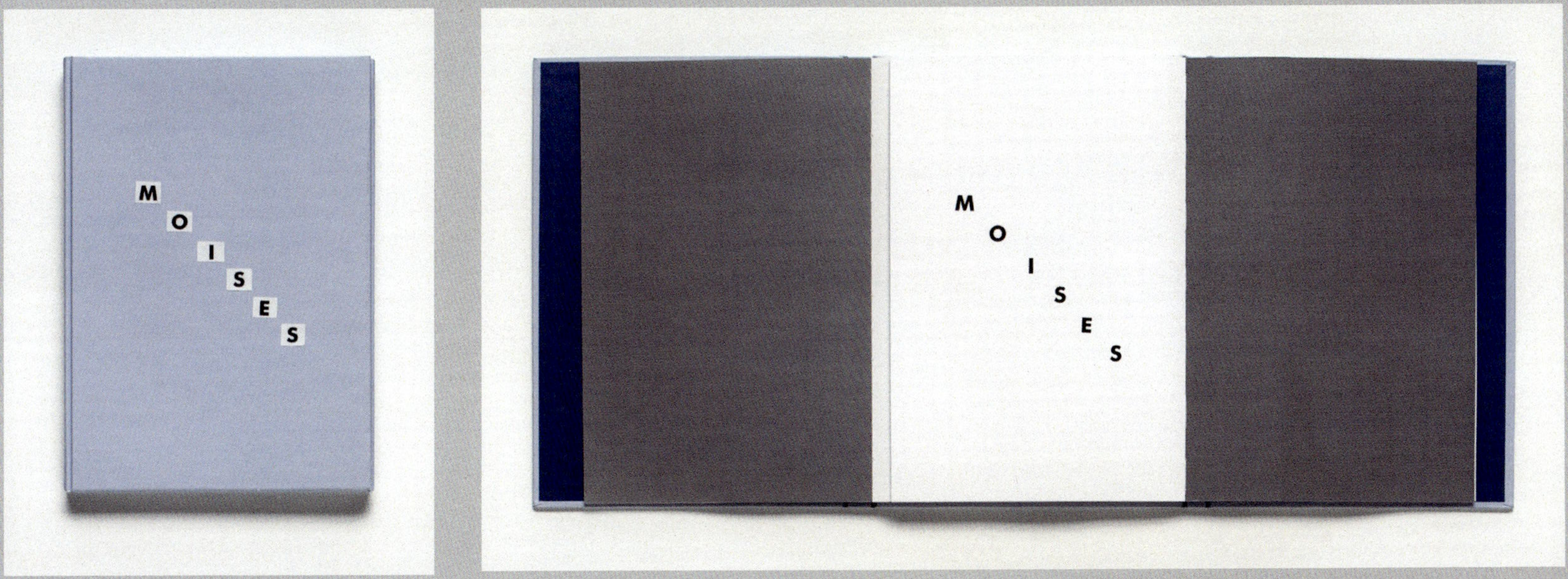

Figure C.1 Cover of Mariela Sancari—*Moisés* (La Fabrica, 2015). Left: front cover. Right: title page, after both sides have been opened. At first an innocuous book, it reveals itself as a lot more complex once the viewer realizes it opens on the left and the right, with interleaving pages

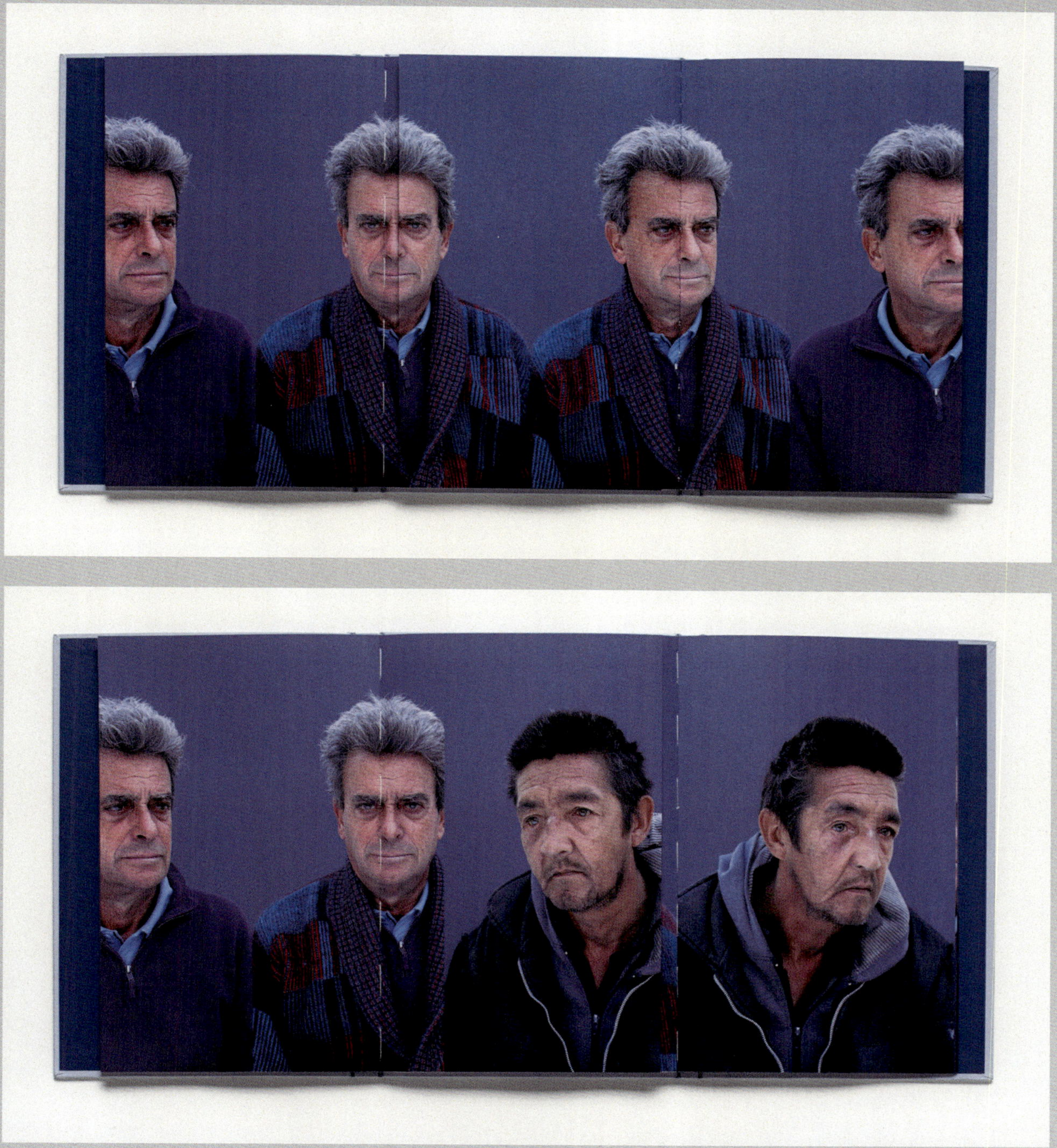

Figure C.2 Top: spread from Mariela Sancari—*Moisés* (La Fabrica, 2015). Bottom: spread immediately following the one shown in the top image. A few things stand out. For a start, the book has been produced (meaning here: bound) very well. The parts of photographs that are on separate pages line up extremely well (note the face of the man second from left in the top image). The use of full bleed makes the experience of looking at the faces more immersive. What is more, the different characters are made to relate to each other through their equal treatment, putting them on equal footing, and inviting the viewer's study, given there are often multiple views of the same or of two men. Note how the saddle-stitched binding of the two sections is visible through the white binder's thread

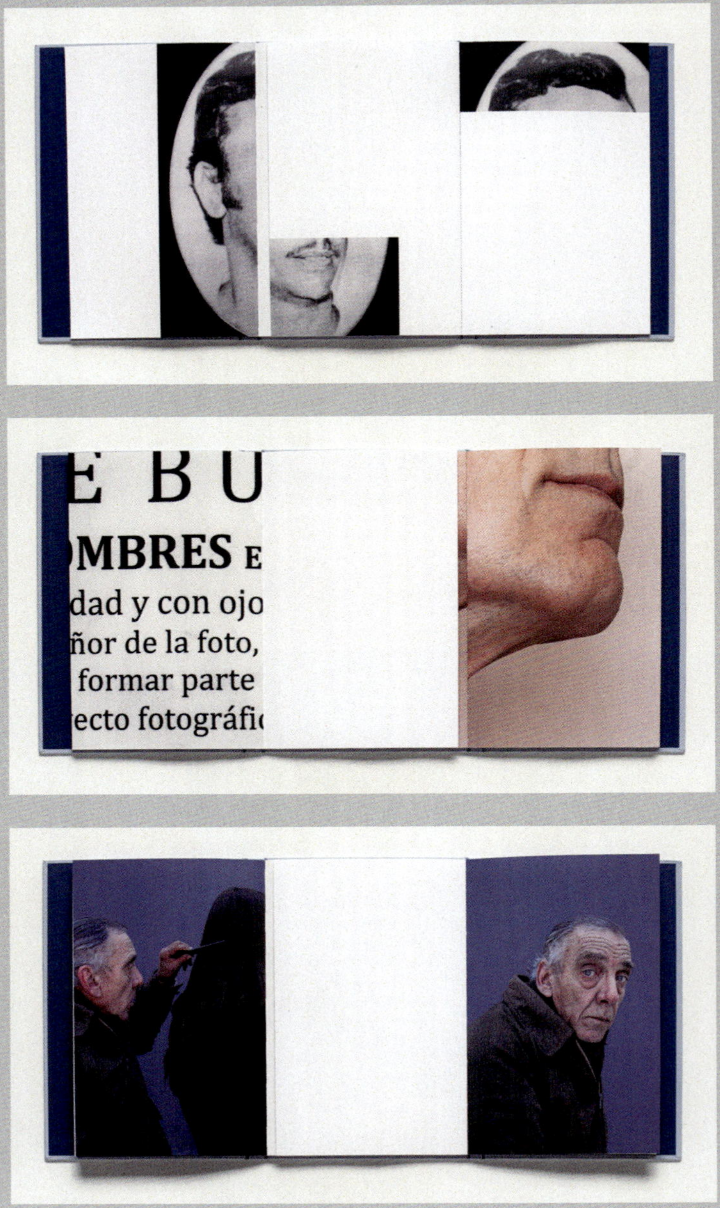

Figure C.3 Three spreads from Mariela Sancari—*Moisés* (La Fabrica, 2015). Besides comparing the different views of different men seen in Figure C.2, the book uses other visual strategies to point at the search for a dead father. The top spread presents fragments of an archival picture of a man (the father), the section containing his eyes and nose missing. The middle spread replicates the process of looking at fragments by showing just the chin of one of Sancari's models opposite text that is equally fragmented (with words such as "dad" or "parte" jutting out). There are other spreads showing just parts of a man's face. The bottom spread contains yet another variant, with a photo of a man looking directly at the camera set against one of him combing a woman's hair. The viewer is made part of the artist's search for her dead father: what might he look like now? And what kinds of interactions would he have with his daughter?

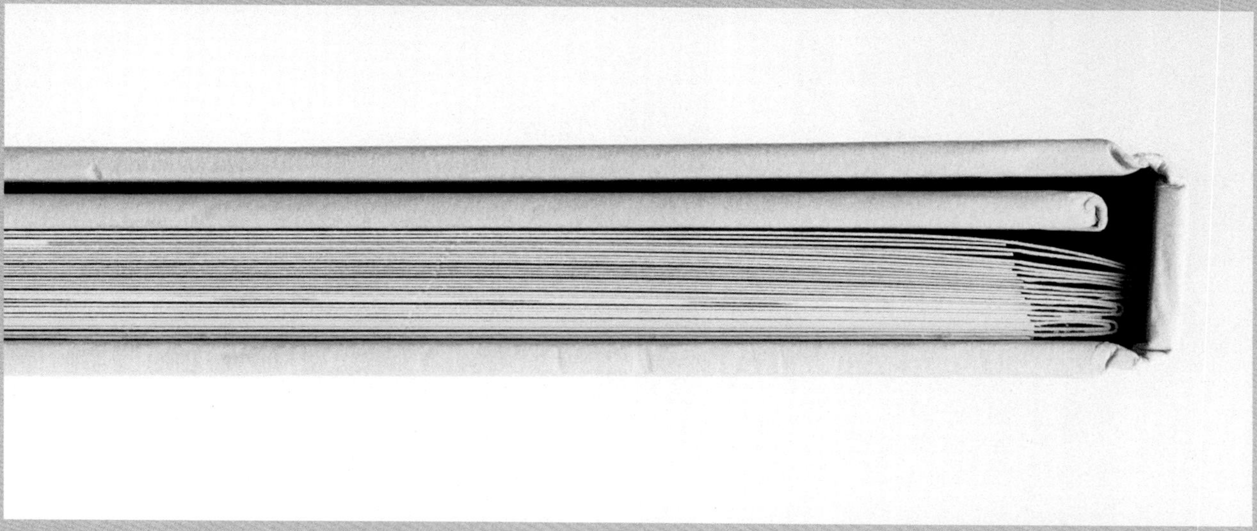

Figure C.4 Two separate interleaving booklets in a single case require careful consideration in terms of the binding. A view from the head of the book shows how the case of the book contains extra space at the spine(s) to accommodate the extra bulk of the book in its center

the images twice, in whichever way they decide to turn back the pages." To reiterate the point, in the most obvious way the physical form of the book (and consequently the way a viewer will have to look at it—there is no other way) becomes a crucial part of the overall concept of the book.

Much like every photobook, the final form of *Moisés* came at the end of a long process. Sancari said she "learned a lot from working with physical dummies, at every stage of the process, as opposed to a file in the computer." The experience of looking through the physical book cannot be replicated by clicking a button on a computer.[1] And the dummies evolved: "In the first dummy, I was trying very hard to 'explain' the story (something I consider to be an obstacle to overcome in my artistic practice), using all sort of different materials, text and images from previous series, to not leave any loose ends. At some point, I realize that in my case, the simpler the idea and its execution were, the better it became." While the form of *Moisés* might tempt one to describe it as complex, it really isn't. It might be more complicated than most photobooks, but the set of basic ideas is very simple: comparisons of similar-looking photographs in two interleaving booklets.[2]

For critic and writer Colin Pantall, *Moisés* succeeds because of the simplicity of its form. "The photographs are quite poignant portraits," he says. "They're very simple too." And the form of the book brings everything together: "It's just so simple, using the idea of unfolding the layers of her father's identity in a very simple and direct manner, and you do it physically. By doing it physically, you look at the pictures. [...]

You *have to look at them*, because you're doing this left–right unfolding" [my emphasis]. Ultimately, he says, "it's getting quite tragic, there are certain amounts of cruelty involved. So it's kind of a recovery. You got all that echoed in the book. It's imaginative. I think that's why this books works. If this were just a normal book it wouldn't work. The design here encapsulates the idea, it connects it, it's not redundant." This then would point at the sweet spot of photobook making, where very simple decisions and ideas lead to a complex and truly immersive book.

Notes

1. Even looking at a video of someone leafing through the book online does not come close to the actual experience of looking at the physical object.
2. The same idea for the physical construction of the book was used in Willeke Duijvekam's *Mandy and Eva* (self-published, 2015), which was designed by Sybren Kuiper.

C H A P T E R 5

From Pictures to a Book: Photobook Design

5.1 Why Design Matters

Having talked with many photographers, students and professionals alike, I'm under the impression that many practitioners view the photobook as a container that holds pictures, and aspects such as layout/design and production are then ornamentations to be possibly added later. Computer software that allows the easy creation of photobooks, whether in the form of *Adobe Lightroom* or *Blurb* templates, reinforces this idea. Given the discussion in Chapter 3, it might already be obvious why this simplistic way of thinking about photobooks is extremely counterproductive. Simple templates are fine if you want to produce a quick album of wedding photographs, say, but they're the worst possible approach to making the kind of photobook that is the focus here.

As a critic, teacher, occasional photographer, and someone who is not a design expert, my view of design is mostly driven by how I view existing photobooks (and, let's face it, everything else around us that is designed—most things are). A designer will obviously approach the topic from a different position, as someone who knows about its many different aspects. Here is designer Beverly Joel's way of making the case: "I think design plays a rather crucial role in the form and structure of a photobook—perhaps more so than with any other visual medium. First and foremost, the format is particularly well suited to the medium—both in size and historical precedence. Working with a designer gives a photographer access to someone whose practice is first and foremost about how best to communicate and present an idea. Those who do a lot of publication design are particularly well versed in understanding how a page works, how to pace information, how text can support an image and vice versa." There is a lot of material to be taken from these sentences. Photography obviously is a visual medium, and many photographers know how to handle it. Photobooks are a related visual medium, but they combine photographs with a lot more, large parts of which require expertise outside of photography: design. Of course, these days it is simple to use existing templates or to learn software such as *InDesign* to "design" a book. But a photographer doing it might just really not be the same as a designer doing it. Joel again: "I find that non-designers are overly accepting of the limited typographic options on their own computers and easily overlook how drastically more refined or considered typographic choices can better communicate the sensibility of a given photo project. A traditional design process is also one that will explore multiple design strategies—I think it's easy for a photographer to go into a project with a single (albeit amorphous) notion of how a book should look. A designer can either refine or blow that notion out of the water—sometimes the exact opposite visual framework is one that most befits a particular photo series and designers are particular apt at helping establish that." Both the aspects of refinement and of enhancement are extremely important. Typesetting a text piece, for example, can be done by anybody. Doing it in such a way that somehow the text becomes a lot more attractive to read is something designers know how to do.

In my own experience, what can make the role of the designer so important is that laypeople such as myself cannot easily see all the different aspects of their work. Just as is the case in photography, beyond the surface level there are many, many details that an untrained eye cannot see in a conscious way, while subconsciously being in awe of it. Good design matters, and to get good design you need a designer. In a sense, the widely spread idea that design can be done by everybody (given it's so simple to buy a copy of *InDesign*) mirrors the idea that everybody is a photographer, given that cameras are now ubiquitous (including, crucially, as part of telephones). However, much like most photographers realize that there is a difference between taking photographs and doing it with dedicated and informed intent, the same is true for design. Readers interested in getting more insight into graphic design might enjoy Craig Ward's *Popular Lies* About Graphic Design* (Actar, 2012), which includes short chapters such as *Graphic Design is Easy*, *All you need is an Idea*, or *The Rules are There to be Broken*. There also is Richard Hollis' *About Graphic Design* (Occasional Papers, 2012), a collection of Hollis' essays and articles, which covers a wide range of topics, including the work of specific designers (for example, Josef-Müller Brockmann or Jan Tschichold), historical trends or developments (for example, *The Modernist Grid*), and general topics of graphic design. Readers eager to see the role of design specifically in the world of books (in general, not just photobooks) might want to consult Roger Fawcett-Tang and Caroline Roberts' *New Book Design* (Harper Design International, 2004), Andrew Haslam's *Book Design—A Comprehensive Guide* (Abrams, 2006), or Sendpoints Publishing's *Art of the Book* (Gingko Press, 2015). Both *New Book Design* and *Art of the Book* cover production aspects as well, the latter quite heavily so.

It is probably fair to say that in the United States, the dominant—or maybe most well-established—model of photobooks is based on Walker Evans' *American Photographs*. It is what I usually refer to as a gallery show on paper: the left-hand side of each spread is kept empty (white), and there is a single photograph on the right-hand side. Whatever variations exist, they mostly revolve around whether or not there are captions and/or page numbers. Of course, there is absolutely nothing wrong with this kind of layout, provided it serves the photography and the book's concept in question (which *American Photographs* obviously does). But it becomes problematic when photographers think of this model as the default, the baseline from which to approach aspects of layout/design and production. Whenever I travel to the Netherlands, photographers and designers there speak of American photobooks as being incredibly boring and as not fully exploring what the medium can actually do. Back in the

United States, photographers and designers speak of Dutch photobooks as overdesigned, with the design making it hard, if not impossible to see the photographs. The truth might lie somewhere in the middle of these two extreme positions, but it also might be a little bit closer to the Dutch than the American side of things.

It becomes very clear that things get complicated when we add personal preferences to the equation. We all have some idea of what we like to see in terms of design when we approach a photobook, regardless of what the book actually is. For example, a lot of photographers strongly oppose having a photograph cross the gutter. In much the same way, I have certain biases for and against specific kinds of design. But when looking at photobooks, what should really matter is not what one wants—either as someone making a book or as someone viewing it, but rather, what the work in question demands. If you are familiar with *Provoke* photobooks made in Japan in the 1960s and 1970s, you will probably realize that these books simply would not work if they had been put together as *American Photographs* was.[1] In much the same way, *American Photographs* would look ridiculous if you strayed from its minimal model. Both *Provoke* books and *American Photographs* work because the layout/design massively supports the photography and the books' concepts in question.

As outlined in Chapter 3, that really is the key of photobook making: every aspect of the book has to support the photography and the book's concept. In other words, layout/design then does not become an ornament to be added later, it instead is an integral part of the book, much like the edit and sequence, and also much like the choice of paper and binding (which I will discuss in the following chapter). Seen in that way, it becomes clear why working with a template often is a recipe for disaster: unless the template somehow happens to be the right one, the danger is that you end up putting the photographs into the wrong container. There is a reason why you store milk in a bottle and cereal in a plastic bag inside a cardboard box. Thus, once you have your photobook concept resolved, the question of design then becomes less of a question of what to do and more of how to do it well (the same applies for production). This is one of the reasons why Dutch photographers work with designers early on. As Donald Weber noted about *Interrogations* earlier, "My dummies and ideas were solidified by the time I even met with the publisher and with Teun [van der Heijden]. But what the designer did (and why I like to work with him) is he sees the graphic or physical representations of the conceptual photographic, narrative and philosophical ideas and can find a graphic language to reinforce that." The situation Weber found himself in is the ideal each photographer should strive for: "Teun understands the work and tried to find the graphic and physical manifestation of your photographic ideas." Given that most photographers are not trained designers, approaching a professional designer early on thus is a good idea.

5.2 The Dutch Photobook

The previous section mentioned Teun van der Heijden, a Dutch designer. Anyone who has followed the world of photobooks not just recently, but going back a few decades, will be familiar with the prominence of books made in the Netherlands (or with a Dutch designer involved). Ed van der Elsken's 1956 classic *Love on the Left Bank* surely would have been a radically different book had Jurriaan Schrofer not worked on it. In fact, this particular designer invented the genre "visual novel" together with the photographer, assembling photographs Van der Elsken had taken of acquaintances and friends into the completely fictional story of a sailor falling in love with a girl, with Paris providing the background. Broadly speaking, design plays a much larger role for Dutch photobooks, making them often look radically different than, say, mainstream US photobooks.[2] As the partnership between Van der Elsken and Schrofer hints at, close collaborations between photographers and designers have a strong tradition in the Netherlands. Rik Suermondt and Frits Gierstberg explain in the introduction to their *The Dutch Photobook* (Aperture, 2012), "this cross-pollination dates back to the period between 1945 and 1968, when photographers and designers were united in a single trade union" (p. 7). While the trade union split into different branches after that, photographers and selected designers stayed in close contact, continuing a tradition that in such a form is unique worldwide.[3]

The close relationship between Dutch photographers and designers has repercussions concerning the actual role of the designer. In contrast to how design is usually approached elsewhere, many Dutch designers pride themselves in becoming involved in many stages. "For me," designer Hans Gremmen says, "it does not matter how we start. It is important to be able to rethink and question everything. If somebody would approach me with a fixed dummy, just looking for a nice typeface for the colophon then I would not do it." We already encountered this vastly expanded role of the designer through Donald Weber's words describing the making of *Interrogations*. This is not to say that a photographer would have to throw everything I discussed up until here out of the window if she or he wanted to work with Gremmen: "What I like when people approach me with a dummy is that there is a clear starting point to talk about. A dummy reflects the ambition of the maker. And it can have elements which I would never have thought about. So it is also fresh for me to see. But—dummy or no dummy—I always want to see ALL the work, all rejected images, contact sheets, texts, thoughts: all of it. This is always very inspiring to see, because it really reveals how people think about their work/project. And it always provides angles to continue working on." So Dutch design is not merely a collection of design elements, many of which are not used nearly as much elsewhere. It also accepts the designer having a much more prominent role during the overall process of the making of a photobook. Regardless of whether you prefer your design more along the lines of, let's say, Walker Evans' *American Photographs* or Donald Weber's *Interrogations* (to use two books sitting at opposite ends of the design spectrum), much can be said for the involvement of a set of specialists other than the photographer during the making of a photobook, regardless of whether it is produced by a publishing house or self-published.

Sybren Kuiper, another very well-known Dutch designer, mirrors Gremmen's sentiments concerning his involvement with a book: "The book is a very particular format. It's not a website, it's not an exhibition. In my opinion you not only need a graphic designer, but a graphic designer who is able to edit your story and use the specific aspects of the physical book. I know that that takes a lot of courage on the part of the photographer, and as a designer you need to earn that trust." As is not hard to imagine, putting that trust into someone who is not a photographer can be hard. But there is much to be gained. Kuiper again: "I once gave a lecture at the photobook festival in Kassel with Ten Golden Rules for photobook design. My rule number three is 'Never listen to the photographer.' The point obviously is that photographers are so involved in their own project, in their own photographs, that they don't have a clear view of it any longer. They get bored with their own photographs, because they have seen them so many times. They tend to remove the best photographs, because they can't see them any longer. Or they focus on small details. You need someone with fresh eyes to see whether the photos actually do what you think they do." To see "whether the photos actually do what you think they do"— there is that strong echo of what I spoke of in Chapter 4.[4] This does not mean that Kuiper insists on essentially making books for photographers: "What works best most of the time is when photographers have tried to edit and make a book themselves a number of times, and are not satisfied with their own result. That's when they arrive at the point where they say 'I thought I could do it. But maybe not. Let's see what you come up with.' However, this is not necessarily always the case. Sometimes photographers didn't try to do any edit at all and are just curious about what somebody else would do with their work. And some photographers have really excellent ideas themselves to work with." This is important to realize for photographers, especially those who are too worried to give other people too much power concerning their book.

5.3 The Role of Design

A designer, notes Hans Gremmen, "brings many practical things to the table, such as knowledge of typesetting, papers, way of binding etc. It sounds like an easy answer, but it is a specialization to make books. It took me ten years of education, and 12 years of experience to get to this point, and although I still make mistakes, I know the most common mistakes and traps when it comes to making books, and know how to avoid these (most of the time)." The designer thus is not necessarily the person who only makes sure the typesetting and margins look fine. An experienced designer knows about the medium and can thus offer a lot more. "I prefer to be involved early enough in the process to have a collaborative dialogue with the photographer." says Beverly Joel. "I'm not interested in just being a production vehicle for already resolved design ideas. I also find that unless you are working with the rare individual who has already been involved in numerous book projects, I'm in a much better position to help navigate the myriad aesthetic and production decisions involved. Often times, photographers have already largely sequenced the body of work at hand, but I particularly love having some input into those decisions as well." In other words, experienced photobook designers know a lot more than merely how to get the margins right.

"But be careful!" advises designer Ramon Pez. "Not all designers are experienced bookmakers, and in the case of a photobook, you must work with a designer who knows how to read the language of photography." This sentiment is especially true for people like Gremmen, who not only designs photobooks but also publishes them under his own imprint (FW:Photography). In fact, much like many other Dutch designers he often looks at photographers' work even when they're not (yet) clients: "With some photographers I have a nonstop discussion about their work for years [...] These discussions result in books, sometimes, but that is not the goal of these discussions. It is more about a mutual interest in each other's view and reflection on things." In an obvious manner, these kinds of discussion are a form of what I discussed in Chapters 3 and 4 where I advised photographers to get other sets of eyes look at their work. A highly accomplished specialist who knows the medium very well but is not a photographer (and thus does not necessarily suffer from the problems many photographers suffer from, a closeness to photography that often gets in the way of developing a concept and/or create edits) can clearly add a lot to a project.

Sybren Kuiper makes the ultimate goal very clear: "I'm not into design as a way of adding extra graphics over the photographs. It's more about telling the story in a physical form that adds to the intention of the story." This is an extremely important point, especially for those for whom Dutch photobooks appear to be too overdesigned: the design is the means to an end, but not the end.[5] Design plays a similar role as the book's concept, the edit and sequence, and, as we will see in the next chapter, production. It helps "telling the story in a physical form that adds to the intention of the story." Seen that way, it becomes clear why design cannot—should not—merely be an afterthought.

Photographers often work on aspects of design, and I acknowledged as much when somewhat artificially separating "layout" and "design" previously. While input from a professional can only make for a better book, many photographers develop a good understanding for how many, if not most of the spreads of their book should be laid out. Imagining, for example, a book along the lines of *American Photographs* in part is a design decision. Playing with the sizes and locations of photographs on a spread clearly is as well. A photographer might not have an eye well trained enough to see whether the sizes work perfectly well and/or whether the margins need to be fixed. But most people know very well that a large photograph at the top of the right page of a spread works differently than a small photograph near the bottom of the left page. The Western tradition of making books revolves around turning pages from the right to the left, and the very relevant parts of books happen to either be located or begin on the right side. So while photographers are often pretty lousy designers as far as details are concerned, in terms of the overall structure of their books they usually have good ideas, ideas that when discussed with other professionals either might get changed, merely slightly improved, or they might remain as is.

Sybren Kuiper sees the design dichotomy as follows: "I think you basically have two kinds of people in the world of photobooks. You have photography connoisseurs, and you have photobook connoisseurs. The photo connoisseur wants a book with a lot of blank space, without distractions. They want to savor the photographs individually. The photobook lovers see the whole project as the end result. The individual photographs have to help the story or narrative, instead of the other way around, which, ideally, then becomes more than the sum of its parts." I'm not sure I fully agree with this, because many books with a lot of white space clearly have a narrative. That said, Kuiper does have a point, given that the role of the individual photographs in a book can be amplified or reduced through design. Another example for an approach where individual photographs become mere elements of a much larger hole is provided by many Japanese photobooks.[6] And ideas closer to the Dutch design model can be found in the history of Western photobooks (outside of the Netherlands) as well, whether it's William Klein's 1956 *Life Is Good & Good For You In New York: Trance Witness Revel*, Sam Haskins' 1964 *Cowboy Kate & Other Stories*, or many other books.[7]

5.4 Approaching Design

Discussions of design can easily become frustrating for those who aren't specialists. It is one thing to be able to create design that works, and quite another to see it at work. Given the vast amount of photobooks that are being produced, anyone interested in making one (in whatever role) should spend quite a bit of time looking at books. The idea should be not to merely become familiar with books (especially the ones that end up in the yearly "best of" lists), or to group them into "I like this" and "I don't like that." Instead, the idea should be to try to understand whether and how they work, to look at how their different elements come together. In terms of design, what usually sticks out is the kind of design one is least familiar with. That kind of design might look overly flashy or minimal (to the point of being absent), but even non-designers can usually understand quite well how the design works to support the work. Or maybe it doesn't. Either way, looking at design that way can help understand its role better. And being familiar with a lot of books also creates a (mental) library of things that might in fact serve one's own work, regardless of whether it's design or production elements. And this, in turn, can then help photographers find designers to work with. Ultimately, you want to work with a designer not because they currently are *en vogue* or because you heard good things about them, but because you have studied examples of their work, and you think their approach can serve your own work well. With photobooks, you will also want to work with a designer who understands the way books are physically made. We will look at the production aspect in the next chapter. Ideally, your designer knows about production, because design can have some serious production repercussions, which, in turn, will influence costs. For example, if you or a designer create a book with lots of gatefolds or multiple types of paper, unless that is done well, costs are likely to explode. "I prefer to have an idea of the budget," notes Kuiper, "because otherwise, I don't know what to aim for." Bells and whistles always come at a price, even when they are seemingly innocent. "So I prefer to know what the production budget is," says Kuiper. Ramon Pez mirrors Kuiper's sentiments: "I prefer to design with a clear limit of budget. Economizing the production is a good practice that leads to better results. This way, we tend to almost naturally enhance the essentials, and the book acquires more strength." For self-publishers, budget considerations are not always fully resolved, and this need not necessarily be a problem. "A lot of the projects I design are split up in two parts," says Kuiper. "First, I design the basic set up of a book or the biggest part of it. My client can get quotes from the printer based on that, and then they know precisely how much money they have to raise. The project then rests for three quarters of a year or a year, and then starts up again when they have money." As a self-publisher, you might end up in this situation especially if you don't know in advance how much you can spend. With publishers, this situation might arise as well—you might find a publisher who accepts your book proposal, asking you to raise (or fork over) money for the production. They might already have a designer they prefer to work with. But still, as a photographer, that is something to discuss with the publisher beforehand: is there a designer? Or are there people to choose from? Not all publishers work in the same way, however. I actually once consulted a photographer who had a publishing contract, but there was no designer. And the photographer had not even thought about that aspect of the book. So we ended up bringing in a designer. Photobooks made with the involvement of a designer simply make for much, much better books.

Notes

1. *Provoke*—subtitled *Provocative Materials for Thought*—was a shortlived Japanese photography magazine published by a collective that included photographers Yatuka Takanashi, Takuma Nakahira, and Daido Moriyama. Its main aesthetic, in Japanese *are-bure-boke* (roughly "grainy–blurry–out-of-focus"), became very influential in Japanese photobook making for a while. Readers interested in more details are referred to *Provoke—Between Protest and Performance*, edited by Diane Dufour and Matthew Witkovsky, Steidl, 2016, for an overview of the movement and *Japanese Photobooks of the 1960s and '70s* by Ryuichi Kaneko and Ivan Vartanian, Aperture, 2009, for details on photobooks made during that period.
2. Readers interested in Dutch photobooks are advised to consult Rik Suermondt and Frits Gierstberg's *The Dutch Photobook*, published by Aperture in 2012.
3. Readers interested in learning more about the history of Dutch photobook design might want to start with Frederike Huygen's magnificent *Jurriaan Schrofer* (Valiz, 2013). As mentioned earlier, Schrofer played a major role in Van der Elsken's *Love on the Left Bank*. Huygen's biography describes in detail the work that predates the book, including the designer's company photobooks (for many of which he hired photographers, including Van der Elsken), plus a very early, different version of *Left Bank*, published in *Drukkersweekblad en Auto-Lijn Keerstnummer*, 1954.
4. The interested reader can find Kuiper's *Ten Golden Rules* at http://www.photonews.de/cms/ wp-content/uploads/2011/11/TEN_GOLDEN_RULES21.PDF, accessed on February, 5, 2016. Please note that Kuiper's rules are based on an approach to photobook making that is common in the Netherlands, but a lot less common elsewhere, namely with the designer taking over vast parts of the editing process as well.
5. Of course, much like there are many badly designed books outside of the Netherlands, you can find them there as well. As you probably can imagine, in that case, they are not

underdesigned (or, worst of all, undesigned), but overdesigned, with design gimmicks overwhelming the photography in question.

6. See *Japanese Photobooks of the 1960s and '70s* by Ryuichi Kaneko and Ivan Vartanian, Aperture, 2009.
7. The interested reader is advised to consult, especially, *The Photobook: A History, Vol. 1*, by Martin Parr and Gerry Badger, Phaidon, 2004.

D. In Focus

Donald Weber—*Interrogations*

The topic of exploitation has been an important part of discussions around photography for a long time. There is, after all, a power dynamic at play: someone with a camera, the photographer, gets to make a decision about how someone else is going to be depicted. Even in cases where consent has been granted, the portrayed might simply not know how she or he will end up looking in the photographs. With consent being absent, the floodgates might open. Discussions of exploitation are usually valid, but frequently they are also misleading. After all, if a photographer takes a picture in a situation in which someone is being mistreated, the resulting photographs might amount to no more than insult being added to injury. And talking about the insult, instead of the injury, runs the risk of both barking up the wrong tree and ignoring an aspect of photography that has been important for a long time as well: bearing witness.

Donald Weber's photographs of police interrogations in Ukraine caused a stir in photography circles when they first appeared. On the internet, the most extreme ones would routinely grace articles, with commentary such as "If you can look at this kind of raw human shame and perverse humiliation without cringing, you're probably a corrections officer or in the CIA" being quite common.[1] How would one go about making a photobook out of these pictures? *Interrogations*, published by Schilt in 2011, demonstrates how: "The idea of the book being that this was to be like a police dossier," says Weber, "a set of files, without being literal. That is why we ended up with the razor like edge of the book and put in a slipcase, in a subtle way, it resembles a dossier without sending a red flag up." This might seem like the most obvious solution, but much like in the case of all good photobooks, getting to the final result involved a laborious process. Dutch designer Teun van der Heijden played a major role in the development of the book. Weber: "Our biggest hurdle was that the majority of my images were centered in the frame, meaning a typical book would have a mean gutter running down the center of all the images. We tried moving the

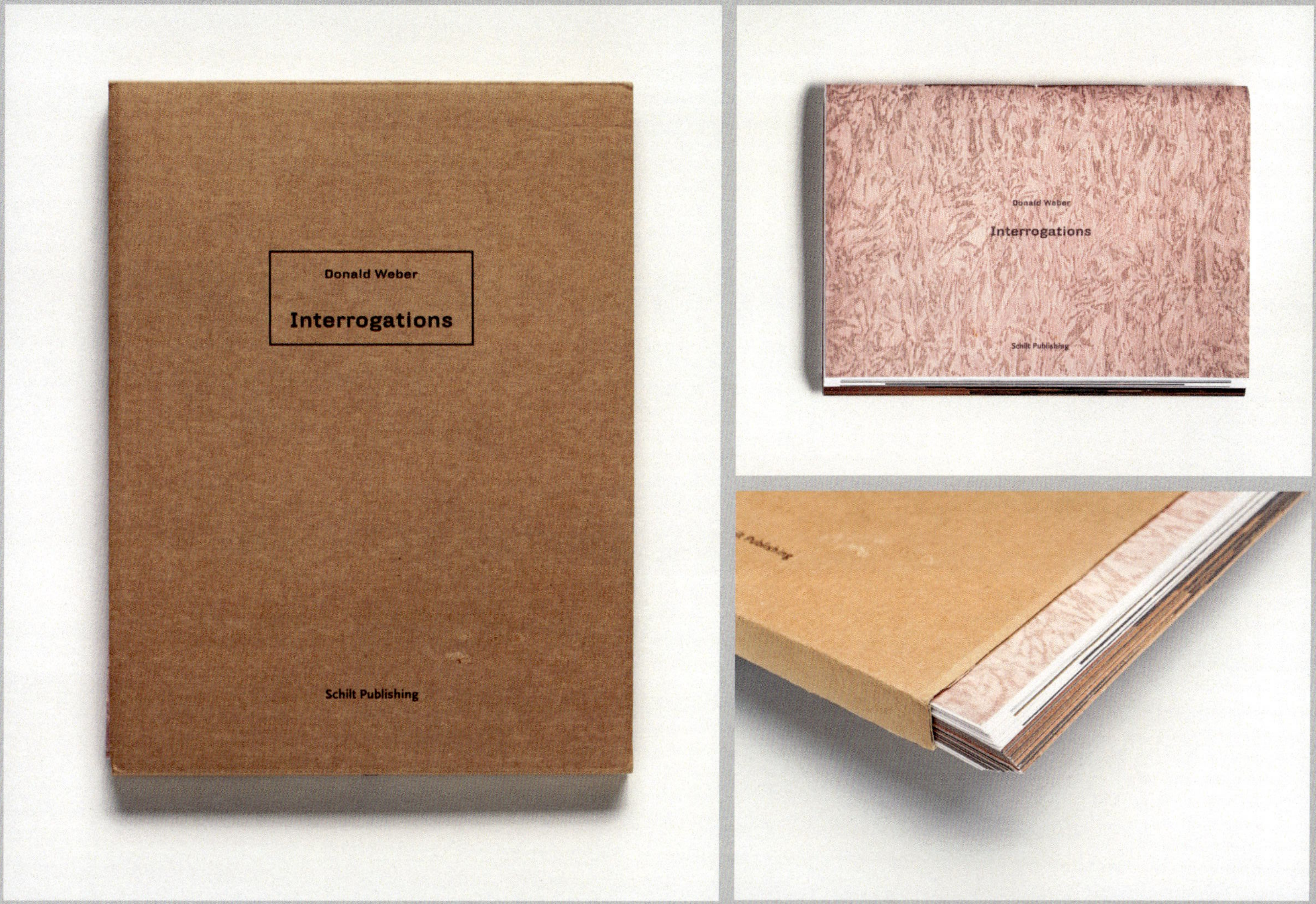

Figure D.1 Left: slipcase of Donald Weber—*Interrogations* (Schilt, 2011). Top right: cover of softcover book contained in slipcase. Note how while the slipcase follows a portrait format, the actual book uses a landscape one. Bottom right: detail of the book's fore edge. The book comprises of a single signature that has not been guillotined at the fore edge. In form, the production of the book mirrors the idea of it being a police dossier

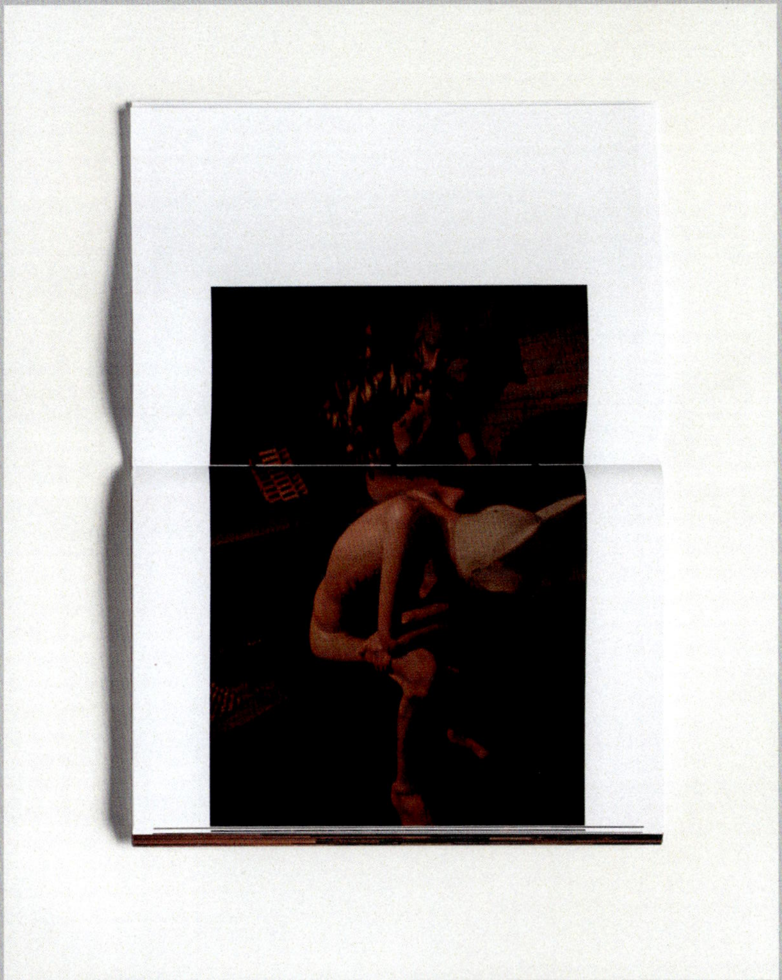

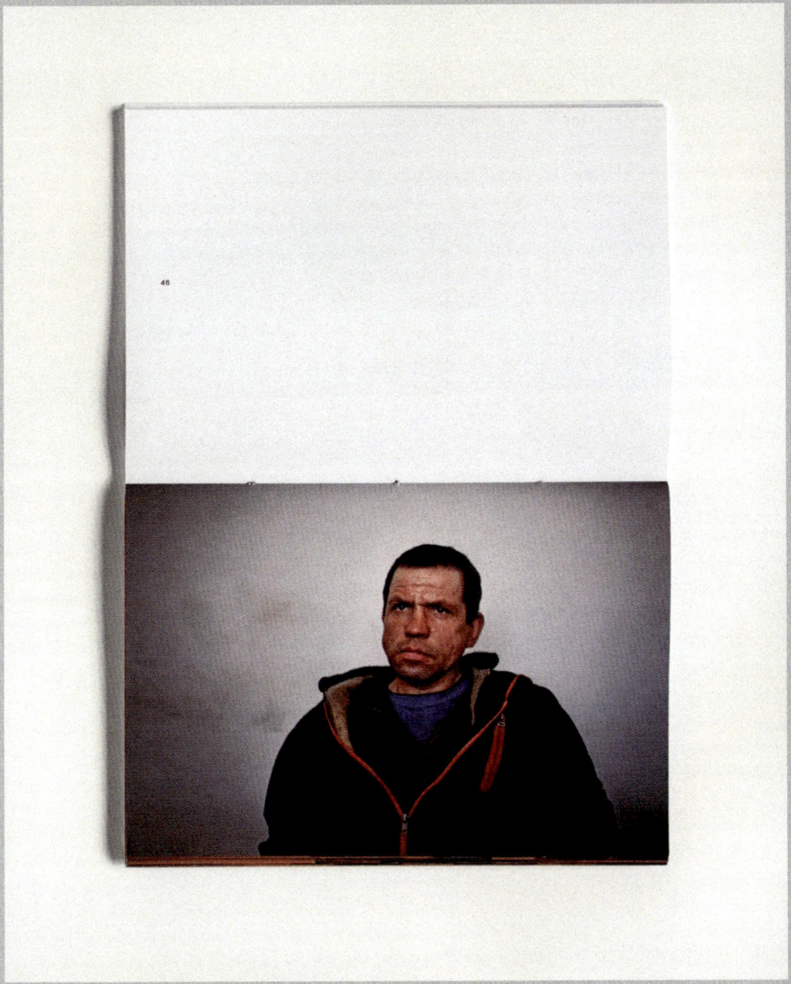

Figure D.2 Selected spreads from Donald Weber—*Interrogations* (Schilt, 2011). Note the calendar-style orientation of the book. Top left: spread from the Prologue. Unlike the main section, the Prologue features a variety of layout choices for the photographs, including, as seen here, images across the gutter. Top right (this page), bottom left and bottom right (following page): spreads from the book's main section. As can be seen, the content of the photographs varies in intensity, with a crescendo towards the most violent images, followed by a diminuendo

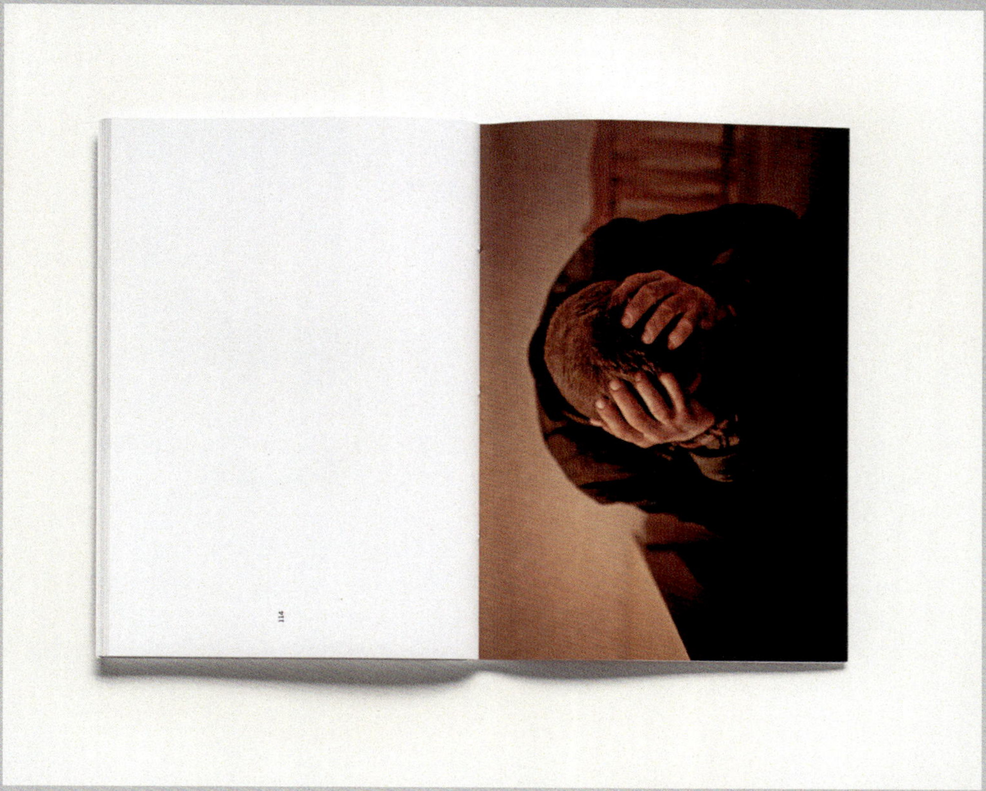
114

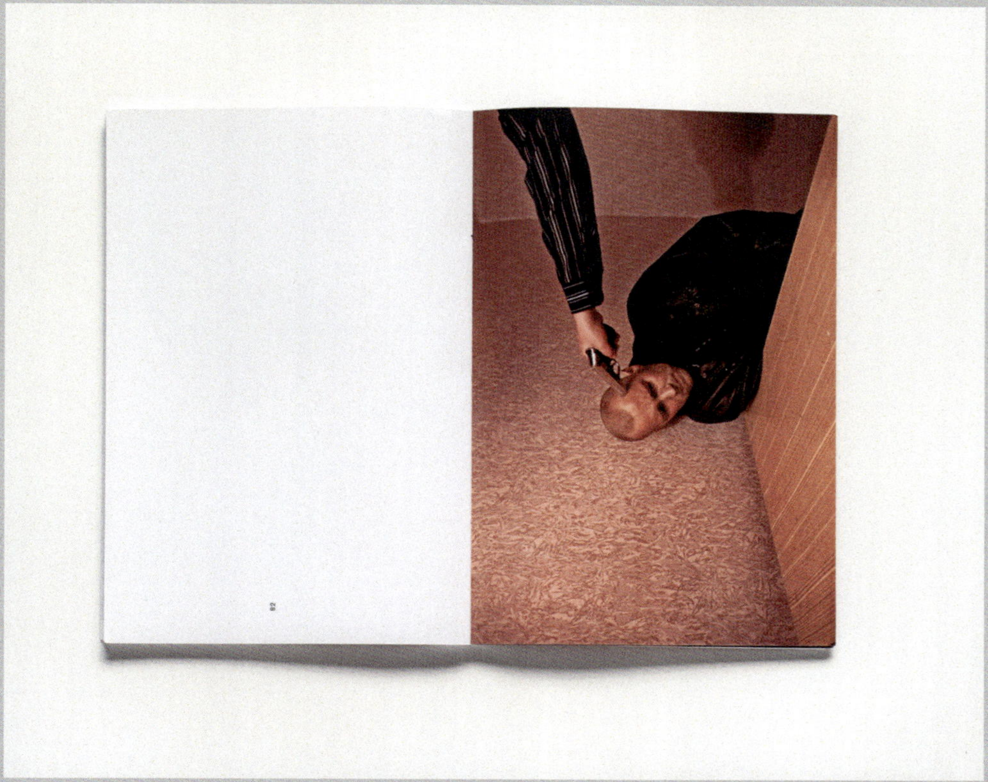
92

images around, slightly cropping, but nothing worked. This is when Teun came up with the idea to rotate the book, 'calendar style,' as he called it. I gave Teun a few parameters, one of them being NO landscape book. So, I found this a clever way to get around my self-imposed restriction of landscape." I think this design decision in part works so well because in a police file, nobody would be too concerned with whether or not the file would have to be rotated to see evidence. While having to rotate photobooks to see photographs was used commonly 100 years ago, it has become a rarity in today's photobook world. But this doesn't mean it can't be used any longer.

Other aspects of the book were found almost by chance, such as paper choices. "We were just making a dummy, Teun took a stack of pages to show me the orientation, and when he folded it over we both realized we loved the edge of the book," says Weber, "and so decided to go this route. This, however, caused a problem in binding, in that there was only one needle in Europe that could puncture this amount of paper in order to stitch the binding, and only a certain kind of paper could be used. It had to be a thick uncoated paper instead of coated to allow the needle to puncture. This was fine, because I wanted an uncoated, matte, textured paper anyway." In other words, while conceptually, many of the choices incorporated into the final book make a lot of sense, some of them were driven in part by sheer necessities of what could be done with the materials, given the intended format of the book and the desired type of binding. As a book, *Interrogations* makes a lot of sense. It does resemble a police dossier, and a prologue forcefully sets the scene for the eventual sequence of interrogation photographs. At the same time, it also shows how a collaboration between the photographer and designer who both were happy to compromise where needed can lead to a successfully realized book.

Note

1. The quote is from a published piece: accessed December 19, 2015, at https://www.vice.com/en_uk/read/donald-webers-interrogations-opens-tonight-at-the-foley-gallery. Needless to say, given that this particular site's visual currency makes many of Weber's photographs look quite tame actually, there is a richness to the statement that appeared to have escaped its author.

C H A P T E R 6

From Pictures to a Book: Production

6.1 The Challenges of Producing a Photobook

If you have made it to this stage of the photobook, where all that needs to get done is to have your desired number of copies printed and bound, what could possibly still go wrong? The sobering answer is: almost everything. If you have made your series of dummies, depending on the amount and degree of work you have put into them you probably have run into some of the problems you might be encountering when producing your final book. The following is a list of common problems that photobook makers frequently run into. Lest you think these problems are limited to self-publishers, most publishing houses are very familiar with them as well. Unlike self-publishers, however, publishing houses usually not only know how to anticipate the problems having procedures to deal with them in place, they also know how to minimize the risk of encountering them.

Problems include (but are certainly *not* limited to) the following:

1. The quality of the printing is bad. This is a very common problem for on-demand printing, where many companies known for their services do not actually print the books. Instead, production is outsourced depending on where the customer resides. Usually, but not always, the overall printing might look thin, and there might be a noticeable color cast across the whole book (regardless of whether it's black and white or color). But the quality of the printing could also be bad if a professional printer is used directly. As we will see later, this problem actually masks a variety of possible underlying problems, only one of which is the printer not doing a good job.
2. The binding has problems. Here are some real stories:
   - A few years ago, I was involved in publishing a couple of photobooks. The first one had to be partly reprinted twice (!) because the binder—a separate company—managed to screw up the very standard binding twice.
   - Around the same time, an acquaintance started his own publishing house, hoping to bring his very first book to Paris Photo, only to find that the binder had trimmed the whole set of books in such a way that the top of each book was missing 1 cm (a little less than 1/2"). Having no other choice, my acquaintance went to Paris Photo with badly

trimmed books, telling potential customers he would only be able to fulfill orders until after he got the error fixed (the whole book had to be reprinted and bound properly).

- A major publisher sent me a review copy, which had the hard cover affixed to the text block upside down.
- Another major publisher sent me a review copy, to let me know a couple of weeks later that the whole book would be redone, because the binding in the first version was too tight. It was. The book was very hard to open.

3. The overall feel of the book is wrong. Anything could be awry in this case, including, but not limited to, the choice of paper, the type of printing, the type of binding, …

The list of, let's face it, horrors here might make it sound as if producing a photobook amounts to a complete nightmare. It's true, it can be that. Some of the aforementioned problems cannot easily be avoided. If the binder screws up the job, there is very little one can do about that other than reprinting the pages and making sure it will get done again, this time properly. Everybody can make a mistake, and there's no reason why the people involved in the production process somehow would not be affected by that. They will be professionals, but they also might make a mistake. For any of the mistakes that might happen the key is not to anticipate what they might be (because experience tells me that something else will go wrong), but to include a sufficient amount of buffer time in the production process to be able to account for possible problems. Don't expect your book to come from the binder perfectly the day before you go to Paris Photo, for example. Just for the record, my acquaintance has since learned a lot from all the various problems he has run into, and he has been able to maintain a successful photobook-publishing business.[1]

Not all the problems outlined here are simply due to innocent mistakes, however. Some of the problems can be avoided by being on top of things during or even before the production process. Being on top of things means being aware of the challenges and being able to deal with the relevant details. In the following, I will discuss solutions to common problems for photobook makers.

6.2 Considering Binding

There exist a considerable number of different types of binding. It's probably safe to say that most people really only become aware of how pages are bound if the binding is radically different from what is usually encountered. But even in the range of binding types frequently encountered, there are important variations. What is more, binding types have repercussions for various aspects of a photobook. In particular, they can restrict the use of images on the actual spreads, the size of a book, the possibility of using thin or thick paper, the possibility of mixing papers, the cost, issues of mass production, whether a book feels "high brow" or "low brow," and more.

In most cases, photographers will not spend much time thinking about the binding, simply because using one of the commonly used types of binding will work. Most commonly used types of binding include perfect binding, Smyth-sewn binding (or anything similar), or stapling/saddle stitching. But even in those seemingly simple cases, there are important facts to consider. Perfect binding is a commonly used and cheap way to essentially glue any number of pages together (making it the ideal binding for telephone books, say). Given the pages are glued together at the spine, perfect bound books don't open fully. If a viewer forces them open, the spine might crack (the book will usually survive, but there will be an ugly crease in the spine, and the book tends to fall open at the crack). With time, the glue will dry out, and the binding will become brittle, so that eventually pages will begin to fall out.

As a side note, it is very important to realize that there is no such thing as an ideal binding. All types of binding put some limits on what can be done with a book. Given that we are dealing with physical materials that change with time, any type of binding might develop problems. So the idea should not necessarily be to try to find a type of binding that will live forever.

Given, also, that perfect bound books can be made cheaply, they are widely used even in the world of photobooks. There is no real reason not to use perfect binding, provided one works around the restrictions imposed by the binding. This is, in fact, the approach a photobook maker needs to take: pick a type of binding that does the job, and work around its restrictions. For perfect binding, the most obvious restriction is that books don't open fully. They won't lie flat. So in almost all cases, images across the gutter are highly discouraged. In fact, anything that gets too close to the gutter (images, text, …) might become inaccessible because of the binding. To give you an example of what we're talking about here, I often have on-demand books made that are 5 x 8" or 6 x 9" in size, perfect bound. For each spread, I make sure that on every page the 1/8" closest to the gutter will be left empty. In fact, if I want an image centered in a 5 x 8" book, I center it on the 4 7/8" wide section away from the gutter. When bound, roughly 1/8" of the page will be taken up by the glue. Whatever slight variations in the binding exist, they are so small that the "centered" image indeed looks centered on the part of the page that is visible. (See Table 6.1.)

These kinds of consideration are fairly simple—provided one is aware of the restrictions imposed by the selected type of binding. Those photobook makers who want to fully produce their own book, including taking care of the binding, will have to have a full understanding of what creating it entails. This process can be fairly simple, such as when a photographer delivers a set of pages to a commercial binder (or even copy shop) to get a perfect bound or spiral-bound book made. The process can also be fairly elaborate, when a photographer decides to do their own binding. Bookbinding started out as a manual process, and it still can be treated as such, either by professional bookbinders or by anyone else. But even when the binding is done by someone else, knowing about its properties is important. Table 6.1 provides an overview of a variety of limitations and/or things to consider for eight different styles of binding, some of them common, others less so. While many boxes are obvious, there are some mays, where something might be possible, depending on the circumstances. Note that Table 6.1 is intended to provide some orientation for those not too familiar with binding. An expert book binder might find ways around some of the restrictions.

Table 6.1 Selected properties and/or restrictions of common and uncommon types of book binding

	1	2	3	4	5	6	7	8
Pictures across gutter	no	no	yes	yes	yes	yes	no	yes
Uses signatures	no	no	yes	no	no	yes	no	no
Maximum page number restricted	no	no	no	no	yes	yes	no	yes
Problematic with thick paper	yes	yes	may	no	no	no	no	no
Mixing different papers easy	yes	yes	may	no	no	may	yes	no
Usually softcover	yes	yes	no	no	no	yes	no	no
DIY-able	no	yes	may	yes	yes	yes	no	yes
Industrial/cheap process	yes	may	may	no	no	yes	yes	no
Mass producible	yes	yes	yes	no	may	yes	yes	may
"Highbrow"	no	may	yes	no	may	no	no	may
"Lowbrow"	may	may	no	no	no	yes	yes	no

Types discussed here: 1=perfect bound; 2=side stitched/stab bound; 3=Smyth sewn; 4="book block"; 5=accordion; 6=stapled/saddle stitched; 7=spiral bound; 8=origami style. See main text for details.

Let's discuss the different aspects discussed in Table 6.1. Pictures across the gutter is an important layout decision. While there appears to exist some disagreement among photographers and photobook viewers as to whether pictures should or should not be allowed to cross the gutter, if you want such pictures, you need to stay away from binding types that are very likely to produce major problems, especially perfect binding and side-stitching/stab binding.[2]

Signatures are an important aspect of book production. Books are printed using larger sheets of paper, which are then folded and cut to produce signatures. Remember, if you take a piece of paper and fold it in half, you get a folio. Add two or more folios together, and you get a signature.[3] By construction, a folio has four pages. A two-folio signature has eight pages. In other words, signatures come as multiples of four pages. If you get a book printed and bound that involves signatures, your book's page number will need to be a multiple of four. Assuming you have text components in your book—you will certainly need the title pages and the colophon—you or (ideally) your designer should be able to create a book with the right number of pages, based on what your printer will produce. You probably do not want your edit to revolve around the idea of multiples of four, but you might have to adjust the overall page count at the very end (this happened to a student book I helped produce—the designer ended up putting the index onto two pages instead of one to avoid having a blank page in the book).

Some types of binding will restrict the maximum number of pages you can include in your book. It's not a huge concern, but if you want to make an accordion, say, a really huge accordion will become incredibly unwieldy, and you'll need a container for it. It's not undoable—see Anne Carson's *Nox*, but it's something to think about. In much the same fashion, there are size restrictions for some types of binding.

The last two rows are labeled "high brow" and "low brow." I'm not attempting to be critical with this. Instead, these labels merely point at the fact that cheaply produced perfect bound books often feel, well, a little cheap. Not that there's anything wrong with that, because that works for many bodies of work. In much the same fashion, a stab-bound book might feel precious simply because of the binding. In most cases, photographers will not need to consider this aspect of their book. But there are cases where it does matter. For example, a book about the punk scene might probably not want to feel too precious, so that the form of the book will be subverting the content.

Any photographer who finds themselves in the position of having to consider a type of binding should probably start out by looking for other books that employ it. Some types of binding are somewhat rare. But for almost all types of binding I can think of I have at least one or two copies in my photobook library (which isn't even that big). For all advanced questions, it's best to consult with an expert, a bookbinder. Bookbinders can be found fairly easily using the internet, and many of them are offering their services for a fee. While this is not a very typical model, photobooks can be and actually are being handmade as well, usually in relatively small edition sizes, starting with just one to a few dozens. Getting photobooks hand bound is relatively expensive (compared with the price an industrial binder will charge), but the difference in price is reflected in the difference in quality.

6.3 Examples of Less Common Types of Binding

It is probably easiest to understand the merits and restrictions of less commonly used types of binding by looking at examples. In each of the cases I am going to discuss in the following, the binding and materials work closely with the books' overall concepts and ideas (compare Chapter 3). This is an incredibly important aspect of photobook making, which I firmly believe in. Even though it is tempting to add bells and whistles to a photobook that are not really necessary, given the main concept—to essentially create a "sexier" product and/or have a larger appeal for collectors—the best photobook is always the one where all aspects closely work together and where all unnecessary things have been avoided. To employ any of the following bindings just for the sake of doing it makes no sense.

One of the simplest ways to bind a book essentially amounts to not binding it at all. This is the type of binding newspapers use, where groups of folded and stacked sheets are added together. Given that most newspapers are fairly large, that they contain a considerable number of folios, and that the newspaper is folded once itself, they typically contain more than one signature—in the world of newspapers, these are the different sections (politics, business, sports, and whatever else). While most people would never think of a newspaper as a book, it essentially is one, however (seemingly) little effort and expense have been spared for its basic production. In principle, there really is no reason why a photobook cannot be produced in much the same way, employing the same type of printing on fairly rough and basic paper (newsprint) and the same type of binding (or lack thereof, depending how you want to view this). Canadian photographer Tony Fouhse adopted this approach for *Official Ottawa*, a newsprint publication (Figure 6.1). The photographs, taken in Canada's capitol, could have easily ended up in a higher end photobook (see Figure 6.2). But Fouhse decided that he wanted to give away the publication for free and that it should have a form that would make that feasible. Thus, the form and production of the publication are driven by the intended function of the publication as much as by how or where images from Ottawa are often seen in Canada, namely in newspapers. In addition, Fouhse explicitly wanted to avoid getting the work out of the regular world of art photography, to reach a new, or maybe different audience. For this, newsprint clearly is ideal, given that it's very cheap to produce. What is more, giving away publications for free is easy: there are lots of public spaces that will accept free publications, for someone interested in a copy to take one. Also, newsprint publications are relatively cheap to produce. Giving away large numbers of hardcover photobooks that cost, say, $10 to make is very different than doing the same with publications that might cost $0.50 per copy. This give-away newsprint model is thus the complete opposite of one where a photographer would produce an expensive item aimed at the small collectors' market. This is not to say that one is better than the other. But especially photographers interested in reaching larger audiences often have more tools at their disposal than is commonly realized.

Instead of using an unbound signature (as in the case of *Official Ottawa*), the folios could simply be attached to each other through the use of staples (or binding cord). We are very familiar with this type of binding via magazines. Unless they are very thick (in which case

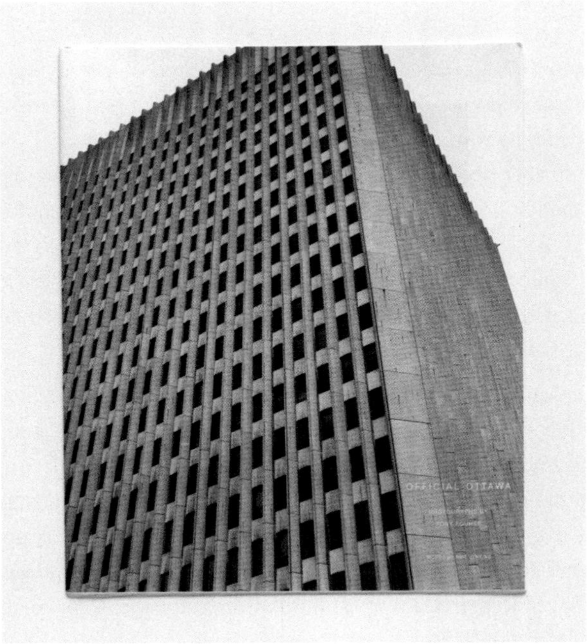

Figure 6.1 Cover of Tony Fouhse—*Official Ottawa* (Straylight Press, 2015)

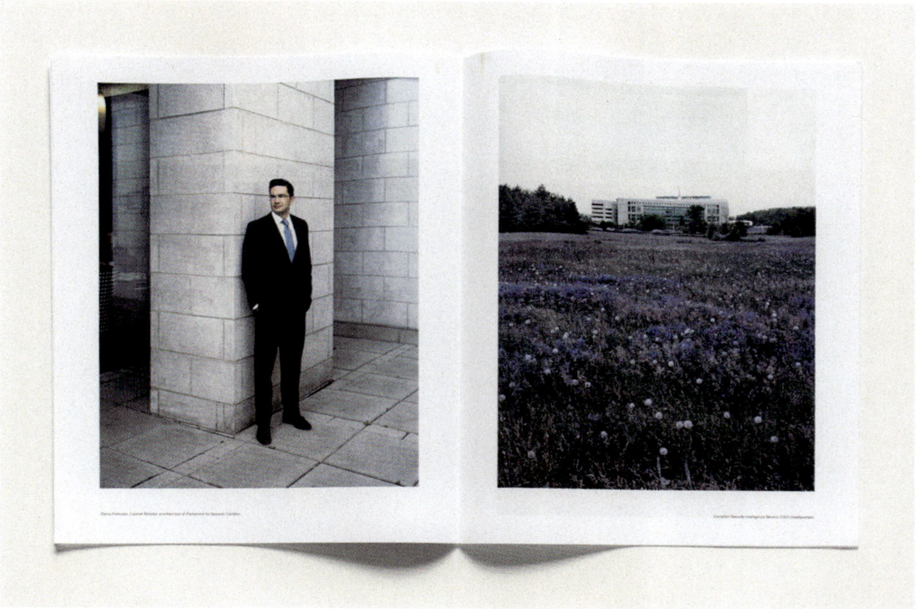

Figure 6.2 Spread from Tony Fouhse—*Official Ottawa* (Straylight Press, 2015)

they are perfect bound), most magazines are a single stapled signature, with the three open parts of the publication having been guillotined to create a straight edge. This is the basic format used for Donald Weber's *Interrogations*, which we have already seen in previous chapters. Intended to mimic in form a police interrogation file (see Chapter 3), the book consists of a single signature with a large number of folios. Instead of guillotining the fore edge, the pages have been kept as is, resulting in pages jutting out more and more towards the center of the book (see Figure 6.5). The book itself is contained in a cheaply made slipcase (Figures 6.3 and 6.5), where the materials themselves support the idea of the police file. But the slipcase also protects the un-guillotined fore edge when the book is stored (or shipped etc.). Figure 6.6 shows a spread from the book—note how the book's orientation makes the viewer look at it calendar style.

The aspect of durability clearly matters for photobooks. All books are made from organic materials. Provided they are being leafed through, their materials will inevitably get old and, much like the human body itself, break down. You might be familiar with this process from old paperbacks, in which the spine of the perfect bound book has become very stiff, typically resulting in it breaking somewhere. This is the result of the glue used decades ago having dried up completely, losing both its flexibility and grip. Where the spine is broken, pages might fall out. While books shouldn't necessarily be produced with their breaking down in mind (unless, of course, there is a good reason for it), it is important to realize that the binding of all books eventually will suffer from problems related to the age of the materials and the physical stresses being put on them through the uses of the book. But there can also be short-term durability issues for photobooks. Unprotected, *Interrogations* is likely to get creased or

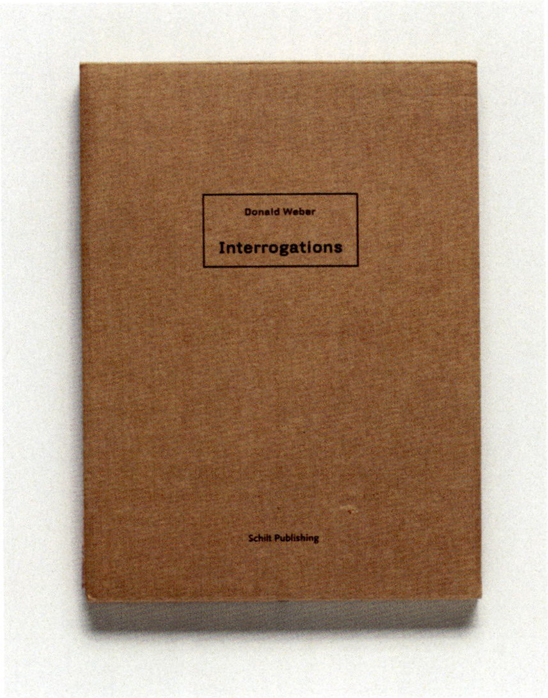

Figure 6.3 Slipcase of Donald Weber—*Interrogations* (Schilt, 2011)

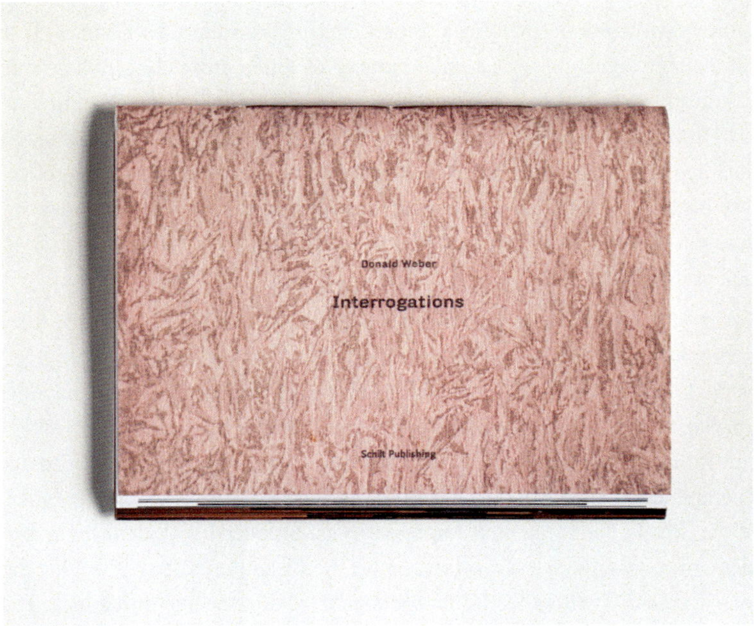

Figure 6.4 Cover of Donald Weber—*Interrogations* (Schilt, 2011)

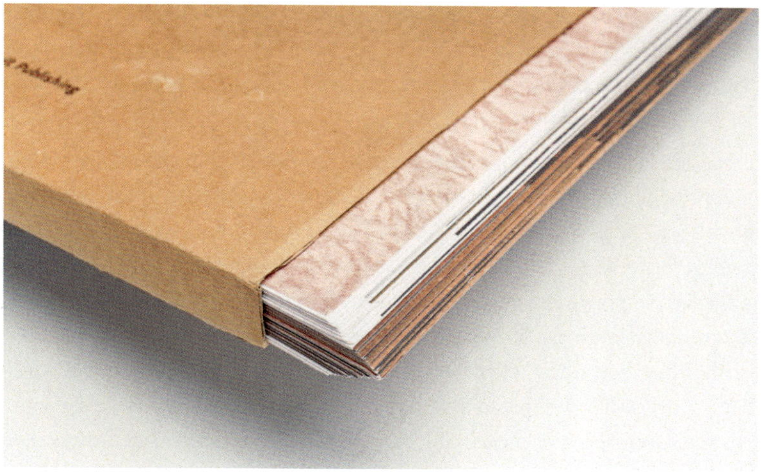

Figure 6.5 View of the fore edge of Donald Weber—*Interrogations* (Schilt, 2011), with the book jutting out slightly from the slipcase (for storage, the book can be fully covered by the slipcase)

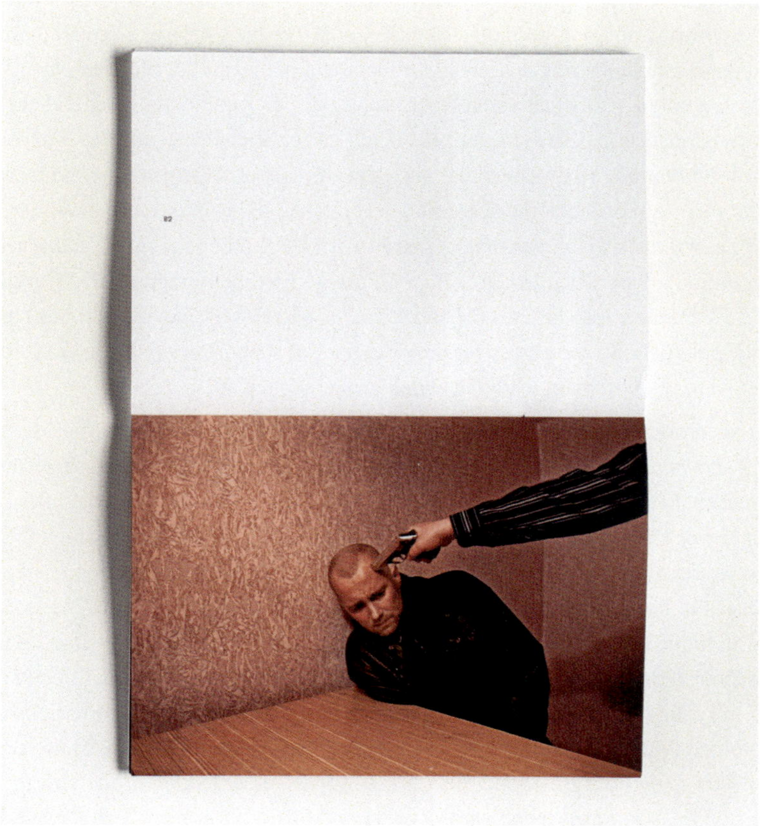

Figure 6.6 Sample spread of Donald Weber—*Interrogations* (Schilt, 2011)

dented at the fore edge easily, given the pages are jutting out towards the center of the book. So the slipcase serves as a way to avoid that, to protect the book itself. What's more, the slipcase also turns the otherwise floppy softcover book into a stable object that can get filed in a bookshelf easily.

Considerations of the types of binding discussed in this section should always come with thoughts about the durability or even outright stability or instability of the resulting book—issues that with regular perfect bound or Smyth-sewn books typically are absent. An extreme case of some of those issues is presented by accordion books (often also called leporello or concertina books). In a sense, an accordion book really is only one very wide page that has been folded up multiple times. As such, it's a very unusual type of book for various reasons. To begin with, it has two sides, a front and a back. You can look through an accordion book from the beginning until the end, and then you can flip it over and repeat the same procedure, assuming there is something printed in the back (which isn't necessarily always the case). If you construct a simple accordion book from a few sheets of paper, using glue or tape, you will immediately notice that such an object is actually quite flimsy. Since there is no spine that will hold the pages together, the book lacks support. The front might easily get skewed against the back. As a result, most accordion books employ a thicker paper stock, to give the accordion more stability, and to prevent the paper from tearing. What is more, accordion books typically come with an additional support structure, much like the slipcase of *Interrogations*. The various support structures I have seen so far include a belly band (a piece of paper wrapped around the accordion, really just a small slipcase, used, for example, for Peter Dekens' *Touch*, The Eriskay Connection, 2012), a slipcase (such as for Richard Avedon's 2002 *Portraits*, published by Abrams), a hardcover the accordion might or might not be attached to (see later), or even a clamshell box the accordion is contained in (as in the case of Anne Carson's *Nox*, New Directions, 2010—please note that *Nox* isn't a photobook, but it's a marvelous use of the accordion). Sjoerd Knibbeler's *Paper Planes* (Fw:Photography, 2015) employs the solution of a hardcover (see Figures 6.7 and 6.8). The accordion is not glued to the hardcover, however (Figure 6.8). So the hardcover provides a lot of support when the book is stored, but it does not restrict the ways in which the book can be looked at.

As an accordion, *Paper Planes* uses as many of the format's possibilities as possible. Figure 6.9 shows part of the photography side of the accordion. A book of paper models of military planes that were never actually built, the photographs do not obey the folds. Instead, they cross them. The object book is folded up not unlike the paper planes, which themselves are folded sheets of paper. In addition, the photography side of the accordion has a different surface than the back, it's semi-glossy. The back, in contrast, which contains information about the individual planes in the form of text (Figure 6.10) is left untreated, exposing a rough cardboard. In addition, a signature of two folios is stapled to the accordion at one spot (Figure 6.11). The folios are facsimiles of paper that might have been used to build a model plane, unfolded to their original states. There are creases and lines visible. Thus, the idea of folding, which underlines the model planes themselves, is contained in the structure of the book itself, in this aforementioned variety of ways. Materials are kept fairly "crude," underlining the basic idea of a paper model plane (as opposed to one made from wood, plastic, or

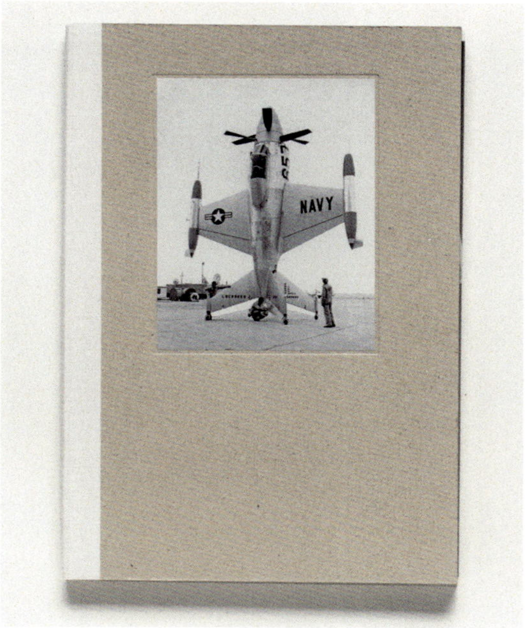

Figure 6.7 Cover of Sjoerd Knibbeler—*Paper Planes* (Fw:Photography, 2015)

Figure 6.8 Title page of Sjoerd Knibbeler—*Paper Planes* (Fw:Photography, 2015); note how the page block is not glued to the case, which features the colophon on the right-hand side

wood). When stored, the accordion looks just like a regular hardcover book. When opened, the viewer can look at the accordion without any possible restrictions that might arise were the accordion affixed to the cover. The seemingly quite simple, possibly at first glance a bit primitive book in actuality is a highly sophisticated object that supports the project's concept.

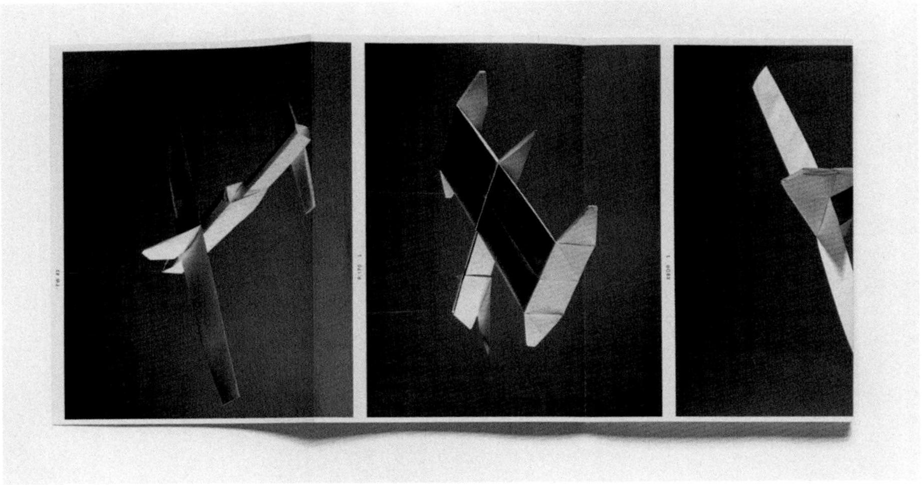

Figure 6.9 Spread from Sjoerd Knibbeler—*Paper Planes* (Fw:Photography, 2015); this would probably be considered the front of the accordion, featuring the photographs

Figure 6.10 Spread from Sjoerd Knibbeler—*Paper Planes* (Fw:Photography, 2015); this would probably be considered the back of the accordion, featuring information about the planes whose paper models are shown on the other side

At first glance, there is nothing unusual about Rafal Milach's *The Winners* (Gost, 2014; Figure 6.12). There is text on what looks like a regular hardcover book, but this is not out of the ordinary. If you look through the book, the layout also is pretty common (Figure 6.13). But there is a twist. As it turns out, all the photographs are tipped in. In other words, they were printed separately and then glued into the book, affixing them at their top edges. Each of them

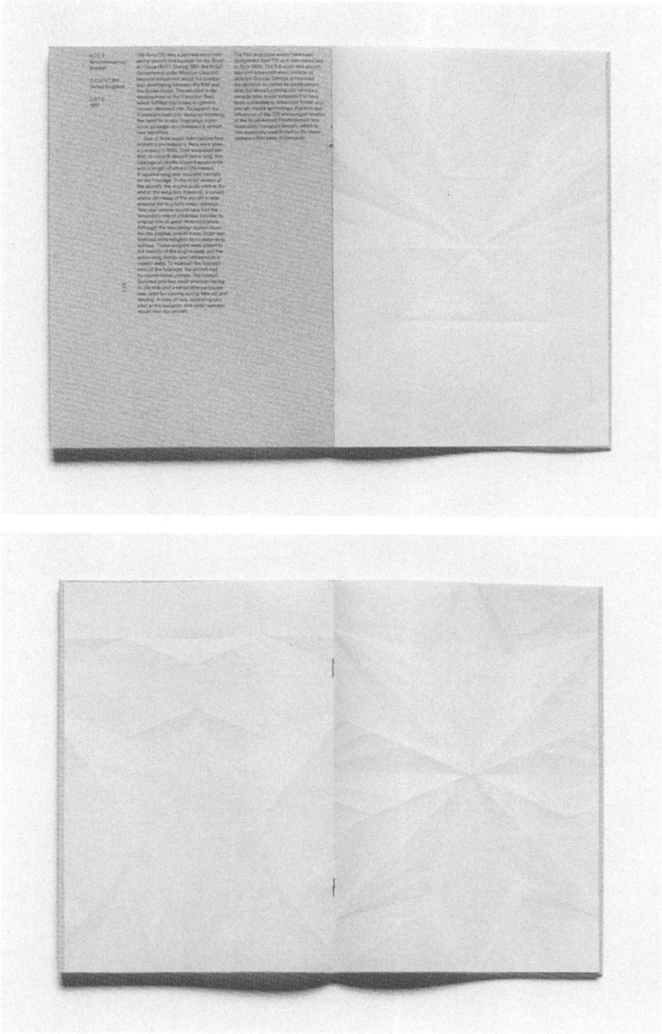

Figure 6.11 Spread from Sjoerd Knibbeler—*Paper Planes* (Fw:Photography, 2015). Two sheets of facsimiles of unfolded paper planes are attached to the accordion with staples. On the top, a view of these pages as they are being encountered. On the bottom, the center spread of these added sheets

can be lifted (see Figure 6.14), to underneath reveal short text about the picture in question. What sounds like a pretty simple—and nifty—production detail, in practice requires a lot more thinking than one might anticipate. For a start, the tipping in of the photographs, which are printed on a thin, semi-glossy paper, requires extra work (which increases production costs). That extra work aside, binding such a book also is not straightforward. If you have ever bought a Moleskin notebook, say, and pasted in pictures or added extra material to it, you will have noticed that the added material will make it bulge. The notebook's spine was constructed to accommodate exactly the number of pages it contains, but not more. To bind *The Winners*,

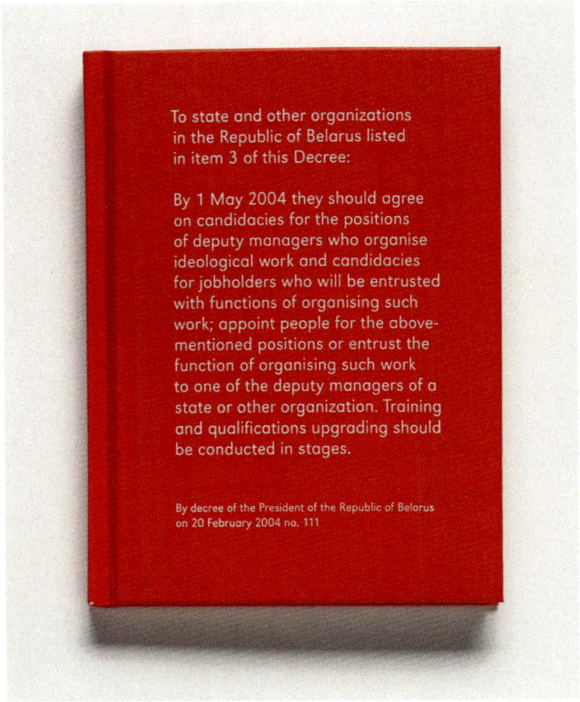

Figure 6.12 Cover of Rafal Milach—*The Winners* (Gost, 2014)

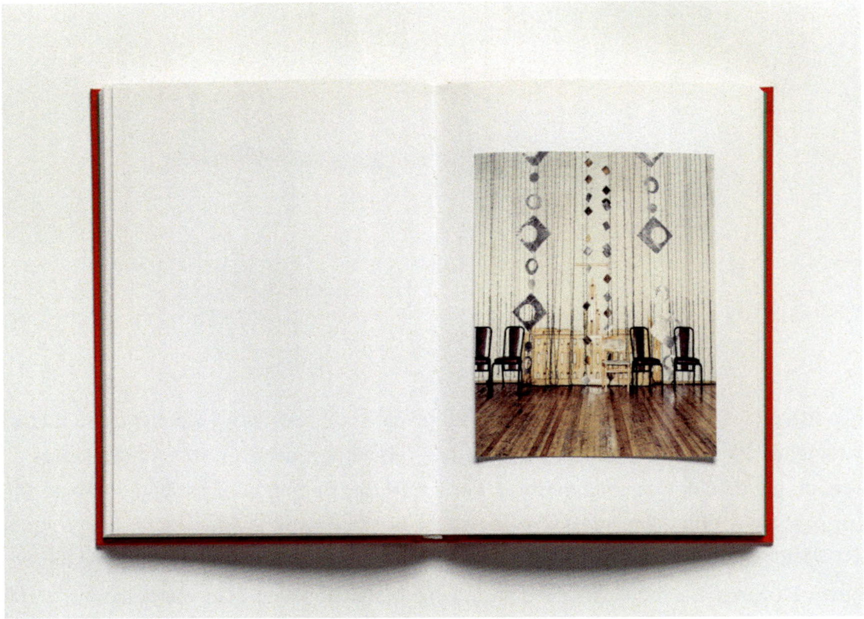

Figure 6.13 Spread from Rafal Milach—*The Winners* (Gost, 2014)

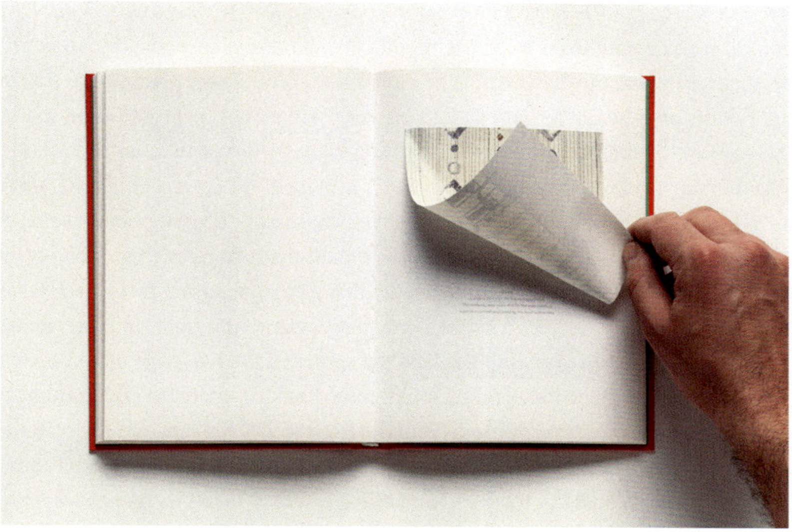

Figure 6.14 Same spread as in Figure 6.13, but with the tipped-in photograph lifted up

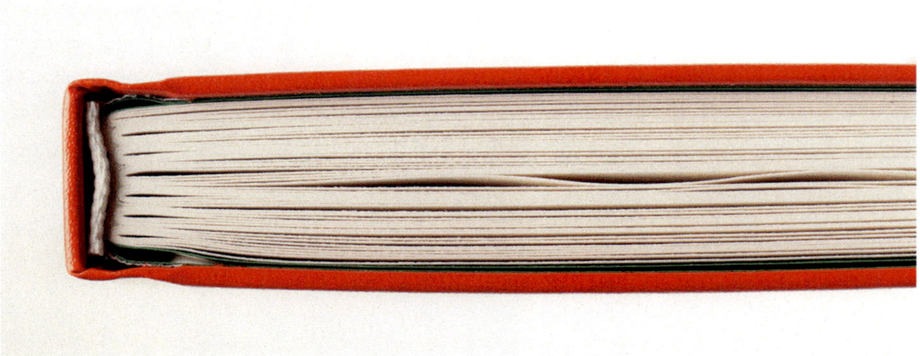

Figure 6.15 View of Rafal Milach—*The Winners* (Gost, 2014), from the head of the book

the additional space needed by the added/tipped-in photographs needed to be taken into consideration. As Figure 6.15 shows, when you look at the book from its head (or tail), you see that the spine's width perfectly covers the width of the bound *plus* tipped-in pages. While this might seem like a very obvious thing to do, in reality when thinking about the production of the book, it's another important detail to take care of, and it requires careful planning (and, probably, experimentation) to make sure the spine's width is just right.

A general rule might simply be that the moment you add bells and whistles to any very basic type of book—thus moving beyond, say, a simple perfect bound or Smyth-sewn book, there are important details to be taken care of. As I will discuss in the next section, a materials dummy is a great tool to find out about such details. These details might affect both the functionality of the book as well as production costs.

As seen in the case of Sjoerd Knibbeler's *Paper Planes* (see Figures 6.7–6.11), photobooks can, in fact, deviate from what one might consider a regular book, one in which there are pages that are turned and that are attached to a spine. While most photobooks stay close to the regular form of a book, deviations can be very interesting, provided they make sense given the concept of the photography in question. *Paper Planes* uses an accordion that is not attached to the cover. Another case in point is provided by Mariela Sancari's *Moisés* (La Fabrica, 2015; Figure 6.16). The photobook consists of two separately bound text blocks, which are glued into the same container and which are made to interleave. The object itself has two front-covers. The viewer gets to open the first (top) one, turning it to the left (just like any other regular book), to reveal a second one that opens to the right. In both cases, Swiss binding has been used: the covers fall flat, and the spines of the two page blocks are exposed (at the right and the left). The viewer then looks at the book by alternatively turning a page to the left and another one to the right. In a similar, reversed fashion, she or he closes the book again, folding a page back from the left or right. What might sound slightly complicated when described with words is actually intuitively clear for a viewer faced with the book.

The combined effect of turning pages to the left and right brings the physical aspect of the engagement with the book more to the forefront. Turning a page becomes more than just that. Instead, it is a very literal unfolding, a revelation of information—mostly photographs—previously hidden. Many of the spreads show multiple photographs of either the same older man (Figure 6.17) or of two different older men (Figure 6.18). Note that the spread shown in Figure 6.18 immediately follows the one from Figure 6.17. In Figure 6.17, the spread is made up of four photographs of the same man. Now, remember that the book consists of two interleaving sections. The gutter of the right section runs though the face of the man shown second

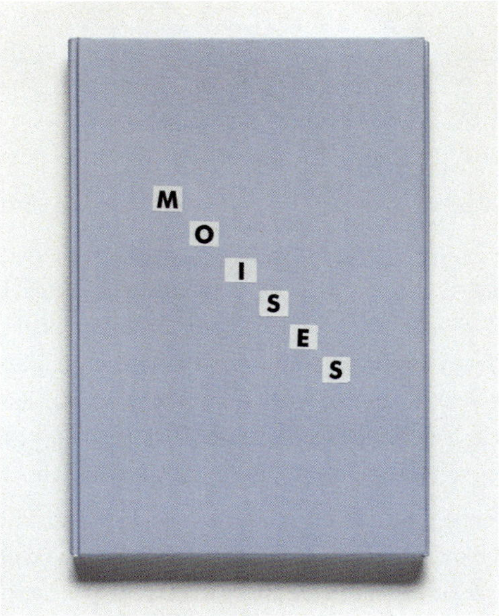

Figure 6.16 Cover of Mariela Sancari—*Moisés* (*La Fabrica*, 2015)

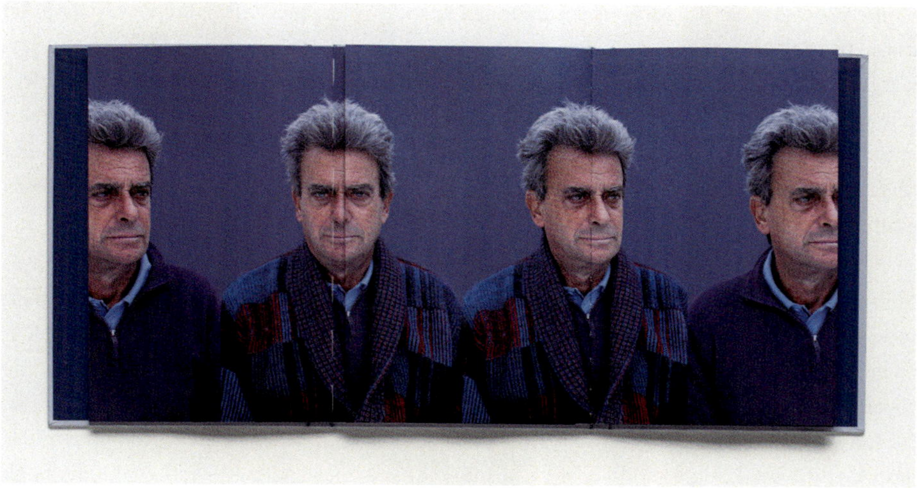

Figure 6.17 Spread from Mariela Sancari—*Moisés* (La Fabrica, 2015)

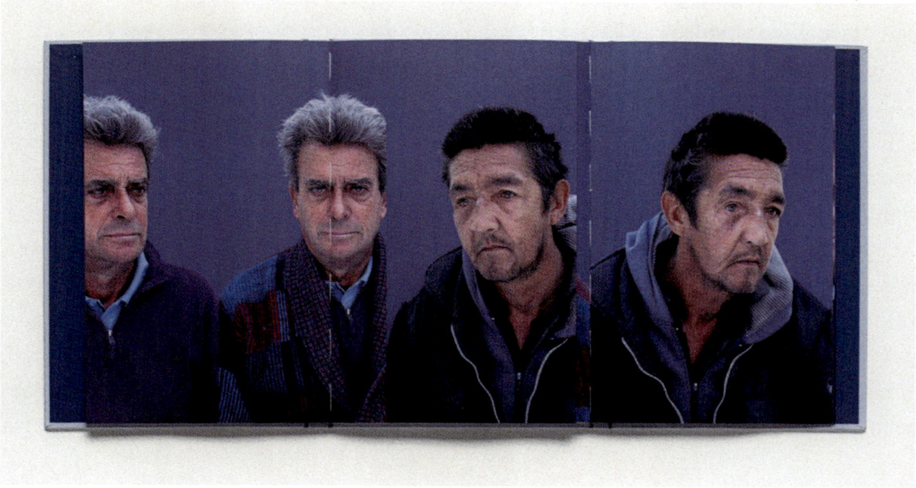

Figure 6.18 Spread immediately following the one shown in Figure 6.17

from right. The gutter of the left section runs through the face of the same man, shown second from the left (this one is a bit easier to make out in the figure, given the white threads used for the binding are visible). The next page that can be turned can be seen to the immediate right of the left section's gutter. Both the edge of the page and that gutter run along the bridge of the man's nose. Note that the book has been constructed very well, so the images line up. Turn the page, and you arrive at the spread shown in Figure 6.18 (in which both gutters are clearly visible, both revealing themselves via the white binder's threads).

One might wonder why such a seemingly complex construction was used to produce *Moisés*, requiring considerable more effort from the viewer. As it turns out, the book centers on the photographer's father, who committed suicide years back. If he were still alive, he would be of the age of the various men depicted in the book. Sancari almost obsessively photographed men her father's age, trying to imagine what he would look like. The book's viewer is made to share the imagined experience of looking at the father through the construction of the book, as more and more faces and aspects of faces are revealed. She or he is made to share the work required to try to solve an unsolvable mystery. The effect of looking at *Moisés* ultimately can only be experienced.

In terms of the production, *Moisés* is somewhat straightforward to produce, but it requires careful precision both concerning how images on the two sections line up (a viewer should see only images and not the fact that there are two separate sections) and how the book is bound. The thickness of the book is determined by the sum of the two sections, plus the cover. For the object to become rectangular, the spine needs to be larger than the spines of the individual sections (see Figure 6.19). If that were not the case the book would not close properly, it would bulge in the center. Needless to say, these added factors make the book less straightforward to produce than any regular book. And, as I noted, more work is required from the viewer. But in both cases, the unusual construction of the book pays off, given that the viewer's engagement with the book not only enriches the overall experience, it becomes part of the discovery that can be had through the pictures.

When I spoke of "regular" books discussing *Moisés*, I had either perfect bound or Smyth-sewn books in mind. As we have already seen, there is a variety of other types of binding, many of which are not used that much in the world of photobooks, thus making them seem unusual. Japanese stab binding is another such a type. This type of binding is not that dissimilar from perfect binding, the difference being that no glue is used, only binder's thread. Another difference is that Japanese stab binding takes up a considerable fraction of each page, which cannot be used for the display of text or pictures. An example of such a binding is provided by Daisuke Yokota—*Linger* (Akina, 2014; Figure 6.20). Figure 6.21 shows what I have just spoken of in terms of part of the page being used up because of the binding: when opened, a section of each page near the spine is fixed together in a block. How and why this is happening might be clear from both Figures 6.20 and 6.22: the binder's thread is woven through

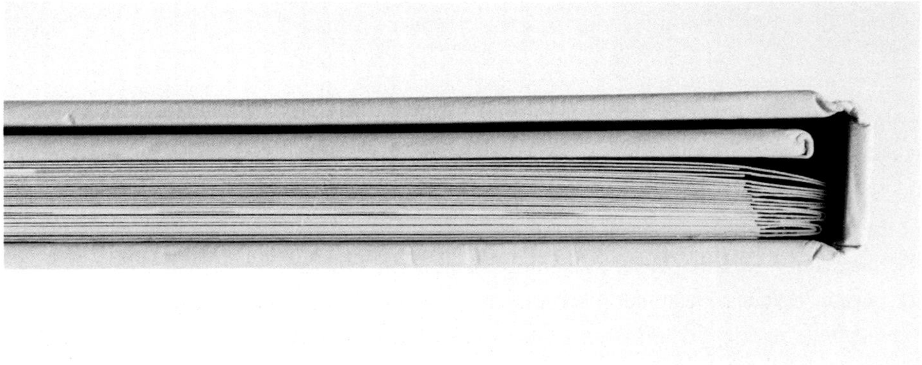

Figure 6.19 View of Mariela Sancari—*Moisés* (La Fabrica, 2015), seen from the head

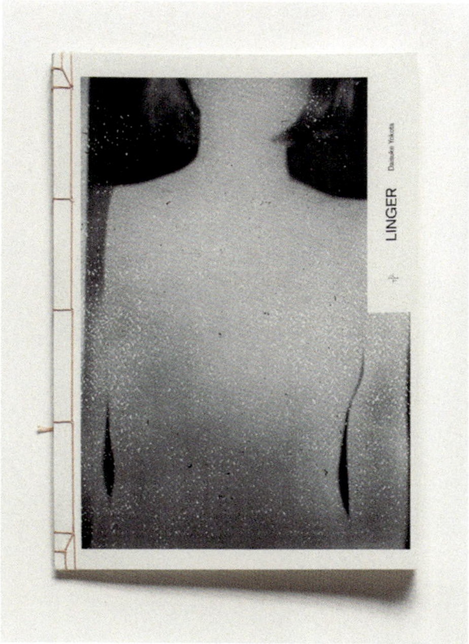

Figure 6.20 Cover of Daisuke Yokota—*Linger* (Akina, 2014)

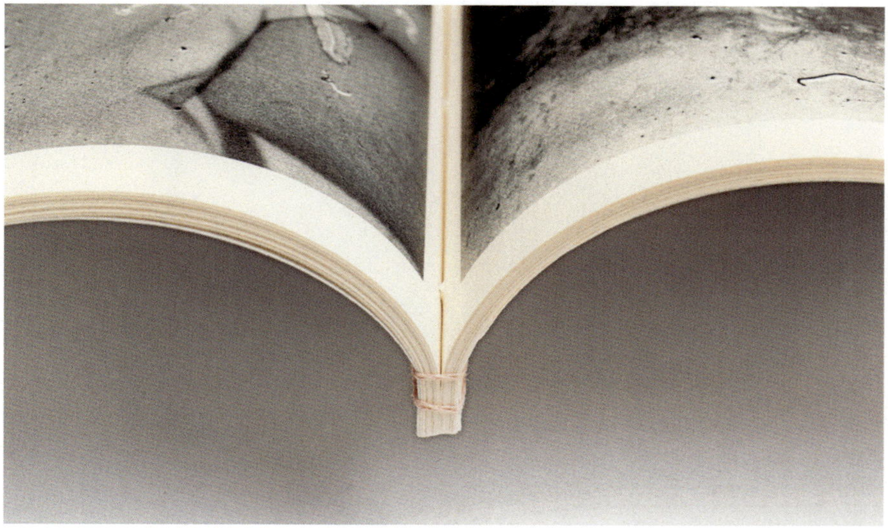

Figure 6.21 Close-up of Daisuke Yokota—*Linger* (Akina, 2014) when opened, looking from the book's tail

holes cut into the pages and around the pages at the spine as a whole. In perfect binding, you get the same effect, but it is less pronounced, with a block formed by the combination of glue and paper. As a result of this type of binding, unless very thin paper is being used, books bound this way do not open very easily. A viewer will have to hold the book with both hands.

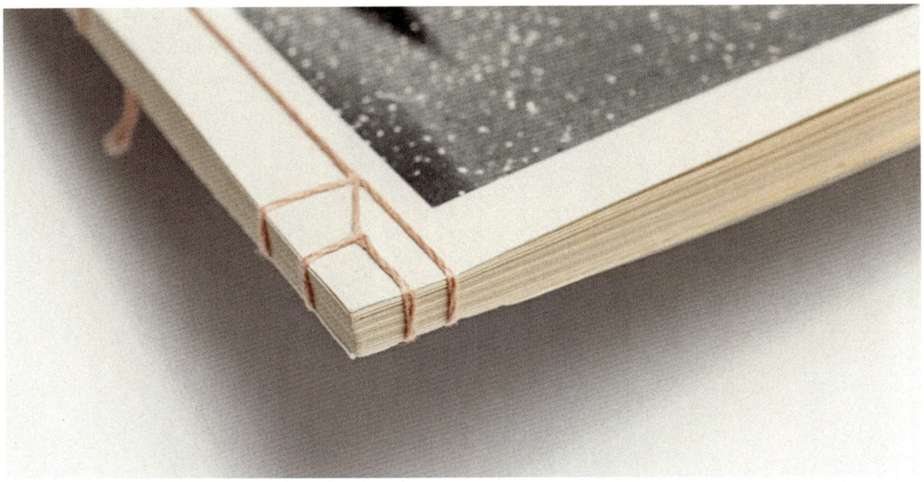

Figure 6.22 View of Daisuke Yokota—*Linger* (Akina, 2014), closed and seen from the tail

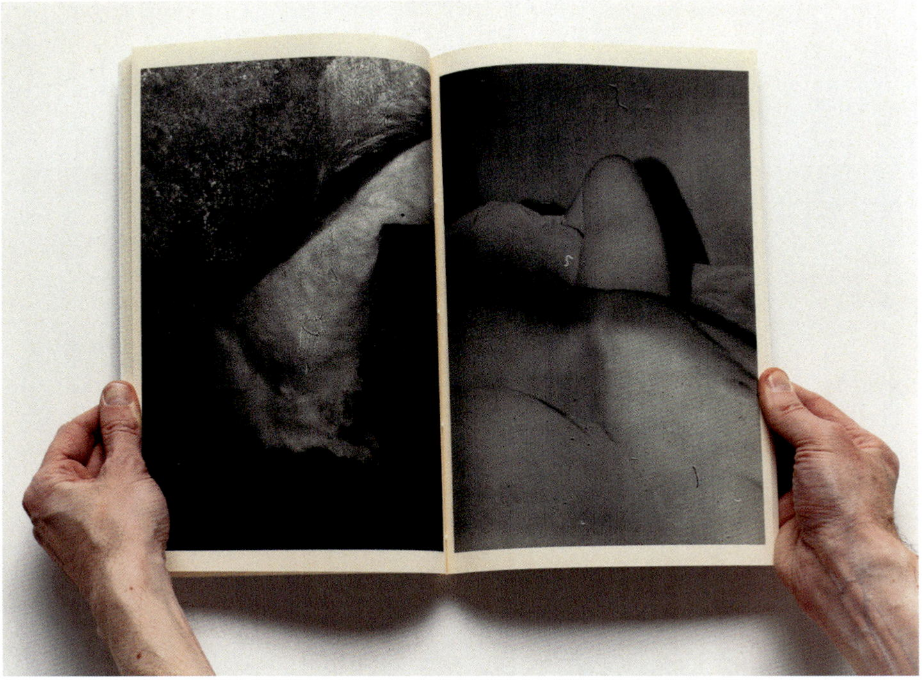

Figure 6.23 Spread from Daisuke Yokota—*Linger* (Akina, 2014)

Looking at such a book on a table is no easy option (see Figure 6.23). Consequently, using photographs that cross the gutter should be avoided.

While the aforementioned facts about Japanese stab binding might make it sound as if this were a type of binding to be avoided, this need not necessarily be the case. For a start, the binding itself is quite prominent—the binder's thread usually remains mostly hidden. Yokota's photographs are intensely process based, so using a binding that reflects that quality is an obvious choice. In addition, as the name indicates, this type of binding has a long history in Eastern Asia (not just in Japan, but also in China), so it makes perfect sense for a book by a Japanese artist.

If one had to come up with the complete opposite of the Japanese stab binding, it would probably be spiral binding, a cheap, industrial process that is equally rare in the world of photobooks. I mentioned the usefulness of spiral-bound notebooks in Chapter 4, while discussing early dummies. But there are not many spiral-bound photobooks being made, for reasons that are not necessarily that obvious, other than, maybe, this type of binding being associated with "cheap" materials. With a little work it needn't be so, of course, as is demonstrated by the book *Island On My Mind* by Irina Rozovsky (Kettler, 2015; Figure 6.24). Anyone who has ever used a spiral-bound notebook will remember that it is fairly easy to tear or damage a page. Consequently, *Island On My Mind* counteracts this problem by using both a thicker paper stock and a double spiral (see Figure 6.25). The double spiral gives the pages less freedom to move. The spirals are thicker than the thin notebook ones and the pages are also more sturdy, which makes pages tearing a lot less likely. In addition to the unusual binding, *Island* also uses a cover page whose size is much different than that of the pages (see Fig. 6.26): it's really just a little flap, with the title of the book given in Spanish. Note that the thickness of the pages not only protects them where they are in contact with the spiral, it also prevents their corners from dog-earing easily.

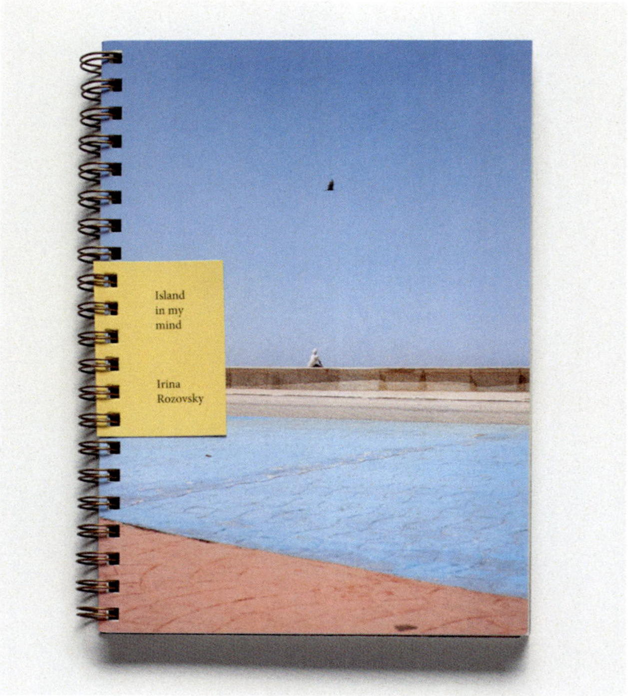

Figure 6.24 Cover of Irina Rozovsky—*Island On My Mind* (Kettler, 2015)

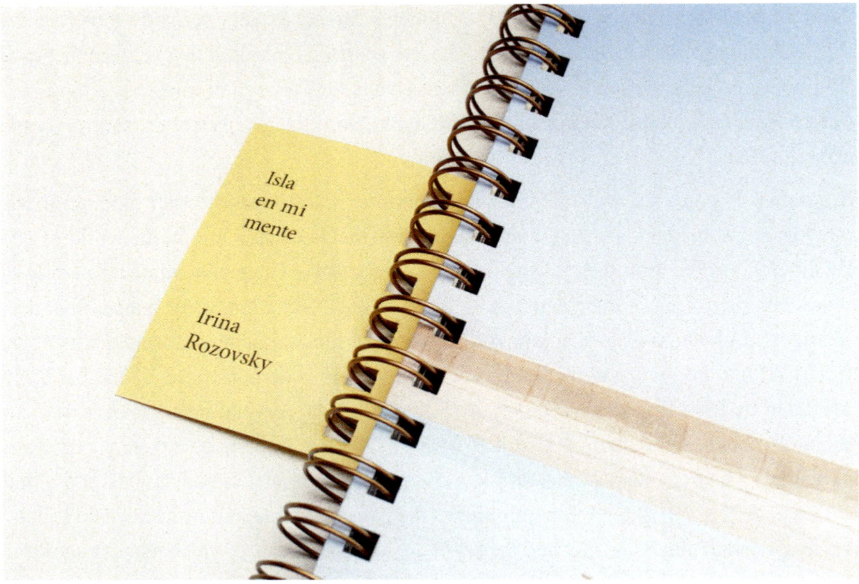

Figure 6.25 Inside cover of Irina Rozovsky—*Island On My Mind* (Kettler, 2015), with the title given in Spanish

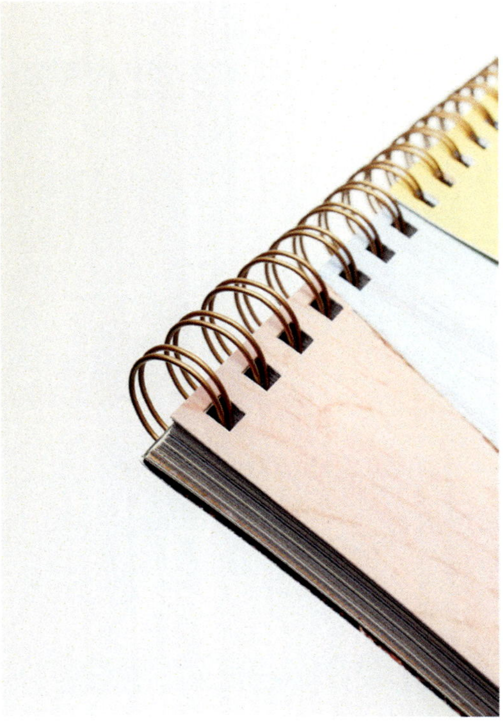

Figure 6.26 Spiral binding of Irina Rozovsky—*Island On My Mind* (Kettler, 2015)

In addition to and one might say in spite of the chosen binding, the photographs in *Island On My Mind* all are used full bleed. As a consequence, the holes punched into the pages to accommodate the binding cut through the photographs. This is already apparent from the cover view (Figure 6.24), which actually shows the small cover flap plus the first picture in the book. It also shows clearly in the spreads (see Figures 6.27 and 6.28). The book's makers pushed the approach to its logical conclusion by even using photographs across the gutter (see Figure 6.28), a decision that, I'm sure, will have made many photographers cringe, especially the more conservative ones. But the format really works for me. The binding adds a bit of grittiness to the photographs, which themselves aren't so concerned with their own preciousness. And as an object, *Island On My Mind* clearly stands out from the crowd, giving it a bit of a cutting-edge feel that, one needs to realize, many photographers will not enjoy seeing. But then as I noted before, no photobook is ever going to make everybody happy. The invasiveness of how the binding is used in this particular case is likely to be offputting for some. It would have been possible to make a book with this type of binding that would not have cut into the photographs. But such a book in all likelihood would lose much of the grit of this particular solution, with the type of binding pushed to its extreme.

These aforementioned books with their different types of somewhat unusual binding are intended to show what can be done with binding. As I noted, like every decision made for a book, the binding must not become an added on gimmick, intended to make the book "sexier."

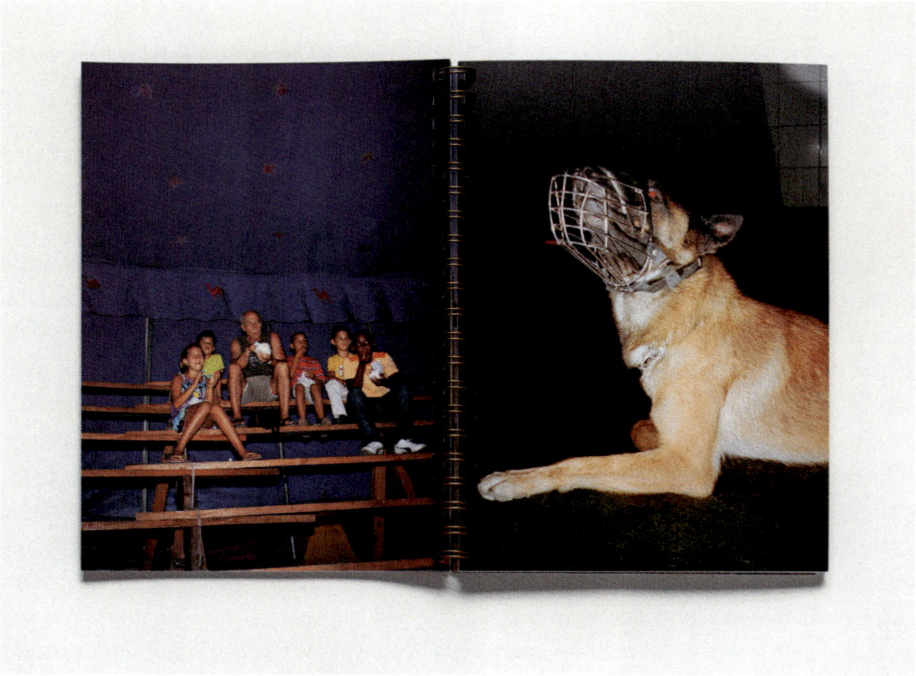

Figure 6.27 Spread from Irina Rozovsky—*Island On My Mind* (Kettler, 2015)

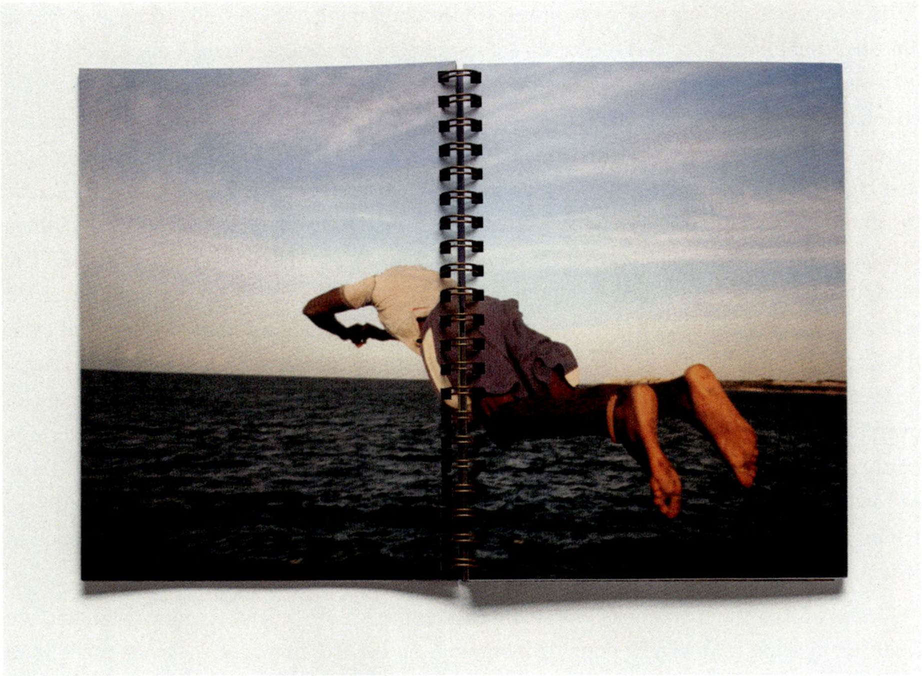

Figure 6.28 Spread from Irina Rozovsky—*Island On My Mind* (Kettler, 2015)

That appeal would only last for a short time. Instead, there has got to be a good reason for the binding, a reason that supports the book's overall concept.

6.4 The Materials Dummy

In earlier chapters, I discussed the importance of working with dummies as demo-style prototypes of the final book. Those dummies all involved including photographs plus an edit/sequence, some layout, some design, etc. But there is another type of dummy that can vastly help a photobook maker, the materials dummy. Let's assume you know the size of your desired book, the number of pages, the binding, the cover type, and all the other materials aspects of the book. You know (or you think you know) that your book is going to have these properties. What is going to prevent you from having a blank book made that uses exactly the kinds and types of material, plus their parameters such as sizes and page numbers? Nothing really. Now, you might wonder why you would want to get a book made that doesn't show any photographs, which might cost you a bit of money? The reason is quite simple. Your materials dummy will provide you with exactly the look and feel of the object itself. You will be able to hold it and see whether the size is right. You will see whether it will feel too heavy or too light. You will be able to experience the binding, the way the pages turn. You will be able to experience what it feels like to touch the paper. And there will be no pictures to distract you. In fact, you could even get a materials dummy made with a couple of actual photographs printed. That way, you would even see the quality of the printing.

In other words, the materials dummy would allow you to check a large part of the production process, before you will actually hand off everything to get the final object made. If your materials dummy shows you that you actually did pick the wrong paper, say (it's too thin or too thick, it's too glossy or too matte, it is too stiff or too flimsy, or whatever other problem you might encounter), then you have a chance to fix the problem before your final book arrives. Chances are, if you get 500 copies of your book made, and you realize that the paper really is completely wrong, you (and/or your publisher) might not have the money (and/or willingness) to trash those 500 books and redo the whole production. Getting a materials dummy produced (or possibly more than one, with improvements being made successively) can save you a lot of headaches, because it delivers the things I started this book out with in the very first chapter, the look and feel of the book. You will want these to be just right. And whatever money you might invest to get a blank book should be viewed as an insurance against future failure (and unhappiness), not as a waste of money.

6.5 Preparing a Book for Press

In light of our earlier discussion of binding, it might be clear why thinking about binding cannot just be an afterthought during the process of making a book—in much the same fashion as incorporating design early is important as I laid out in the previous chapter. In part this is because of the restrictions bindings place on the physical properties of a book: do these restrictions serve the work in question? But there is another aspect to binding, namely economics. In an ideal world, all photobooks would be hand bound by a master bookbinder. In reality, such an approach is only feasible in a very small number of cases, given the high costs involved. Binding a book always costs money, so these costs must be part of the overall budget available for the book, regardless of whether a publishing house produces it or whether it is self-published. "Publishers are leery of getting involved with complex bindings that involve too much hand work," says Sue Medlicott, a book producer with decades of experience helping books get made. "To execute a complex binding is expensive, and you don't necessarily want to pour money into that at the expense of the image reproductions. It's a balancing act between concept, execution and costs." Established publishing houses tend be well aware of this balancing act. Self-publishers or those interested in starting a new publishing venture can—and should—learn from that: take your available book budget, and really see how much money you want to (or can) make available for the various items that might come up. Note that "cheap" types of binding are absolutely not necessarily bad. Spiral binding is a simple and cheap industrial process, but it can make for great books, and the same is true for perfect bound books. It is for these reasons that Medlicott says that "when we receive mock ups of photobooks, we always look at the binding first, then work backwards." In the sense of what a photobook ultimately is, an object, this approach makes perfect sense. For photographers, this might be very counterintuitive, given they start out with the photographs.

As I have pointed out at various stages before, none of the various elements that are added to the pictures should overwhelm them. Everything should serve the final product, the book. But the book is the sum of its parts, and these parts have to be carefully considered.

On-demand bookmaking, as great as it can be, often powerfully demonstrates how adding photographs into a rather limited set of containers results in bad books. Editing and sequencing issues aside, the resulting objects often not only lack character, they also can be off. I personally think that on-demand perfect bound softcovers tend to be fine, given that they can be made easily, and they accommodate any number of pages. But hardcovers often don't quite fit, in part because their outer shells, the hardcovers, are not custom made for each book (which would be too expensive). So I have seen quite a few books where the spine of the book was considerably larger than the block of pages. Add to that limited options for the available paper, and it's no surprise that so many on-demand photobooks look and especially feel the same. This is not to say that there is no room for on-demand publishing. But at the time of this writing (early November 2015), the quality of on-demand publishing is unable to reach the kind of quality most photographers might want to aspire to.

One of the most common problems with photobooks, however they are being produced, involves the quality of the printing. There are different aspects to consider here. To begin with, the printing might be flat and thin, essentially sucking the life out of the photographs. While this is a common outcome of on-demand printing, certain photobook publishers produce similar output. Color casts, in contrast, mostly show up in on-demand books.[4] Color casts, such as every photograph looking a little bit too green or magenta, affect both color or black-and-white images, and one can debate which case is more irritating. Even when using the "profiles" offered by on-demand printing services, such casts often are hard to avoid. It would be straightforward to argue that with on-demand printing, you get what you pay for, and there really isn't much need to discuss them any further at this point.

That said, getting a book that has the right colors is always going to prove to be a considerable challenge. Apart from not considering aspects of binding, another aspect of production that photographers often run into too late is the quality of their image files. Printing presses operate in CMYK, and photographers tend to be aware of that, given they have to buy those usually expensive ink cartridges for their printers. Many photographers know that proper color calibration in their studios is very important, so that what looks fine on the computer screen doesn't look very different when it comes out of the printer attached to said computer. But this still does not guarantee that those files will then translate into good results once everything is taken to a professional printing house. "With a good set of separations and some knowledge about your printer and their press profiles," says Medlicott, "you should be able to go anywhere in the world to print a book." But this often tends not to be the case. Medlicott: "If the photographer's studio is not used to supplying large files and match prints that accurately represent their work, they should talk to a professional separator or prepress company that can help supply a printer with suitable material." Various former students of mine have gone on to get their books printed professionally, either as their own publishing house or with a publisher, and, in many cases, even the most advanced digital wizards ended up having to talk to a professional separator, someone who knows from long experience how to properly translate RGB mage into CMYK ones that work with the chosen printer. “If you’re going to spend any extra money on any stage, get the prepress right .... and invest in an ink-on-paper proof as well,” says Medlicott. “This should happen at an early stage, when you can review technique and how the images look on the paper that’s been tentatively selected to print on. The hard work happens well before you step up to the press to produce the book.” Can’t things be fixed if the photographer works on press, while the pages are printed? As it turns out, while that approach might have worked OK in the past, today it’s a bad idea. “With the technology as advanced as it is today,” says Medlicott, “there’s very little one can do on press to correct images. If I have one piece of advice, it’s to get a professional to work on the separations and get to a point where Epson prints, or wet proofs, are matching their expectations.” Proper preparation for the final step of the process is thus key, much like it should be at any stage of either making a book or preparing for a gallery show.

If at any stage there are problems to be solved that are beyond the photographer’s expertise, make sure experts are being brought to the project, whether as designers, production people, or separators. Photographers who think they know how to cover the problems still might want to consult with experts—unless they have successfully produced a book, avoiding the various pitfalls I discussed earlier. On-demand printing and the presence of inkjet printers in photographers’ studios might make it look as if printing a book is simple and straightforward, but it might not be at all—unless you know exactly what you’re doing. Today’s world of book printing roughly divides into older (and very high-end) technologies such as offset printing and newer, digital technologies (using, say, HP *Indigo* or Kodak’s *Nexpress* digital presses). For digital technologies, photographers might be able to work out problems in their own studios, using printer-supplied profiles. This process might simply include the same steps as when working with an in-office printer: working through color calibrations in a set of iterations. Many companies offering digital printing will supply a printed proof either as part of the deal or at a relatively small extra cost. In the case of offset printing, however, at least consulting with a professional separator in all likelihood is the best option.

Either way, files need to be prepared properly, a topic that is beyond the scope of this book. There is no shortage of books covering digital file preparations. A very good example is provided by Jeff Schewe’s *The Digital Print: Preparing Images in Lightroom and Photoshop for Printing* (Peachpit Press, 2013). In addition, there are also numerous video tutorials available online, on sites such as *YouTube*.[5]

Photographers (or publishers) who are in need of a lot of input might consider hiring a production person such as Sue Medlicott. What you will get for your money is the following: “As a production person I get involved at various stages. Sometimes the artist calls directly, other times it’s a designer or an institution. There are generally three components to any project: budget, schedule and quality. It’s a balancing act, but we try and figure out where we can get *the best quality for the value* and have it *fit within the expected delivery dates. There are compromises all along the way*. But this is a healthy discussion to have and can only improve the book. For instance, does the project really need 20 fold outs when six perfectly, and logically placed fold outs would suffice?" Note the three sections I highlighted: "the best quality for the value," "fit within the expected delivery dates," and "there are compromises all along the way." While self-published books often might be flexible concerning their delivery dates (unless a book has to be done for a major book fair, say), the other two are extremely important. They hint at the fact that the compromises involved in photobook making result as much from the restrictions placed by the medium itself as from the fact that budgets typically tend to be limited. In fact, to make something work within specific constraints often helps creating a much better end result.[6]

6.6 Photobook Budget

Given the many factors in the process of making a photobook that involve money, looking into the details of a budget should be on top of the "to do" list. A commonly used approach to the budget deals with it as an afterthought. A photographer decides about the book she or he wants to make, maybe even with an idea of how much it might cost to make it, and unforeseen costs then inflate the total, creating unnecessary headaches. Alternatively, one could start out with the budget, slice it into the various bits (more of that later) and then work out the book. Of course, a photobook should get developed based on what the photography in question needs. Starting out by thinking about money is likely to offend the artistic sensibilities of many people. But as we have seen in the chapters leading up to and including this one, without compromises photobooks can't be made. And money plays a big role in this, regardless of whether one is working with a publishing house (where the total amount of money to be spent simply is fixed) or self-publishing. Unless you are independently wealthy or are thinking of a very cheap production (aka a zine), you will have to either make or at least consider making some compromises concerning your book. The fact that some of these compromises are dictated by money might just be a good thing: art without restrictions or obstructions is often incredibly problematic. And the budget constraining your photobook really is not that different than the aspect ratio of your chosen camera: you just have to work with it.

In the following, I want to outline the various items that might factor in the overall budget of a photographer's book. Their relative allocations might vary from book to book. For example, a friend might be a designer, and you don't have to pay her or him because you return the favor in other ways. Or you want to hire that world-famous designer, and you're happy to spend a significant amount of money on design. The point in the following really only is to provide a list of all the items that need to be thought about, to make sure there is money in the final budget for the ones that apply. This can mean that the overall budget arises out of summing up all costs (and then having to somehow raise it), starting from the total available budget and making sure all relevant items can be covered, or any kind of variation of that. So these are the points to consider:

Editing: It is not unusual for photographers to hire an experienced editor for their work, if, for example, none is provided by a publishing house. Such professionals provide their services for a fee.

Text: Text can play many roles in a photobook. Often, an additional essay (or possibly more than one) might help enhance the book in various ways. For example, the name of a well-known author can provide additional cachet for the book, possibly even expanding its original target audience beyond the world of photography. Writers might work for free, but usually a photographer will have to pay for the production of an essay.

Design: If a publishing house does not work with in-house or associated designers, as already discussed a photographer is well advised to hire a designer for the book. Much like in the case of a professional editor or writer, a designer will have to be paid.

Production—Management/Packaging: Specialists such as Sue Medlicott offer invaluable expertise for the production of a photobook. They will expect payment for their services.

Production—File Preparations: If the photographer is unable to produce suitable files for the printing of the book, a professional separator will take care of this problem. She or he will have to get paid.

Production—Printing: In an obvious way, the printing of the pages costs money. This money includes the cost of the paper, plus the costs of producing the plates (in the case of offset printing) or whatever other costs are associated with the printing. In all likelihood, the press expects to get paid for the number of hours it works on the job.[7]

Production—Binding: Once the pages have been printed, they will have to be bound by a professional binder or binding house. This adds costs in the form of materials and time spent on the job. Any aspects of binding that go beyond what can be done by machines will inflate the costs considerably.[8]

PR: Having, say, 500 copies of a book is one thing. Getting these 500 copies sold often is quite another. Publishing houses often have mechanisms in place to promote their books, or they work with distributors that will do that job. Self-publishers are completely on their own. In either case, given that there are hundreds and hundreds of photobooks made, getting possible buyers to notice a book will require considerable efforts. One solution is to hire a PR specialist who will take over promotion. That person will have to get paid. In addition, a number of books will have to be made available to be handed out as press or PR copies to publications or individuals who either express interest in the book, or who the photographer thinks should see the book. Given that press copies are not sold, their costs have to be factored into the budget (or into the price of the books that are being sold).[9] Other ways to promote books include participating in a photobook fair, such as Offprint in Paris, the New York Art Book Fair, the photobook market at Unseen Amsterdam, or any of the other numerous fairs and festivals. While being present at a festival is a great way to make a book visible, there can be considerable costs associated with it, which include travel, accommodation, and whatever fee a festival might charge for a table or booth.

Note that as a self-publisher, a photographer has to not only take care of all aspects of the book's making, she or he will also have to cover all costs that are being incurred. A publishing house might be willing to cover all costs, but it is more likely that the photographer will be asked to contribute some amount of money. I discussed that aspect in Chapter 2. Given the contents of this chapter provide an overview of the many different costs that can be associated with the production of a photobook, it should not come as a surprise that many publishing houses simply cannot afford covering all costs.

Notes

1. Things can go very wrong even after a photobook has been produced successfully. It is not uncommon for shipments of books to be held up in customs for very long periods of time (months). So let's say you ship your books from Germany to the US for the New York Art Book Fair, only to find they never arrived. Instead, they're stuck somewhere in customs limbo. Or your books arrive, but the package got severely damaged, leaving you with copies of the book you cannot sell.
2. Conceptually, perfect binding and side-stitching/stab binding are really the same type of binding: you place a stack of pages on top of each other, and you glue them together in the former case, or you sew or staple them together in the latter case. The gutter problem becomes more apparent in the case of side-stitching/stab binding, but it's really just the same for perfect binding.
3. If you insist on it, you can call a folio the simplest signature.
4. I'm giving on-demand printing services a pretty bad rap here. But I have been trying them over the past few years, and I actually do use the most commonly known one all the time. I use on-demand Indigo printing when the quality of the resulting printing does not matter much, for example either when working with appropriated photographs taken from the internet (with cell phones being the source cameras, colors often are all over the place) or when making books with faux Polaroids created on my iPhone with the app *Polamatic* (again, the colors of the images are so wonky to begin with that a slight color cast essentially is almost impossible to notice). I have also used Indigo printing for faux tintypes (also made with an iPhone), and I found that printing them in color produced a somewhat better image than when using black and white. In the tintype case, the choices were images that had a slight color cast versus images that were very thin on the pages, with the line screen clearly visible. I ended up hand varnishing the faux tintype book by applying a thin layer of varnish on each image, which not only added depth to the shadows, it also made each picture look slightly different, as if there were different emulsions in them.
5. The same is true for book binding as well. I once taught a class on photobook making, at the end of which a student showed up with a homemade book. When I asked her where she had learned how to bind a book—which included sewing signatures and adding a hard case—she told me she had "simply" watched a tutorial on *YouTube*.

6. This point is forcefully carried home by Lars van Trier's *The Five Obstructions*, a film that should be required viewing for photographers.
7. This is another reason why file preparation is crucial: while problems possibly can be fixed on press, this will take time, and it will thus add to the costs incurred by the printing.
8. This is the main reason why publishing houses often will not be willing to add bells and whistles such as, for example, gatefolds to a book. Gatefolds usually require work done by hand, which creates considerable additional binding costs.
9. Shipping press copies adds further costs, especially if books are being sent abroad.

E. In Focus

Sjoerd Knibbeler—*Paper Planes*

As discussed especially in Chapter 3, every aspect of a photobook needs to be in support of its underlying concept, with the concept tied to the photographs. To find the right translation of a photography project into book form often is a tricky task. But sometimes, the seemingly most ingenious solutions can also be the most obvious ones. For his project *Paper Planes,* Dutch artist Sjoerd Knibbeler built and then photographed folded paper models of military planes from all over the world that had never made it into the full production stage. Given the resulting photographs essentially constitute a typology, it would have been simple to produce a book along the lines of, say, Bernd and Hilla Becher's *Typologies of Industrial Buildings* (MIT Press, 2004). That, however, is far from what *Paper Planes,* the book (Fw:Photography, 2015), ended up looking like.

Paper planes and photobooks have the most basic underlying material in common, paper. What is more, paper is being folded in both cases, with paper planes obviously employing much larger and more elaborate amounts of folding. The type of book that probably contains the largest amount of folds is the accordion (sometimes also referred to as a leporello or concertina book). In principle, an accordion book is a single sheet of paper, folded multiple times.[1] The multiple folds in an accordion allude to the folds in a paper plane. *Paper Planes* employs an accordion book for its content. The photographs are printed on what probably will be considered the front of the accordion.[2] For each plane the back contains information about its history. Front and back are separated not only by content, but also in form, with the back showing a rough, untreated cardboard surface.

While the information about the individual planes on the back is kept on individual sections of the accordion, the photographs wrap across folds.[3] This wrapping forces the viewer to fully engage with the accordion, given that for the photographs, the individual sections do not act as simple pages. In addition, a separate signature consisting of two folios with facsimiles of paper previously folded was stapled to the accordion, which not only further drives home the point of the multiple uses of folded paper (both in the planes and the book), but which also demonstrates a simple way to complicate the simple structure of the accordion.

Both conceptually and in form, *Paper Planes* thus uses the very properties of its book format to allude to the aspect of folded paper that underlies the model planes built (and photographed) by Knibbeler. At the same time, the bells and whistles are kept at a strict and consistent minimum. The viewer is thus never led to believe anything was merely used for the sake of adding gimmicks to a book about paper planes.

Notes

1. In reality, accordion books tend to be assembled from multiple parts that are attached to one another. This usually happens for a variety of reasons, mostly production issues. Using a single very long page often simply is unfeasible. In addition, gluing sections of the accordion together often results in the pages being thicker (stronger) and thus there is more of it. The stability of the accordion is a crucial problem for these types of book: given they lack the support of a spine, they can be easily skewed, resulting in tears (which, for this type of book, essentially threaten the whole structure).
2. Unlike any other type of book, by construction an accordion book has a front and a back.
3. The aspect ratios of the photographs and the individual sections of the accordion are different, 1:1.25 versus 1:1.4 (A4).

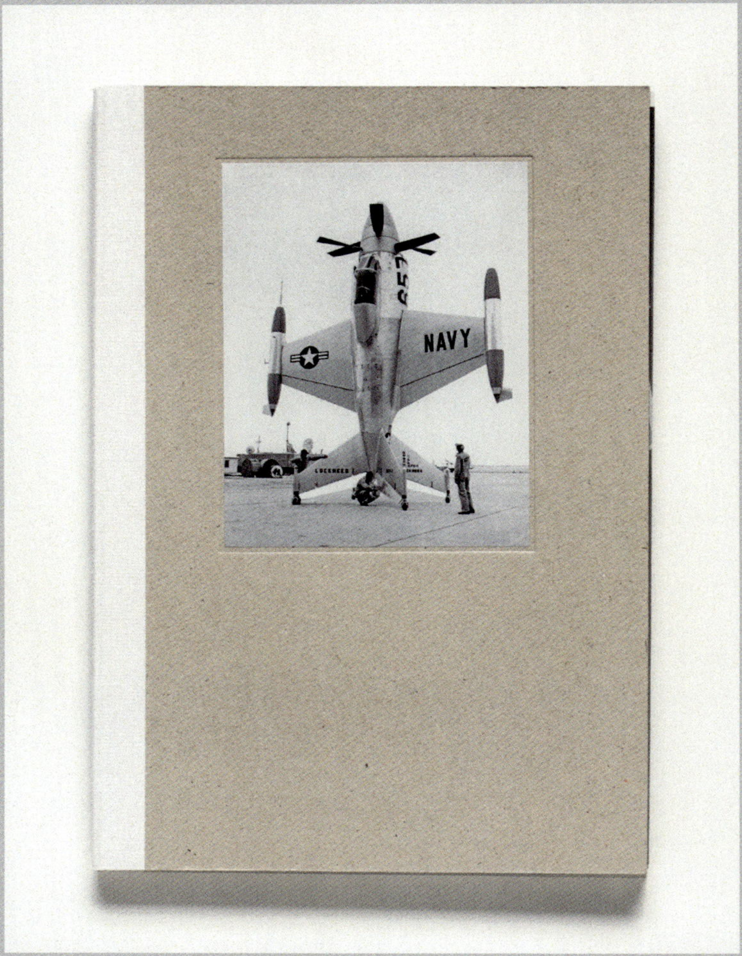

Figure E.1 This page: Cover of Sjoerd Knibbeler—*Paper Planes* (Fw:Photography, 2015). Following page: the inside of *Paper Planes*. As is clearly visible, the page block is not attached to the hard case.

The page block's first page and parts of the inside of the cover double as space for the book's title and the colophon (which can be seen on the very right hand side of the cover)

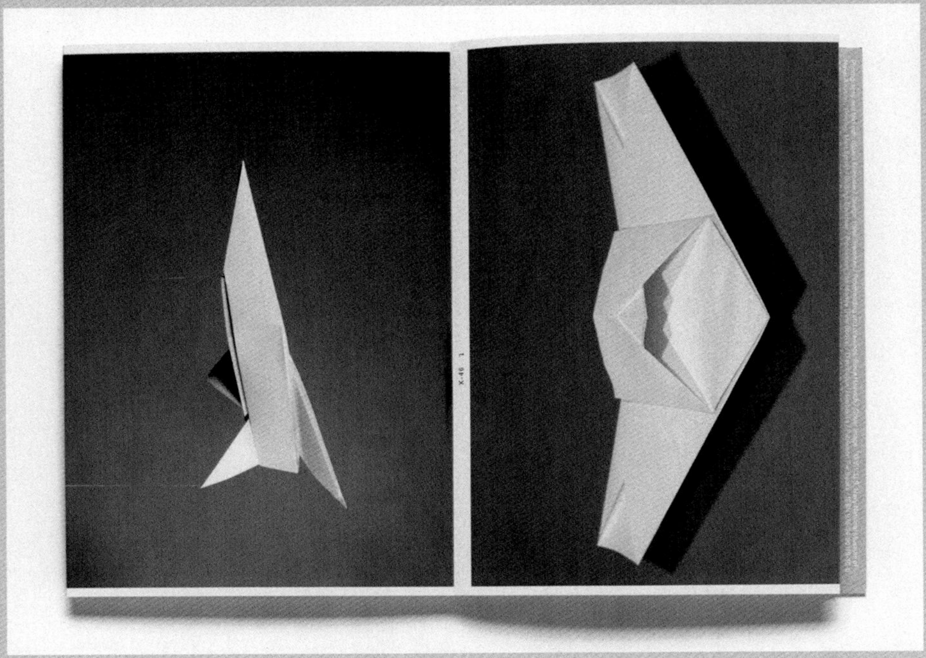

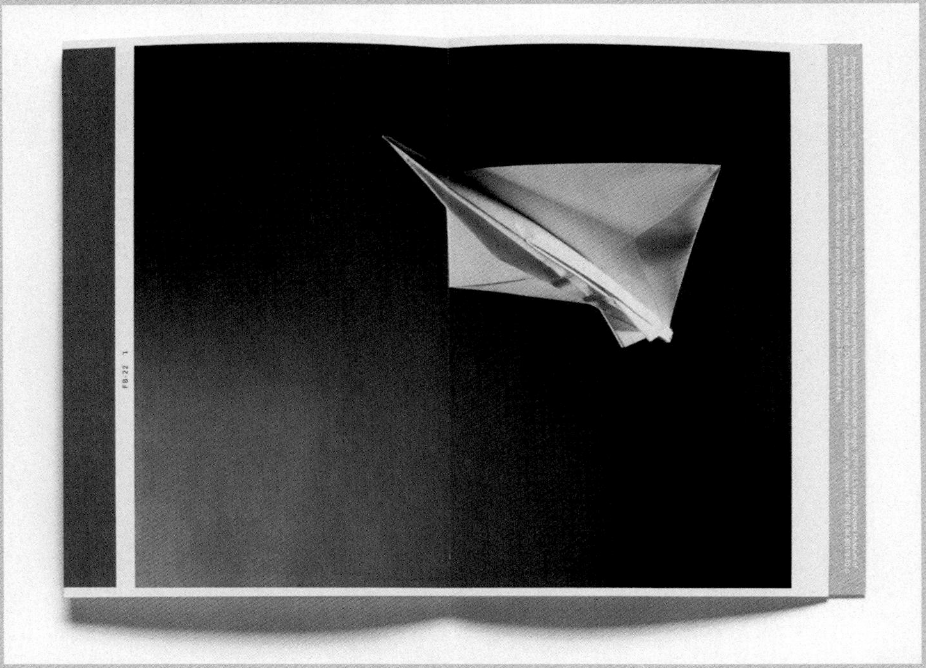

Figure E.2 Interior spreads from Sjoerd Knibbeler—*Paper Planes* (Fw:Photography, 2015). Top and bottom left (this page): spreads from the front, showing photographs of the model planes. Note that the photographs are not always constrained to the individual sections of the accordion. Instead, they wrap around the folds. Top and bottom right (following page): spreads from the back. Unlike the photographs,

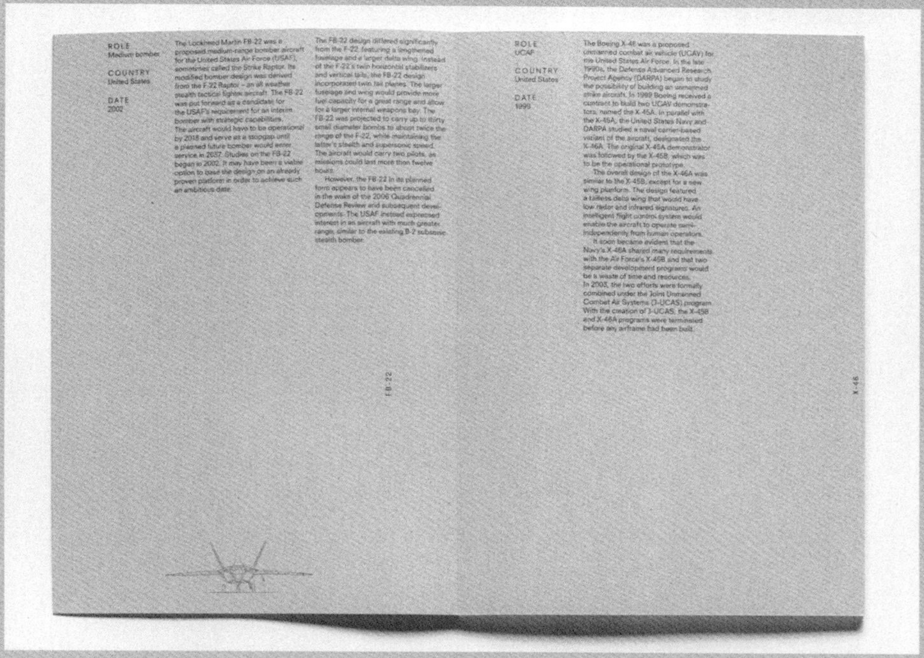

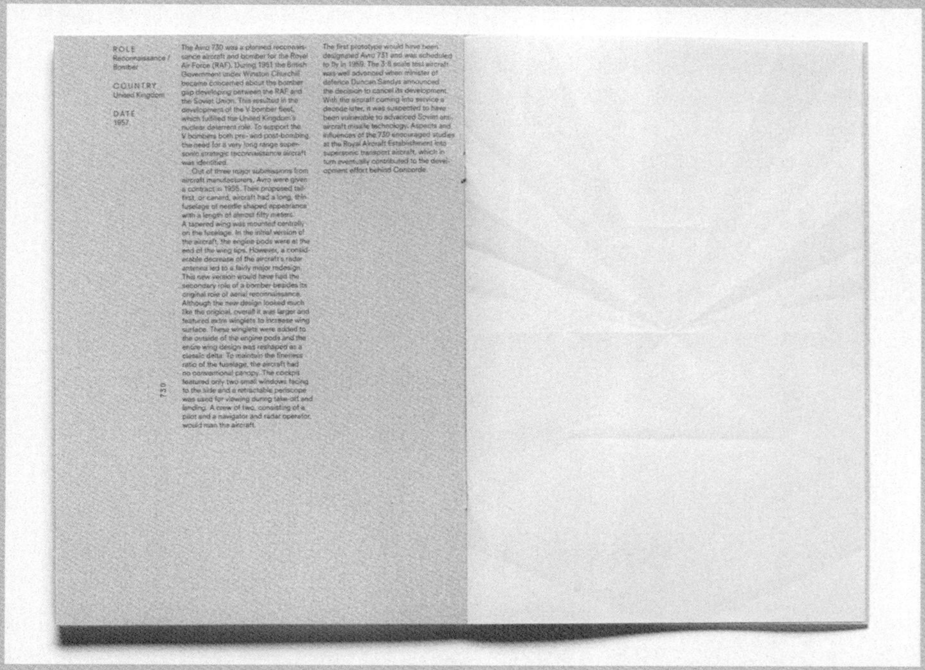

the text for each individual plane is contained in a single section of the accordion. In the bottom right image additional, stapled-in sheets are visible, facsimiles of unfolded sheets of paper, presumably previously used for model making

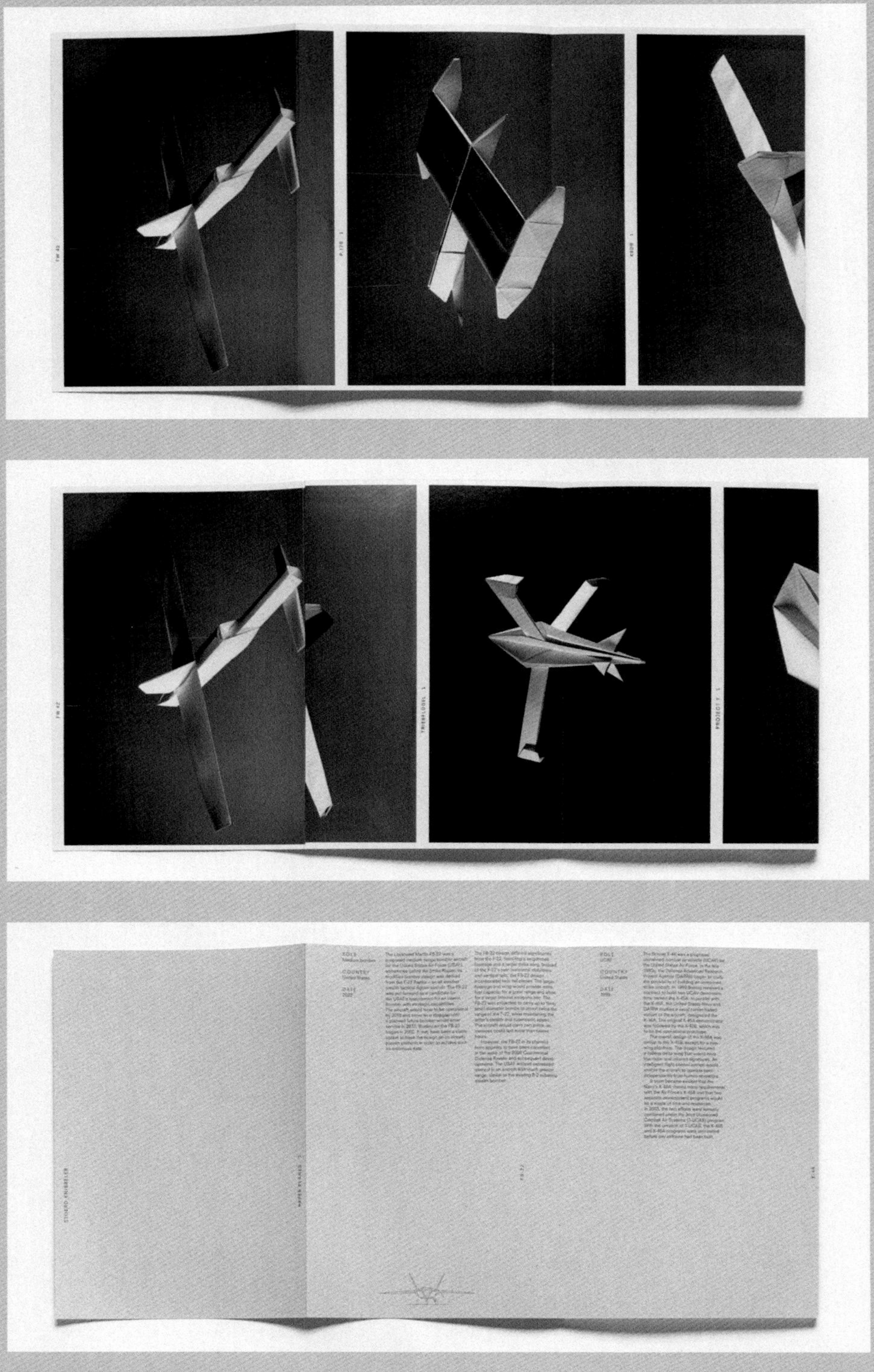

Figure E.3 Interior spreads from Sjoerd Knibbeler—*Paper Planes* (Fw:Photography, 2015). While an accordion can be treated like a regular book, of course, it is also possible to unfold larger parts, as has been done here. Note how in the middle panel the accordion was unfolded in such a way that two photographs overlap. The use of the accordion format allows the viewer to do that. Here, formally the overlap of the photographs makes for an interesting juxtaposition

CHAPTER 7

How to Make a Photobook (in 17 Rules)

In the following, I am going to summarize the content of the preceding chapters through a set of rules. As is always the case with rules, they are only useful if they are being understood for what they are. There can be—and will be—exceptions. But especially those not very experienced with making photobooks might want to initially stick to the rules, to then break them later.

Rule #1: Have a Good Answer for: "Why does this Book Have to be Made?"

Don't get me wrong: I love photobooks, and I can't get enough of them. That said, there are already thousands and thousands of photobooks in existence. Given the time, effort, and money that a photographer will have to invest into the making of their own photobook, I very firmly believe that she or he has to have a very good answer to this question. Of course, to a large extent having a good answer is crucial, given the competition. Given there are so many photobooks in existence already, do we really need one more?

The key to finding a good answer for this question is to rephrase it: "what am I going to contribute that doesn't exist in this form already?" Working out a good answer for this question should, in fact, be part of working on the underlying body of work in question. After all, in photography everything is related. No photography project should exist just for its own sake. There will have to be a good reason for it, regardless of whether it's successful or not. Part of the reason why there are so many bad photobooks out there is because making a photobook has become a bit of a fad. You have to have a photobook, simply because you're a photographer. Not so! Not so at all! If making a photobook doesn't make sense for a photographer, they are under no obligation to make one.

In other words, every photographer interested in making a photobook should make sure that the artistic bar is as high as possible, and that it then is being crossed. This, and only this, might help the book succeed.[1] If the bar is placed high, and the book crosses it, it is likely to add something to the larger conversation in photography that is being fueled by this strange and strangely exhilarating medium.

Rule #2: Do Your Research

Given you now know that your book has to be made, the absolutely best state to be in when starting work on a photobook is to be fully aware of all the necessary decisions. Realistically speaking, for most photographers, especially those engaging with the process for the first time, that is unlikely to be the case. But that needn't be a source of anxiety. Even if one is unaware of the kinds of decision that might have gone into the making of somebody else's photobook, looking at books that way, studying them, can vastly help to gain a better understanding of the medium.

For anything one encounters in all likelihood some decision had to be made, whether it's paper choices, design, the book's size, or whatever else. Of course, the decision process is going to be inaccessible (unless one manages to speak with the photographer, designer, publisher in question). But one can still try to understand the reasons behind some particular choice. For example, why might the book be so small? Or so large? What might the reasons be, given the book's content, and—crucially—does this work? A viewer might come to the realization that they can't think of a good reason. This could mean that the reasons are not immediately clear, maybe because of a lack of experience on the part of the viewer, or that there aren't any good reasons. There are, after all, many books that have problems. On top of that, the question of personal tastes, of personal preferences looms in the background. But anyone taking all of this into consideration can learn a lot about photobooks by looking at them carefully. This means looking at the full package, the photography inside as much as the object and the way it is made.

Another reason for studying photobooks this closely is that inevitably, they will register somewhere on the spectrum of one's own personal preferences. It is important to find out why one reacts to a photobook the way one does: what is being done right here for things to work so well? Or what is not working? And if something is working well, that can—or maybe should—then result in a note being made, regardless of whether it concerns a type of paper that feels especially nice, a smart solution for the way the editing and sequencing work with text, the type of binding, or whatever else there might be. I know people who will buy a book—all types of book, not just photobooks—if it makes use of something they could conceive of using later themselves.

While building a reference library might feel like a bit of an excessive solution for most photobook makers, having some references inside the medium is tremendously important. The idea is not simply to know each and every book that is being published.[2] Instead, it is to be aware of as large a number as is possible and feasible, while developing a deeper understanding of them. The more you know about photobooks, the easier it will be to approach the making of your own.

Rule #3: Avoid Shortcuts

Photobooks, like all books, come with a beginning and an end. But still, there is only so much their makers can do to control how viewers will engage with them. The same is true for this book. I don't know whether you have read the preceding chapters to arrive here, or whether you have skipped some—or all—of them, to read this chapter first. If the latter is the case, please realize that any of these rules might not make as much sense as they will otherwise. To fully understand the rules and where they are coming from you will have to be familiar with the content of the preceding chapters.

This rule of avoiding shortcuts probably might apply for many, if not most, other human activities, especially if the intent is to do them well. They certainly apply for the medium of photography itself, even without the component of photobook added. Being a photographer inevitably entails having to deal with a fair amount of tedious activities that require work and dedication. Taking a shortcut might reduce the amount of time spent on something. But it usually is unlikely to yield a result of as high a quality as when more time is being spent. Certainly, the same is true for photobook making. Avoid shortcuts. All of the various aspects of photobook making require careful and attentive consideration. It is very likely that taking a shortcut will affect the final product in a detrimental way. For example, sloppy files might result in the photographs not looking as good as they should in the book. Ignoring aspects of design will make the book look bad, amateurish, unattractive, and so on.

If, as can easily be the case, the making of a photobook creates a seemingly overwhelming amount of work, a likely solution is to enlist (aka hire) professionals who are not only trained to deal with their field of expertise (for example, a designer), but who also can do the job in the fraction of time, while delivering vastly superior results. This immediately leads to Rule #4.

Rule #4: Photobooks are Made Through Collaboration

I don't know a single photographer who is able to combine the roles of photographer, editor, designer, and production expert at the same high level. And there is absolutely no reason why a photographer should simultaneously be an expert editor, an expert designer, and an expert production person. This would be an unrealistic expectation. Consequently, to make a successful, high-quality photobook, a photographer should be prepared to work with a team of experts:

- While photographers should be able to successfully create meaningful edits of their work, having access to at least one other set of eyeballs is very important, regardless of whether that other person is a hired editor (who might take over editing the book) or another expert who is willing and able to provide honest, open feedback.
- While the easy availability of programs such as *Adobe InDesign* make it tempting to design the book without any expert input, the reality is that most photographers simply aren't very good designers at all. Unless a photographer has training in graphic design, she or he should access a designer during the making of a photobook.
- Printing photographs on an inkjet printer connected to a computer at a high level of quality is one thing. Getting the same files printed on a professional printing press is an entirely

different matter. Especially if large amounts of money are going to be spent on a book, photographers should consider talking to an expert in separations to make sure their source files are of adequate quality.

- While most photographers have some idea what they are looking for in their desired photobook, they typically lack the breadth of knowledge of bindings and materials that professional production experts or (most) publishers possess. Thus, consulting with such specialists is very important.

With added experts, the group of people working on the book will expand from solely consisting of the photographer. When working with a publishing house, there probably will be experts available (this depends on the publishing houses in question). Making good use of these experts is very important for a photographer. In particular, fighting the advice given by the experts in all likelihood might cause major problems. After all, unlike most photographers publishing houses have ample experience with publishing books, and they might insist on something for very specific reasons.

In Aperture's *The Photobook Review* #009 (Fall 2015), the idea of the collaboration between partners is being stressed in a series of conversations with photobook makers. "First and foremost," notes Roberto Salazar, a typographer and editor, "collaboration is based on the notion that nobody possesses a 360-degree view—not of their own practice, nor those of others. I have an aesthetic and technical bias; however, my subjectivity is only relevant within the context of collaboration. As such, I'm able to enrich a project by adding to the gene pool, as it were."[3] Photographer Rob Hornstra chimes in: "If you are not capable of leaving your comfort zone, I'm afraid you will end up with a mediocre book."[4] In other words, making a photobook through a collaboration has a lot to do with one's comfort zone. One might think one knows all the possible solutions or answers, but the reality is that nobody really does.[5]

Self-publishers will not find themselves in the same luxury position of having a publisher provide a team. Instead, they will have to take care of each and every aspect of the photobook production themselves. While adding experts is likely to incur additional costs, the benefits of working with experts outweigh these costs easily. In the case of a zine in an edition of ten this might not matter much. But over the past few years, self-publishers have been making photobooks designed to compete with those produced by major publishing houses in terms of style, production quality, and artistic aspiration. Often, such projects have to come with considerable budgets. In such cases, for example it would be utterly foolish to spend a lot of money on printing a book at that fancy German printer everybody is using right now, while trying to save money on making sure proper file separations have been done. Given that self-publishing in part has been greatly aided by the internet, it is important to realize that team building for a book can follow the same ideas. "Modern teams that are formed for specific projects are increasingly heterogeneous," says designer Ramon Pez, "and they can be based in different countries, meeting on the internet." In other words, you don't necessarily have to have all people in the same room, allowing you to work with a much larger variety of experts than who might be available locally.

Once a photographer is prepared to work with a team, that team and its work have to be organized. It is usually a good idea to get the team work started earlier than later. Pez again: "It is more useful to start a photobook from the start with the team of designers, editors, and/or writers, illustrators. Especially in cases where the narrative structure and the contents are complex." This echoes Salazar's earlier comment about nobody having a 360-degree view of everything. Getting the team together and involved early adds possibly fruitful expertise and opinions, and it brings every member of the team to the same level right away.

Rule #5: Every Photobook Should Have a Budget

Regardless of whether a photographer is working with a publisher or not, there should be a very clear understanding of the costs. There are publishers that will cover all the costs. But very few photographers will find themselves in that position. In all likelihood, photographers will be asked to contribute to the costs of making a book. Of course, self-publishers will have to cover all costs. So anyone interested in making a photobook should start out by carefully thinking about how much money they have available, and about how that money might have to get allocated to the various items that have to be covered.

"It's a rare project where budget does not come into play," says designer Beverly Joel. "While the choice of typography and image placement are largely immune to cost considerations, the trim size and page count certainly are affected. Paper choices, binding (hard vs. soft cover), and other materials like the binding cloths, printed endpapers, use of varnishes can all greatly impact the overall feel and presence of the book." With a team involved (see Rule #4) this might immediately become clearer, as different members of the team will have an effect on different parts of the book (and thus budget—there certainly will be ample overlaps, though).

Budget considerations play a role regardless of how large or small the amount of available money might be. Joel: "Occasionally, larger budgets can mean the reproduction quality improves while a limited budget allows a greater emphasis on a more aggressive or 'present' design that can't rely on pristine image separations. There's always a bit of a balancing act with it, and more often than not, budgets are pretty constrained." Ultimately, constraints are good, since they enforce the finding of possible solutions. They foster creativity. But of course, they also require the ability to compromise (we'll get to that in Rule #8).

Rule #6: Everything Has to Be in the Service of the Book

In a sense, this rule is a variant of the rule that photobooks are made through collaboration. Whereas Rule #3 deals with the process of making a book, this version addresses the final object, the book itself, the end result of the process. Everything has to be in the service of the book. Each and every element of the book has to work in service of what the book is supposed to do, with the book always being more than the sum of its parts. This means that each and every element of the book has to be tailored to work in perfect support of the whole, with no element getting undue preference over all of the others. To be more precise:

- The edit and sequence of the photographs have to be done with the book in mind. A book is not the same as an exhibition, and there will have to possibly be tough decisions made about pictures to include and, more crucially, exclude.
- The design of the book has to provide an important part of the visual framework of the book. Good design will make the experience of looking at the book more pleasurable, while at the same time not putting itself into the center of attention. Underdesigned and overdesigned books should be avoided.
- The materials and production of the book also have to be in service of the overarching concept of the book. Using precious materials for a book on, let's say, a punk concert in all likelihood is going to create a cognitive dissonance for the viewer: why is this book presented in such a precious way when its content is aiming to convey a feeling of raw energy?

This leads directly to Rule #7.

Rule #7: There Has to be a Good Reason for every Decision Made

This rule might sound like something incredibly obvious, but it's not at all. As Rule #6 makes clear, during the making of a photobook, a lot of decisions have to be made. Which pictures are going to be included and excluded? How large is the book supposed to be? What type of paper should it be printed on? What binding should be used? Etc. Etc. Etc. Each and every one of these questions represents a decision that has to be made. There has to be a good reason for each decision made. And that reason, ultimately, will tie in with the main concept of the book and possibly to some extent with the budget. Saying "I like" whatever was decided on is not a good enough reason. We all like all kinds of things. But do these things actually make sense in every single specific context? For example, a photographer might really enjoy books printed on thick paper. That's great. But if there is a thick paper to be used for the book in question, there will have to be a good reason beyond the photographer's general preference for thick papers. Will the book work with thick paper? If yes, that's great. If not, there is no good reason to use thick paper, and a different choice will have to be made. This leads to Rule #8.

Rule #8: Be Prepared to Make Compromises

It's hard to imagine going through life without being aware of the fact that there will have to be compromises. Most people simply can't have it all, and that's good. This is certainly true for the process of making a photobook. There will be countless compromises to be made, many of them ultimately being no big deal. There might be no place in the sequence for a photographer's favorite picture. A book might have to be a little bit smaller than planned because of the size of the sheets used by the printer. A book might have to have fewer pages. Or more pages, and so on.

Compromises usually have to be made for a variety of reasons. For a start, collaborations without compromises rarely ever work. Beyond the very nature of collaborations, compromises come at different points during the process of making a photobook. Any decision based on the book's concept might feel like being a compromise, but that's not really the case. Whatever creative solution a photobook demands, it should get. That's not a compromise, it's a necessity. Actual compromises will instead be posed by budget or production considerations, which, in turn, can percolate down to other aspects of the book. Insisting on a solution that is not feasible makes sense for a while—maybe there is a way around a problem after all. But if such a way around a problem cannot be found, a compromise will have to be made. In the end, a compromise will not lead to the end of the world. Instead, it will lead to a book that can actually be made—as opposed to the fairydust one that, alas, only exists in someone's imagination. A somewhat different way to approach this rule is the following.

Rule #9: Aim for the Perfect Book, then Make the Best Possible

It would be great if that perfect photobook could be made. If only … As Rule #8 makes clear, there will have to be compromises. They're not the end of the world. The perfect photobook often simply is not feasible, not doable, not financeable. So it's good to know what the perfect solution for a given photo project might be, to then be flexible enough to work towards the best possible solution, given the constraints. This is important when making a book with a publishing house, given that few publishers are interested in prolonged arguments with photographers. It is also important for self-publishers, especially given that initially, there will be nobody else available who will easily point out the constraints. As we saw earlier (Rule #4), given that making a photobook should be a collaborative effort, identifying constraints and working around them is much easier in a team than as a one-person group.

Rule #10: There Is No Such Thing as the Perfect Photobook

While the previous rule mostly deals with how to physically realize a photobook, there is another, more fundamental realization to be had. For many photo projects, there are different ways of making a photobook around them, with one way not necessarily being better than any of the other ones. In other words, that one perfect version of the book might not exist. So instead of trying to find the perfect photobook realization, it is often better to create as best a version of one particular solution as possible. I teach in an MFA photography program, and I have come across students who would endlessly obsess over what the perfect book might be, without getting to actually making something for a long time. That is not a good idea. Instead, commit to what looks like the best solution, and then really make it work. The best that can happen is that you end up with a very good photobook, maybe even a great one. In that case, does it matter that it might not be the perfect solution, given it's not even clear what that perfect solution would be? Probably not. The worst that can happen when developing a book that way is that at the end of the process (when having a very advanced dummy), it turns out the book doesn't work. However frustrating that might be, in all likelihood having spent so much time with the book will immediately lead to another incarnation that works. Making a photobook is not the same as assembling a puzzle or a model kit, where one knows in advance what the pieces are, and what the end result will have to look like. Whatever one encounters during the creative process of making art never is a waste of time. Never.

Rule #11: A Photobook Plays more than One Role

Regardless of whether its makers have considered this aspect or not, a photobook always plays more than one role:

- It first and foremost is the very specific creative, artistic expression of a photography project in book form.
- But a photobook also is a product that exists in some marketplace (unless it is not for sale). There are different, almost separate marketplaces for different books. Some books find their ways into chain bookstores (online or offline), while many others are sold online, in specialty bookshops, and/or at photobook fairs. And then there are books made for the collectors market. Anyone making a photobook should think about where their book will be positioned and what this might mean.
- Independent of the previous two aspects is the one of a photobook being a promotional item for a photographer, regardless of whether that was intended or not. A book might fall into the hands of a gallerist, a curator, a photo editor, or whoever else, and they might decide they want to work with the photographer, given they enjoyed the book.

All photobooks play these different roles, regardless of whether this was intended or not. One particular role might be the intended one. But it would be a mistake to ignore the other roles. In fact, treating a photobook as having these different roles helps working on it, because it will help to make decisions.

Rule #12: Keep Your Audience in Mind

I have the feeling that many photographers will baulk at accepting this rule. Shouldn't a photobook be the perfect artistic expression of some photography project? Well, sure. We have, however, already seen that there will have to be compromises, and that aiming for the perfect book might not be the best idea. But there is more. Even if it is feasible to make that gorgeous perfect book, who will buy it if it will have to be sold for $150? Are the people who will be willing and able to pay that amount of money—in all likelihood wealthy collectors—the audience of the work? If yes, that's fine. If not, there's a problem.

This problem occurs frequently with photobooks, and I often think many photobook makers don't think about it much. The price point of a book has direct repercussions. In much the same way, the way a book is produced has repercussions. For example, a luxurious book about poverty might have a lot of people wonder about the cognitive dissonance at play there. What this boils down to is that the book's concept should dictate every aspect of it, including how it is positioned on the marketplace.

Marketplace aside, if a photobook is overly obtuse and difficult to understand, it will have a hard time competing with other books. Maybe the book needs to be that obtuse and difficult. That's something to think about before making the book, so that there are no surprises when the book is out. So photobook makers really want to keep their audiences in mind.

Rule #13: Don't Approach Editing and Sequencing as if They Are Dark Arts

Many photographers have considerable problems with editing, let alone sequencing their own work. It needn't be so. Even outside of the context of photobooks, being able to make a good edit of one's photographs is extremely important. Editing and sequencing are not dark arts, however, mysterious activities that can only be performed by the select few who might or might not have access to extrasensory perceptions. While it might seem bewildering to see how an experienced editor creates a coherent set of photographs out of a large group almost effortlessly, to a large extent the seeming lack of effort is based on experience. And that experience has usually been gained through many years of editing work.

The truth is that editing and sequencing can be learned. To a large extent, editing is based on recognizing form and content, and how said form and content then might create meaning, given specific contexts, and given a viewer's preconceptions. To learn how to edit one's work starts with giving the photographs full attention, to see how their form and content work, and to then discard those that fall short. Running an edit by another experienced person (or maybe a few—but not too many—people) is a good idea. That way, the feedback from the other person can help see where the edit might fall short, and this then should inform the next iteration of the edit.

Editing and sequencing usually are not activities that can or should be performed once. Instead, an edit grows with time, it changes with time. Repeated work on an edit might take a lot more time, but it also makes things a lot easier for a photographer, given solutions can be found with time. With time, things tend to fall into shape—assuming the photographer is willing and able to give the process time. Even experienced editors usually do not create edits and sequences for a book in an afternoon. So, let's move onto Rule #14.

Rule #14: Allow the Process of Making a Book to Take Time

Rushing through the process of making a photobook is a very bad idea. Every aspect might take time, and it's OK if that is the case. It's absolutely OK to work on an edit and sequence for months, to get to the point where things really work. Many of the problems posed during the course of making a photobook are unlike simple mathematical problems that can be solved easily. Allow for the process to take time. And if there is a deadline for the book, do not allow the deadline to dictate the outcome. Instead, be comfortable with delaying the publication of the book if there is not enough time to find a good solution for a problem (while, of course, keeping in mind that compromises will have to be made).

Assuming there is a team working on a book, there are likely to be iterations in the process. The process can then undergo what Ramon Pez describes as "continuous feedback": "Limits lead us to look for new solutions that open doors to new ideas that then have an important influence on editing, design, choices of narrative." While a book ultimately is an inorganic entity, the making of it probably should be organic, with—seen on larger time scales—a clear evolution towards a good whole, while on a shorter timescale there might be leaps, there might be false starts, or dead ends etc. Exploring the options, trying things, is crucial. Without giving the process the time it needs, it is unlikely to work well.

Rule #15: Always Work with Physical Objects

Photobooks are physical objects, and the viewer's interaction with the book determines to a large extent what she or he will get out of it. Consequently, during the process of working on a photobook, produce physical objects to handle. For example, when a photographer is at the stage where there is a first sequence, buy a simple spiral-bound notebook, have small (and cheap) prints made, and stick them into the notebook with removable double-sided tape. This first dummy will immediately reveal whether the sequence really works in book form, however cheap and simple and maybe even clumsy the actual object might be. Turning the pages, seeing pictures on pages, one after the other, is very different than seeing them lined up on a table, or seeing them on "pages" in a PDF on one's computer. Physical dummies are invaluable tools during the process of making a photobook. In much the same fashion, a materials dummy can be produced to experience what the book might feel like, given the various decisions concerning size, materials, binding etc.

Rule #16: All Aspects of Photobook Making Are Important

Rule #4 (about collaboration) already hints at something a lot of photographers have a hard time accepting: all aspects of photobook making are important. It is tempting to worry about editing and sequencing, to then come up with some basic idea of what the book should look like, asking a designer to get involved, and to then have the book printed and bound somewhere. That might work, but there is no guarantee that it will.

For a start, design should not be an afterthought, like a label that gets added later. Design already enters through the type of image layout on the individual spreads. And the production of a book is no separate entity, either. To a large extent this is because whatever the desired book is supposed to be, it has to be produceable, meaning it has to be technically feasible. And the budget has to be able to cover the costs of the production. All too often, photographers come up with elaborate books that are prohibitively expensive to make. It's a good idea to be ambitious. At the same time, one needs to be realistic. This means that involving a designer and a production person early on is a good idea. There might not be the need to hire a production person, but someone will have to be able to talk to a printer and binder to assess the costs and feasibility of a planned book.

As Rule #8 states, be prepared to make compromises. Ideally, obstacles should be run into early. If it turns out that an elaborate design is much too expensive to produce, it's much better to find out early on in the project than late, when there's only that last step left, getting things printed and bound. So the more a book project takes shape, the more stress should be put on its non-photography aspects, design and production. There are different ways of how a photographer might go about this. If a production person is hired, she or he might start backwards, working from the budget and the desired object (in all likelihood trimming the production down, to arrive at something that is realistic). A photographer might start out with editing and sequencing and simple dummies, to add on experts or expert advice later. As long as all relevant aspects of the process of making a photobook are being considered in such a way that none of them becomes an afterthought the number of likely obstacles is probably going to be manageable.

Rule #17: Don't Worry about Money

This might end up being the infuriating rule, given how it is phrased. If you want to make a photobook, in all likelihood it is going to cost you money, usually quite a bit of it. So how can one *not* worry about money? I'd be the last person not to be sympathetic concerning worries about money. What I really mean to talk about with this rule is that you want to think about the money you need beforehand. Do not expect to get your book published for free (it's probably not going to happen), and don't expect to be making money with the book (it's probably also not going to happen).

There's a joke I've heard from different photobook makers, and it goes something like this: "You can have a little money after making a photobook—if you started out with a lot of money." In most cases, photographers will be required to bring some, if not a lot of money to the table when making a photobook, even when working with a publisher (it's obvious in the case of self-publishing).

If you don't have the money needed to make a book, you basically have two options. Either simply don't do it, or find ways to raise the necessary money. In terms of finances, there are countless more profitable ways for a photographer than making a photobook. Making a photobook is going to be a financial investment, and there is no guarantee it will work out.

So this rule amounts to different aspects: Accept that photobook making will cost you money. At this point in time, that's the reality of photobook making. What is more, accept that you are unlikely to make much, if any money from your book. Once you have committed to making a photobook, having raised the money in whatever way, make sure to stay within your budget, but let go of any financial expectations.

This also means that if the amount of money you need to raise is going to give you more than just a headache, take a step back and think carefully about whether you can and want to afford this investment. In an artistic sense, making a good photobook always pays dividends. In a strictly business sense, those artistic dividends might come at a financial loss. But then making a photobook is not any different than, say, taking photographs. You will have to buy a camera, a computer, and a lot of other things (material and immaterial), without knowing beforehand whether or how the investment will be worth it. Approach thinking about money and your photobook in the same way.

Notes

1. Obviously, there's no guarantee that *any* book will succeed.
2. This is a problem I run into with students frequently. Many of them will be aware of every "cool" or hyped photobook published over the course of the past few years. But most of those students do not have a deeper understanding of how to approach and understand these books. The quantity of the books you know only translates into a higher quality of your understanding if—and only if—you spend the time to study the books.
3. Quoted from Taco Hidde Bakker, *One Plus One Is Three*, in *The Photobook Review* #009, Fall 2015, p. 11.
4. Ibid., p. 12.
5. And, unfortunately, there are enough bad photobooks out there to prove this point.

Reference Materials

Martin Parr and Gerry Badger, *The Photobook: A History, Volume I* (Phaidon, 2004)

Martin Parr and Gerry Badger, *The Photobook: A History, Volume II* (Phaidon, 2006)

Martin Parr and Gerry Badger, *The Photobook: A History, Volume III* (Phaidon, 2014)

Martin Parr and Gerry Badger's three-volume series of books have become indispensable tools for those interested in the history of the medium. At slightly over 300 pages each, the books contain a plethora of information about a wide range of books. Volumes I and II cover the medium's history, starting with the very earliest examples of photobooks, all the way to the contemporary photobooks. Given the first two volumes' focus mostly on pre-contemporary photobooks, Volume III adds a lot more information about photobooks that were more recently made. The real strength of the series probably lies more in its historical introduction to the medium. Compared with the first two volumes, the most recent addition to the series feels a little light.

The general outline for each book is a set of chapters, some of them based on historical periods, others on thematic considerations. An introduction lays out the general theme of each chapter in detail. Afterwards, each book is covered rather briefly, with a relatively small number of sample spreads and a brief comment. The three volumes thus offer a great starting point from which to explore the medium in more detail using other sources.

Alessandro Bertolotti, *Book of Nudes* (Abrams, 2007)

Fotostiftung Schweiz, *Swiss Photobooks from 1927 to the Present: A Different History of Photography* (Lars Müller, 2011)

Horacio Fernandez, *The Latin American Photobook* (Aperture, 2011)

Horacio Fernandez, *Photobooks: Spain 1905–1977* (RM, 2014)

Mikhail Karasik, *The Soviet Photobook 1920–1941* (Steidl, 2015)

Martin Parr and Wassink Lundgren, *The Chinese Photobook* (Aperture, 2015)

Verna Posever Curtis, *Photographic Memory: The Album in the Age of Photography* (Aperture, 2011)

Andrew Roth, *The Book of 101 Books* (PPP Editions, 2001)

Rik Suermondt and Frits Gierstberg, *The Dutch Photobook: A Thematic Selection from 1945 Onwards* (Aperture, 2012)

Ivan Vartanian and Ryuichi Kaneko, *Japanese Photobooks of the 1960s and '70s* (Aperture, 2009)

Any of the books listed in this section can serve as supplemental material for the Parr/Badger series. Most of the books focus on a particular region, occasionally with an element of time added. What is more, their presentation often deviates a little from the standard terse fare offered by Parr/Badger.

The Book of 101 Books could and maybe should have become the standard for looking at photobooks, but it's sold out and not widely available. Used copies sell for hundreds of dollars.

The Dutch Photobook and *The Latin American Photobook* closely follow the Parr/Badger model, both in terms of the amount of information given for each photobook, and the organization of the whole book. In contrast, as its title indicates, *Japanese Photobooks of the 1960s and 70s* focuses on a very specific period of time for photobooks produced in Japan, and each book is presented in much more detail, both in terms of the amount of text and the number of spreads reproduced. *Swiss Photobooks from 1927 to the Present* is probably the most exhausting book about photobooks, with very long and detailed essays about each photobook.

It might be personal bias, but one difference between the books mentioned in this section is the overall quality of the material covered. While they're relevant in their given context, many of the photobooks covered in either *The Latin American Photobook* or *Swiss Photobooks from 1927 to the Present* simply aren't very interesting books. In contrast, both *The Dutch Photobook* and *Japanese Photobooks of the 1960s and 70s* are highly recommended additions to Parr/Badger, because they do not just add geographical focus, but their photobooks also focus in on aspects that are highly relevant (design and a particularly important part of the history of photography for the Dutch and Japanese books, respectively).

Two exceptions to the Parr/Badger-type books are provided by *Book of Nudes* and *Photographic Memory.* As its title indicates, *Book of Nudes* focuses solely on photobooks containing images of the nude human form. The book is organized historically, and it provides a unique and quite interesting view of different cultural periods using photobooks of the nude as a vehicle. *Photographic Memory* deals with a type of photobook not covered in this book, albums. As books, albums are very interesting objects, and the author makes it very clear why they deserve to be studied much like monographs.

German language only:

Manfred Heiting, *Deutschland im Fotobuch* (Steidl, 2011)

Manfred Heiting and Roland Jaeger, *Autopsie, Band 1: Deutschsprachige Fotobücher 1918 bis 1945* (Steidl, 2012)

Manfred Heiting and Roland Jaeger, *Autopsie, Band 2: Deutschsprachige Fotobücher 1918 bis 1945* (Steidl, 2013)

Russian language only:

Mikhail Karasik, *Great Stalinist Photographic Books* (Kontakt-Kultura, 2007)

Mainly Japanese language:

Nobuyoshi Araki, *Anarchy Photobook Mania* (Izu Photo Museum, 2012)

None of the books covered in this section contains much—if any—English text, so they simply are inaccessible for those who cannot read German, Russian, or Japanese.

Deutschland im Fotobuch [Germany in the Photobook] roughly is the equivalent of, say, *The Dutch Photobook*, with the exception that it covers photobooks made about or centering on Germany, instead of focusing on books made in Germany. The two-volume *Autopsie: Deutschsprachige Fotobücher 1918 bis 1945 [Autopsy: German-Language Photobooks from 1918 until 1945]* presents an overwhelming overview for that period, with very academic writing and possibly too much information for anyone other than a serious scholar.

The plethora of spreads reproduced in *Great Stalinist Photographic Books* is highly usable, given Parr/Badger contain a good introduction to the topic of propaganda books. Many of the Soviet books covered somewhat briefly in Parr/Badger can be found here. Given that design played a huge role for these books, even just as visual source material the book is quite useful. I have not seen *The Soviet Photobook 1920–1941*, but from what I hear it's a revamped and expanded English-language version of this older book.

Nobuyoshi Araki has literally produced hundreds of photobooks, so it makes perfect sense to devote a whole book to his oeuvre alone. A relatively small paperback, *Anarchy Photobook Mania* gives a good overview of this particular photographer's output. The book contains some English text in the form of essays about the photographer's importance, and the overview pages are bilingual. What is more, it is picture heavy, giving many examples of Araki's images. As an example of what a single photographer can achieve, it's most impressive. Needless to say, those who are offended by nudity or the depiction of sexual acts might want to stay away from it.

Imprint: Visual Narratives in Books and Beyond (University of Gothenburg/Hasselbladstiftelsen, 2013)

This bilingual book (English/Swedish) features essays/interviews by/with four authors (Gerry Badger, David Bate, Bettina Lockemann, Michael Mack), two of which sections—Lockemann's essay and the interview with Mack—make this a recommended buy for those interested in the more theoretical side of photobook making.

Dewi Lewis and Alan Ward, *Publishing Photography* (Cornerhouse Publications, 1992)

Solidly immersed in a publishing world that now has vastly changed (especially with the advent of online book selling, digital printing technologies, and the recent wave of self-publishing), the book still offers quite a few very useful pointers, provided from the point of view of a publisher. Many of its details are specific to the UK (such as pricing/discount rates etc.), and they might not apply any longer at all. Most of the descriptions of the process of making a book still apply, though.

(Please note this list represents books I own and/or have been made aware of at the end of 2015.)

The Photobook Review (Aperture, biannual)

Unlike the above publications, Aperture's *The Photobook Review* is a biannual journal that comes with the eponymous magazine. Each issue is guest edited by someone from the larger world of photobook making, and it typically centers on a broader theme.[1] Featuring interviews, book reviews, and in-depth articles, *The Photobook Review* is required reading for anyone interested in the world of photobooks.

Note

1. An overview of all existing issues is available at http://aperture.org/pbr/.

Index

Note: Page numbers followed by 'f' refer to figures, followed by 'n' refer to notes and followed by 't' refer to tables.

D

E

F

G

H

I

J

K

L

M

N

O

P

R

S